Memorial Tributes

NATIONAL ACADEMY OF ENGINEERING

NATIONAL ACADEMY OF ENGINEERING
OF THE
UNITED STATES OF AMERICA

Memorial Tributes

Volume 3

NATIONAL ACADEMY PRESS
Washington, D.C.   1989

National Academy Press • 2101 Constitution Avenue, NW • Washington, DC 20418

Library of Congress Cataloging-in-Publication Data

(Revised for vol. 3)

National Academy of Engineering.
Memorial tributes.

Vol. 3– imprint: Washington, D.C.: National
Academy Press.
1. Engineers—United States—Biography. I. Title.
TA139.N34   1979   620'.0092'2   79-21053
ISBN 0-309-03482-5 (v. 2)
ISBN 0-309-03939-8 (v. 3)

Printed in the United States of America

CONTENTS

CONTENTS

FOREWORD

THIS IS THE THIRD VOLUME in the series of *Memorial Tributes* issued periodically by the National Academy of Engineering to honor the deceased members and foreign associates of the Academy. Publication of this volume contributes to the observance of the twenty-fifth anniversary of the founding of the NAE on December 5, 1964. It is intended that these volumes will stand as an enduring record of the many contributions of engineering to the benefit of humankind. In all cases, the authors of the tributes had personal knowledge of the interests and engineering accomplishments of the deceased members and foreign associates.

The National Academy of Engineering is a private organization established in 1964 to share in the responsibility given the National Academy of Sciences under its congressional charter signed by President Lincoln in 1863 to examine and report on questions of science and engineering at the request of the federal government. Individuals are elected to the National Academy of Engineering on the basis of significant contributions to engineering theory and practice and to the literature of engineering or demonstrated unusual accomplishments in the pioneering of new and developing fields of technology.

Alexander H. Flax
Home Secretary

Memorial Tributes

NATIONAL ACADEMY OF ENGINEERING

STUART LAWRENCE BAILEY

1905–1984

BY ALEXANDER H. FLAX

STUART LAWRENCE BAILEY, former president of Jansky and Bailey, Inc., and vice-president of the Atlantic Research Corporation until his retirement in 1970, died on August 11, 1984, at the age of seventy-eight. Bailey was known for his outstanding personal contributions and pioneering work in three main areas: (1) the development of air navigation radio aids; (2) radio signal propagation measurements, which were applied to the design and location of broadcasting stations; (3) the development of transmission standards for service and interference in AM and FM radio and in television broadcasting.

Stuart Bailey was born on October 7, 1905, in Minneapolis, Minnesota. He received a B.S. in electrical engineering from the University of Minnesota in 1927 and an M.S. in electrical engineering the following year. As an undergraduate, he was active on the staff of W9XI, an experimental radio station at the university. During his graduate work, Bailey was the chief engineer of radio station WLB, which was owned and operated by the university. It was also during these years at the University of Minnesota that Bailey met C. M. Jansky, who was later to play a major role in his professional and personal life.

Bailey spent three years (1928–1930) in Minnesota working for the U.S. Department of Commerce as a radio engineer in the Lighthouse Service and Airways Division. In 1929 he went to Panama to install two automatic marine radio beacons, one at the entrance to Cristobal Harbor and the other at Cape Mala, 120 miles south of Balboa.

In 1930 his former professor C. M. Jansky contacted him and together they founded Jansky & Bailey, Inc., which pioneered many advances in radio technology over the years. It completed some early work on directional antennas and helped map UHF educational television networks for twenty-one different states. Between 1938 and 1946 the company built and subsequently operated the nation's third—and Washington's first—FM radio station, W3XO, which is WINX-FM.

Stuart Bailey was president of Jansky & Bailey, Inc., from 1953 to 1959, when the company was acquired by Atlantic Research Corporation. He continued working for Atlantic Research until 1970, when he retired as the vice-president and general manager of its electronics and communications division. He continued working as a consultant to the firm for the next ten years.

Stuart Bailey was an excellent organizer and the leader of numerous engineering projects and investigations. He displayed exceptional leadership and organizational skills during World War II in connection with radio frequency anti-jamming practices. After the war, he was a member of various advisory committees dealing with color television, radio propagation, and telecommunications in general.

During World War II Bailey was put in charge of all government contract work performed by Jansky & Bailey, Inc., a great deal of which was done under the U.S. Office of Scientific Research and Development. This work involved a detailed study of all the factors that affect mobile, short-range radio communication, a study of the effects of hills and trees as obstructions to radio transmission from 4 to 116 megacycles, and a detailed analysis of electronic equipment to determine those characteristics that are important to its operation by the armed services.

In addition, under a Signal Corps contract, Bailey supervised the firm's work on the measurement of many existing and proposed radio antennas for use by the armed forces. He participated in determining the levels of vulnerability to radio transmission jamming of particular pieces of U.S. and captured enemy equipment and also helped to develop methods of reducing the vulnerability levels. In June 1947 Mr. Bailey received a citation from the secretaries of war and navy for his contributions to the U.S. Office of Scientific Research and Development.

Bailey's outstanding achievements included his work for IBM Corporation on the "radio-electric typewriter" in the late 1930s and his assistance to Bell Telephone Laboratories in its selection of the National Radio Astronomy Observatory site in Green Bank, West Virginia. During the 1950s he worked on the Dual-ex system of mobile radio teletype digital record communication (the genesis of the Teleproducts Test Equipment Division, which has become a division of Atlantic Research Corporation). He assisted in the development of transmission standards for the broadcast industry in cooperation with the Federal Communications Commission and also supervised a multiyear tropical signal propagation measuring program in Thailand for the Advanced Research Projects Agency of the U.S. Department of Defense.

Stuart Bailey was active in the Institute of Electrical and Electronics Engineers (IEEE), becoming an associate member in 1928, a member in 1936, a senior member in 1938, and a fellow in that same year. He served as the treasurer of IEEE in 1948, 1961, and 1962 and was elected its president in 1949. He was also a member of the board of directors from 1943 to 1955 and from 1961 to 1962.

Mr. Bailey was an active participant in numerous industrial, governmental, and international committees relating to FM transmission standards, television, propagation in all ranges of the spectrum, and proposals for regulation. He was consistently well prepared and well informed on the issues, and as a result, he was always an active, intelligent contributor. The work of these committees invariably pertained to highly technical matters, the sense and an understanding of which Bailey was always able to convey in clear, concise language, thus commanding the respect of his fellows.

Stuart Bailey served on the executive committee of the U.S. National Committee of the International Scientific Radio Union. He was chairman of the American Standards Association Sectional Committee on Radio (C-16) from 1953 to 1954 and a member of the board of the Engineer's Joint Council from 1964 to 1966. He was elected to the National Academy of Engineering in 1973 for "outstanding pioneering work in radio signal propagation measurements and their application to station design and location." Other honors bestowed on him included the Outstanding Achievement Award from the University of Minnesota in 1956 for "leadership in development of radio and television." The university further recognized him as a "worldwide leader in the development of radio and television, ever striving to perfect the standards of radio engineering."

Just before being hospitalized in 1984, Stuart Bailey attended the IEEE's centennial celebration in Boston, where he received the Centennial Gold Medal Award for "extraordinary achievement deserving of special recognition." Bailey was a member of Sigma Xi, Tau Beta Pi, and Eta Kappa Nu. In addition, he belonged to the Cosmos Club and the Broadcast Pioneers. He was a registered professional engineer in the District of Columbia.

Stuart Bailey has been described as a man who loved life and lived it to the fullest. He was a gentle man and treated his employees with a respect that inspired their confidence and loyalty. His family meant a great deal to him, and he maintained strong ties with them. His wife, Carol Sue Bailey, died in 1980. He is survived by his brother Richard Bailey and sister Dorothy Thomas.

Stuart Bailey will be remembered fondly by the numerous friends he maintained through his professional, church, and civic activities.

This tribute is based on biographical materials that appeared in the professional, technical, and general press. It was written by the NAE Membership Office under the editorial direction of the academy's home secretary.

Jack A. Baird

JACK ANTHONY BAIRD

1921–1986

BY IAN M. ROSS

J ACK ANTHONY BAIRD, who, during more than ten years of his career at AT&T and Bell Laboratories, guided the planning of engineering for the world's largest computing system—the U.S. telecommunications network—died May 23, 1986, of a coronary occlusion at the age of sixty-four. Far ahead of his time, he implemented the necessary combination of operations research, technical planning, and technology assessment so AT&T and other organizations could cope with the demands of large, complex electronic communications systems serving both civilian and military purposes. Jack Baird brought good judgment and good sense to the practice of systems engineering, thus paving the way for modern-day data networking and the computers it links.

Jack Baird's professional affiliations included being named a fellow of the Institute of Electrical and Electronics Engineers (IEEE) in 1969; he was also named a member of the Newcomen Society in North America in 1970 and a member of the National Society of Professional Engineers' industry advisory group in 1981. He was elected to the National Academy of Engineering in 1971. At the academy, he was an active member of the Committee on Telecommunications from 1974 to 1978 and served as chairman of its study panel involving the U.S. Department of Commerce's Office of Telecommunications.

His service to the U.S. government earned him much respect. During his tenure at Bell Laboratories, Jack served as a member of the Special Panel on Common Carrier/Interconnections for the Computer Science and Engineering Board of the National Research Council. After his retirement from AT&T in 1983, he served actively as the chairman of the National Research Council's National Security Telecommunications Policy Planning Environment Committee (National Communications System) and as a member of the Voice of America's Radio Emergency Advisory Committee.

Jack Baird was born on May 27, 1921, in the small rural town of Omaha, Texas, the population of which was then, as now, less than 1,000. He was the only child of Harry and Allie Baird. His grandfather was the town doctor and served as Jack's role model, inspiring him to work diligently and think pragmatically while solving problems. As a teenager, Jack was a ham radio operator at a time when such activity was considered extraordinary.

He graduated from Omaha High School in 1939 (as the class valedictorian) and entered the Electrical Engineering School of Texas A&M University, from which he graduated with a B.S. in 1943. He then married his childhood sweetheart, Louise Taylor, also of Omaha, and joined the U.S. Navy as a radar maintenance officer. He served from 1943 to 1946, spending almost two years on destroyer escort duty in the Pacific. After his discharge, Jack was hired by Bell Telephone Laboratories, thus fulfilling a boyhood dream.

Working in Whippany, New Jersey, Jack spent several years in the development of military radar and communications systems. As a member of Bell's technical staff, he helped to develop the first radar system for freighters sailing on the Great Lakes. He also developed the first postwar high-altitude bombing system.

At the same time, he pursued graduate work and received his M.S. in electrical engineering in 1950 from Stevens Institute of Technology in Hoboken, New Jersey. He then returned to Texas A&M under the G.I. Bill and was awarded a Ph.D. in electrical engineering in 1952.

On rejoining Bell Laboratories, Dr. Baird resumed military development work with particular emphasis on the application of transistors and other solid-state electronic devices. He advanced rapidly from supervisor to department head to assistant director, until he eventually became director of military systems development in 1958, only six years after returning to Bell Labs.

During this period, Jack's projects included the first application of transistors to digital computers. His pioneering work began with TRADIC (Transistorized Airborne Digital Computer), which evolved into LEPRECHAUN, a radically new computer that was developed for programming and logical-design research on digital computers for military real-time control applications. At the same time, Jack was also responsible for the development of the first transistorized mortar shell proximity fuses.

As a director, Jack was involved in the development of the digital computer for the Nike Zeus anti-ICBM (Intercontinental Ballistic Missile) system, which later was successfully demonstrated at Kwajalein Island in the Pacific Ocean. Jack presided over an enormously demanding cooperative effort that combined the specialized skills of a wide range of AT&T talents plus those of some fourteen major subcontractors and hundreds of other small subcontractors.

In 1961, as director of military switching development, Jack supervised the development of a major circuit and message switching network sponsored by the U.S. Army Signal Corps—Project UNICOM, which was eventually known as the Defense Automatic Integrated Switch (DAIS) system. The development of the system was carried out under the direction of Bell Laboratories with International Telephone and Telegraph Corporation (ITT) and Radio Corporation of America (RCA) as associates. This work resulted in the first demonstration of an electronic time-division switch, the fundamental concept that is now used in multiplexing and switching of digital transmission signals. The foremost contribution of the project was its demonstration of the feasibility of very large, flexible, real-time, stored-program systems for strategic communications. Many of the system's principal features have since been realized in operational systems.

In 1964 Jack Baird was appointed executive director of switching systems engineering at Bell Laboratories. This new post brought with it the responsibility for all switching systems studies and systems engineering of electronic and electromechanical switching systems in the Bell system. As executive director, Jack initiated significant efforts in long-range planning for the switching of local and long distance signals.

Two years later, he became a vice-president at Bell and assumed responsibility for three systems engineering divisions: transmission, switching, and data. At that point, he was directing long-range planning for the entire Bell system, planning that involved digital transmission, traffic analysis, data and video telephone services, and advanced switching systems. He held that post until 1973 when he became vice-president of engineering at AT&T. At the time of his retirement in 1983, he was vice-president of network planning and design at AT&T, as well as chairman of American Bell International, Inc. In addition, he was a member of the boards of Illinois Bell and Bell Telephone Laboratories.

During his thirty-seven years in the Bell system, Jack Baird's competency in many systems engineering areas was often demonstrated by his assignments involving heavy burdens of technical management. Despite his realization that such duties would limit his individual contributions to his field, he always accepted the challenges and undertook the tasks that his country and his company asked him to perform.

Jack Baird was the antithesis of a flamboyant executive, preferring instead to guide his subordinate colleagues into flourishing careers as they benefited from his counsel. He was a quiet, unassuming, yet incredibly talented engineer whose work continues to serve millions of people around the world. Meanwhile, he never forgot his roots and frequently visited his friends and family in and near Omaha, Texas. He was a devoted and strong husband to his wife Louise and a firm, active father to his two sons, Robert and Glen.

ROBERT ALT BAKER, SR.

1907–1982

BY JOHN W. SIMPSON

Robert alt baker, retired executive vice-president of the Public Service Electric and Gas Company of New Jersey, died on December 8, 1982, at his winter residence in Stuart, Florida. He was a pioneer in the field of steam power plant design, particularly in relation to the use of high steam pressure and high temperatures and the application of computers to automatic control. He was also one of the electric utility industry leaders in the introduction of nuclear energy for electric power generation.

Robert Baker was a native of Reading, Pennsylvania, and graduated from Lehigh University in 1930 with a degree in electrical engineering. After graduation, he joined Public Service Electric and Gas Company of New Jersey as a cadet engineer. He subsequently moved steadily through a series of assignments and was named vice-president in charge of electric operations in 1965 and vice-president of combined electric and gas operations in 1968, a position he held until he became executive vice-president. After his retirement from the company in 1974 and until his death, Bob was an associate of Overseas Advisory Associates, Inc., of Detroit, Michigan, an energy management consulting firm.

Robert Baker was active in a number of professional organizations. His activities included being named a fellow of the Institute of Electrical and Electronics Engineers, the Instrument Society of America, and the American Society of Mechanical Engineers. He became a member of the National Academy of Engineering in 1967. Also in 1967, he was presented with the George Westinghouse Gold Medal by the American Society of Mechanical Engineers; in 1973 he was awarded an honorary doctoral degree in engineering by Lehigh University. He was the author of numerous engineering papers.

Bob Baker achieved an important and notable position in the field of steam power plant engineering, particularly in the areas of design and construction and in the operation of many units incorporating pioneering concepts. Examples of some of the innovations that were envisioned and designed under his leadership include the first power generation unit in the country to use steam at a temperature of 1,100°F, the first central station unit to employ austenitic steel piping, and major use for the first time of the Croloy 16-8-2 welding electrodes.

Joint studies with manufacturing engineers and utility staff, including Bob, resulted in the first use of what was to become a common arrangement in the industry: cross-compound, 3,600-rpm steam power generation elements, with high-pressure elements on one shaft, the reheat turbine on a second shaft, and identical low-pressure elements on each shaft driving identical half-size generators and boiler feed pumps. Bob also assisted in the development of large hydraulic couplings for boiler feed pump drives and was among the first to use main unit shaft-driven boiler feed pumps.

Other important pioneering areas of Bob Baker's work included his activities in automating steam plants and his contribution to the development and application of large gas turbines for electric peaking and emergency service. Under his guidance the largest such unit in the world was installed at Sewaren, New Jersey. The unit makes unique use of large aircraft jet engines as its power source and is capable of developing full power from a cold start in four minutes. In addition, Bob, together with other associates, had the vision and gave impetus to the work that led to the development of a large pumped storage project and to one of the largest mine-mouth generating stations in the world.

Robert Baker was an early leader in the introduction of nuclear energy for the production of electricity. He was also a leader in implementing the concept of constructing complete nuclear power plants in a factory and then floating the plants to their final locations.

He was particularly instrumental in his company's ordering of four such units, which in turn permitted the concept to be developed, a factory to be built, and a construction permit to be issued by the Nuclear Regulatory Commission. Unfortunately, a lack of projected load growth did not permit this project to proceed to completion. The concept was developed to a sufficient degree, however, that it may well prove to be a leading method of generating electricity at some time in the future.

Thomas Baron

THOMAS BARON

1921–1985

BY MONROE E. SPAGHT

THOMAS BARON, who retired in September 1981 as president of Shell Development Company, died in Houston, Texas, on May 20, 1985, at the age of sixty-four. He was born in Budapest, Hungary, on February 15, 1921, but came to America in 1939.

He attended De Paul University, after which he continued his education at the University of Illinois, obtaining a B.S. (1943) and a Ph.D. (1948) in chemical engineering. He also served in the U.S. Army from 1944 to 1946. After receiving his doctorate, Dr. Baron remained at the University of Illinois, first as an instructor in chemical engineering from 1948 to 1949 and then as an assistant professor in the same department until 1951.

In 1951 Dr. Baron joined Shell Development Company in Emeryville, California, as a chemical engineer. In 1955 he became assistant head of Shell's Chemical Engineering Department and was named head of that department in the next year. He held that position until 1961. After an assignment with the Shell Chemical Company at its synthetic rubber plant in Torrance, California, Baron moved to Houston, Texas, in 1965 as vice-president of Shell Development's Exploration and Production Research Division. In 1967 Thomas Baron became president of Shell Development Company, then an organization of nearly 2,000 people. He held that position with distinction until his retirement in 1981.

During his thirty-year career with Shell, Dr. Baron received several awards and distinctions that showed the high regard of the chemical engineering profession for his contributions and accomplishments. He received the Alan P. Colburn Award of the American Institute of Chemical Engineers in 1952 and the Institute's Professional Progress Award in 1961; in 1973 he was elected a fellow of the institute. He also received the American Academy of Achievement Award in 1962 and the University of Illinois College of Engineering Alumni Honor Award for Distinguished Service in Engineering in 1967. At various times, he served on advisory councils at Princeton and Stanford universities and was a consultant to the U.S. Army Chemical Corps from 1949 to 1951. In 1977 Thomas Baron was elected to the National Academy of Engineering.

The above paragraphs record the impersonal facts that describe the career of Dr. Thomas Baron. Yet, there is much more to be said about this outstanding man.

When Tom joined our organization, I was president of Shell Development Company with offices in Emeryville, California. It was my pleasure to see him through the following years and to witness firsthand much of his work. It was evident to all of us from the very beginning that he was a most outstanding engineer, indeed.

In his years at Emeryville, Dr. Baron made significant contributions to chemical engineering theory and practice in fluid dynamics—specifically, to the areas of organic chemical reactions relating to both the petroleum and chemical process industries, of combustion phenomena, and of multiphase separation processes. He successfully found solutions to complex problems in these areas by the use of applied mathematics. His publications, most notably those concerning the design of catalytic reactors and turbulent flame theory, are classic contributions to the literature.

Most significant in these later years, however, was his personal direction of, inspiration to, and leadership in broad fields of industrial research that he perceived were necessary for his company. These fields included such diverse areas as (1) extractive technologies (petroleum exploration and production; coal extraction, benefication, and upgrading; shale oil extraction; and tar sands technology); (2) basic chemical and engineering exploratory work; and (3) process research and development in the oil and chemical products sectors.

Thomas Baron was highly respected by his colleagues. Writing about him some years ago, one of his senior people expressed that respect in this way:

Dr. Baron is totally committed to scientific excellence, and insists on professional excellence among those who work for him. He uses his own manifold talent in scientific, intellectual, and artistic matters to excite the imagination and inspire the efforts of scientists under his leadership. His own scientific accomplishments in mathematics, physics, and chemical engineering stand as an example of the excellence which he inspires in others. His dedication to scientific excellence is based on his firm conviction that the welfare of his company, the industry, and the nation demand such excellence from all who work for them. His intense commitments are tempered by a sense of fair play, human understanding, and judgment which enable him to place the inevitable pressures into a proper perspective.

Thus, there has passed from the human scene another distinguished scientist. The world is better for his having been with us, and all of us who knew and worked with him will always carry happy and respectful thoughts of that association in our hearts.

Dr. Baron is survived by his wife, Marjorie; his mother, Mrs. Maria Baron; and two daughters.

Richard C. Bellman

RICHARD E. BELLMAN

1920–1984

BY SOLOMON W. GOLOMB

*O*n *Friday, May 11, 1984, "A Celebration of the Life and Accom-plishments of Professor Richard E. Bellman" was held on the Los Angeles campus of the University of Southern California. His col-leagues and friends from around the world gathered to share their memories of this remarkable man. Some of their comments were pub-lished by the university as "A Tribute to Richard Bellman." We can-not include them all in this volume, but the following excerpts pro-vide an indication of the extraordinary impact Dick Bellman had in his life and work.*

RICHARD BELLMAN was a towering figure among the contrib-utors to modern control theory and systems analysis. His in-vention of dynamic programming marked the beginning of a new era in the analysis and optimizations of large-scale sys-tems and opened a way for the application of sophisticated computer-oriented techniques in a wide variety of problem areas, ranging from the design of guidance systems for space vehicles to pest control, network routing, and speech recog-nition.

Richard Bellman was born in Brooklyn, New York, on Au-gust 26, 1920. He received a B.A. from Brooklyn College in 1941 and an M.A. in mathematics from the University of Wisconsin in 1943.

As part of his service in the U.S. Army, he spent two years

23

at Los Alamos, where he was a member of a group in the Theoretical Physics Division headed by Dr. R. Marshak. Leaving Los Alamos in 1946, he entered Princeton and completed his work toward a Ph.D. in a record time of three months.

In the immediate postwar years, Princeton was a center of defense-motivated research activity in nonlinear differential equations. As a graduate student at Princeton, Bellman became a member of an inner circle of young mathematicians led by Professor Solomon Lefschetz. His doctoral research under Lefschetz resulted in his first major work, entitled *Stability Theory of Differential Equations*, in 1946. This work was subsequently published as a book by McGraw-Hill in 1953 and is regarded as a classic in its field.

After staying on the faculty of the Mathematics Department at Princeton from 1946 to 1948, Bellman left the east coast to become a member of the faculty of Stanford University in 1948 and then joined the newly established Rand Corporation in Santa Monica, California, in 1953. At Rand, he became interested in the theory of multistage decision processes, which was then emerging as an important problem area in the control of both small- and large-scale systems. His invention of dynamic programming in 1953 was a major breakthrough in the theory of multistage decision processes. This breakthrough set the stage for the application of functional equation techniques in a wide spectrum of fields extending far beyond the problem areas that provided the initial motivation for his ideas.

In addition to his fundamental and far-ranging work on dynamic programming, Richard Bellman made a number of important contributions to both pure and applied mathematics. Particularly worthy of note is his work on invariant imbedding, which by replacing two-point boundary problems with initial value problems makes the calculation of the solution more direct as well as much more efficient. His work on quasi-linearization and its applications to system identification has led to many results of a practical nature in the study of nonlinear systems.

In recent years, Bellman's research activity focused increasingly on the application of mathematics to medicine and biological sciences. His interest in these and related areas reflected his strong conviction that mathematics should not be content with being a beautiful castle with no bridges to the real world. There was a time when Bellman's outspoken criticisms of the elitist attitudes of the mathematical establishment were greeted with hostility and derision. Today, when pure mathematicians are experiencing difficulties in finding suitable jobs, many of those who disagreed with Bellman will concede that he was right.

Bellman left the Rand Corporation in 1965 to join the faculty of the University of Southern California, where he held joint appointments as professor of mathematics, electrical engineering, and medicine—appointments he held until his death on March 19, 1984. A prolific writer, he authored over six hundred published research papers, approximately forty books, and several monographs.

Richard Bellman's fundamental contributions to science and engineering won him many honors and worldwide recognition. Prominent among these are the following: first Norbert Wiener Prize in Applied Mathematics, awarded in 1970 jointly by the American Mathematical Society and the Society for Industrial and Applied Mathematics; first Dickson Prize from Carnegie Mellon University in 1970; the John von Neumann Theory Award bestowed in 1976 jointly by the Institute of Management Sciences and the Operations Research Society of America; and the 1979 Institute of Electrical and Electronics Engineers' Medal of Honor in recognition of the invention of dynamic programming.

His honorary degrees include the doctor of science of the University of Aberdeen, Scotland, in 1973; the doctor of laws of the University of Southern California in 1974; and the doctor of mathematics of the University of Waterloo, Canada, in 1975. He was elected a fellow of the American Academy of Arts and Sciences in 1975, a member of the National Academy of Engineering in 1977, and a member of the National Academy of Sciences in 1983. [*R. E. Larson and L. A. Zadeh*]

In celebrating his life here today, let us also celebrate his good humor and his steadfast determination to produce, to achieve, to give, and to give joyfully, in the face of circumstances that would have overwhelmed and crushed men of lesser caliber. In these superb human qualities, as in his creative work, I firmly believe that Dick Bellman has lived on a level at least the equal of Beethoven. [*Roger Jelliffe*]

Of his great contributions, I think that he would feel that the students he inspired were among the most important; through them his ideas go on and will be expanded to meet the needs of expanding technology and human need. The only function that Richard Bellman could not bound was his own energy and imagination. [*Fleur Mitchell*]

The measure of a man is the number of people whose lives he has influenced and the contributions he has made. Dick Bellman not only influenced the lives of many people, but he had the rare genius to be able to contribute to many fields. [*Alan Rowe*]

Someone said that the Soviet Union is not just another country—it's another world, another planet. And it, indeed, is. But the stars, we might say, continuing the metaphor, are the same on every planet. They shine for everyone and everywhere. Dick was, and is, such a star. His influence in the Soviet Union is deep and profound. His works penetrated many areas of Soviet academia, industry, and economy in general. From the academic point of view, there is not a single university that does not offer courses based on Dick's works. Hundreds of papers continuing Dick's ideas are published annually in Soviet journals. It is hardly possible to find a researcher in the quantitative sciences and engineering unfamiliar with, at least, the term "Dynamic Programming."

Dick's name is probably cited more at Soviet scientific meetings than at American ones. As an indirect proof of this, let me just mention that Dick was invited to be the main speaker at the first, and only, International Congress of Mathematicians held in Russia, in 1966. More than ten of his books have been translated and published in the Soviet Union. No other American scientist has been given such honors in the USSR.

This is one of the trademarks of Dick's creative work: Truly a mathematician of the twentieth century, he viewed a computer as a tool as well as an important source of mathematical work. His results are always practical and easily applicable. Probably, this is why his mathematical discoveries have important engineering implications in such areas as system science, control, communications, bioengineering, etc. The depth and importance of problems considered, the practical applicability, and the timeliness of his works, this is what, in my view, made the largest impact and defined Dick's influence on Soviet science.

Dick gave all of us, his students and friends in every country throughout the world, an ultimate example of scientific creativity and success, personal courage and strength, friendly devotion and support. [*Semyon Meerkov*]

He was contemptuous of the established order and intolerant of mediocrity. He was strikingly handsome, brilliant, and a master of both the spoken and the written word. Clearly, he was a man of towering intellect and almost equally towering ego. But what I could see was that behind the facade of arrogance and bravado was a man who was capable of great kindness, a man who was decent, straightforward and generous in the extreme.

He died at peace with himself. But his ideas will continue to live, and so will the fond memories of all of us who knew him not only as a brilliant thinker and arrogant personality, but, more importantly, as a man of great nobility of character and a warm, thoughtful, caring human being. [*Lofti Zadeh*]

At the time of his death at age sixty-three, Richard Bell-man had just completed his autobiography, *The Eye of the Hurricane*, World Scientific Publications, Singapore, 1984. He is survived by his wife, Nina; his son, Eric; and his daughter, Kirstie.

MAURICE ANTHONY BIOT

1905–1985

BY RAYMOND D. MINDLIN

MAURICE ANTHONY BIOT died on September 12, 1985, while he and his wife Nady were reading at home in Brussels, Belgium. By the time of his death, he had built a distinguished career of research, teaching, and consulting that spanned a broad range of science and technology centered in classical mechanics. His work extended from the most highly theoretical and mathematical problems through experimental studies to practical applications and patented inventions. He was active in his field until the day of his death.

My old friend Tony Biot was born in Antwerp, Belgium, on May 25, 1905. His early college training was at the University of Louvain in Belgium, from which he received a bachelor's degree in Thomistic philosophy in 1927. Then, in rapid succession (at only one-year intervals), he collected mining and electrical engineering degrees and a doctorate in the sciences—with enough time to spare to complete the curriculum at the Louvain Institute of Economic Sciences.

Within another year, after emigrating to the United States, he earned a doctorate in aeronautical sciences from the California Institute of Technology. It was also at Caltech that he began his long, fruitful association with Theodore von Karman.

After leaving Caltech, Biot held teaching positions at Harvard University's Graduate School of Engineering (1934–

1935), the University of Louvain (1936–1937), Columbia University (1937–1946, interrupted by his two-year enlistment in the U.S. Navy beginning in 1940), and Brown University (1946–1952). Subsequently, he became a consultant, working mainly with the Cornell Aeronautical Laboratory, Shell Development Company, and the Mobil Research and Development Company.

I first met Tony Biot more than fifty years ago during a summer session at the University of Michigan, where he had stopped on his way from Caltech to Harvard. In those days, young engineering teachers of his age from all over the United States converged on the Ann Arbor campus each summer, where they were taught the theory and applications of solid mechanics by Stephen Timoshenko and, occasionally, by H. M. Westergaard and R. V. Southwell. In the fall, these young men (there were no women in attendance at that time) went back home to spread the solid mechanics "gospel"—new to this country—among their own students. Tony Biot was well beyond this stage, however; by 1934, he had already published some two dozen research papers in this area.

In the 1930s, while most of us were concerned about simple steady-state vibrations, Tony had already published some of his pioneering works on the response of structures to transient disturbances. While we were struggling with the elements of the theory of elasticity, he had already begun to publish his nonlinear, second-order theory accounting for the effects of initial stress and large rotation. When we were first being introduced to the mysteries of photoelasticity, he was already an old hand, having published papers on experimental techniques and applications to thermal and shrinkage stresses by means of mathematical analogies.

In addition, Tony's first few papers on soil mechanics (involving foundation pressures and consolidation) had appeared by this time, as had his works on fluid flows and electromagnetic wave propagation. By 1935 he had been awarded a number of patents ranging from a steering linkage for automobiles to the now well-known scheme of aircraft navigation based on the establishment of fixed-interference patterns of radio waves.

From the early 1930s until the time of his death, Biot continued to make notable advances in the fields he had entered at the beginning of his career. His early interest in fluids and aeronautics led to his later work in transonic and supersonic aerodynamics, the three-dimensional theory of airfoil flutter, and the introduction of matrix methods and generalized coordinates in aeroelasticity. He applied his ideas of mechanical transients to the design of earthquake-resistant buildings, to aircraft landing gear, and to the sound emitted from stringed musical instruments.

His initial papers on soil consolidation blossomed into his general mathematical theory of porous media with applications to geophysical prospecting and well logging. His ingenious solutions of problems involving the reflection of electromagnetic and acoustic waves from rough surfaces are outgrowths of his early interest in radio waves.

Tony Biot's initial work on thermal stresses developed into a major advance in irreversible thermodynamics. His conceptions of generalized free energy and entropy displacement vectors made it possible to establish variational principles on which he based his new methods for the solution of problems in heat conduction, diffusion, thermoelasticity, thermoviscoelasticity, and chemical reactions. He published an extensive review of this work in *Advances in Applied Mechanics*, (vol. 24, pp. 1–91 [New York: Academic Press, 1984]). In addition, his longtime interest in the nonlinear effects of initial stress and the inelastic behavior of solids culminated in his mathematical theory of the folding of stratified rock, complete with its amazingly detailed physical verification, both in the laboratory and on the geological time scale.

Tony Biot's accomplishments did not go unrecognized. He was awarded the Timoshenko Medal of the American Society of Mechanical Engineers in 1962 and the Theodore von Karman Medal of the American Society of Civil Engineers in 1967. He was elected to the Royal Academy of Sciences of

Belgium in 1966 and to the U.S. National Academy of Engineering in 1967. In 1983 he became the seventh recipient of the Acoustical Society of America's honorary fellowship. In celebration of his seventy-fifth birthday, the Indian Institute of Technology dedicated the fourteenth volume of its *Journal of Mathematical and Physical Sciences* to him, listing his reports, patents, and research publications as well as his three books: *Mathematical Methods of Engineering*, coauthored by Theodore von Karman (New York: McGraw-Hill, 1940); *Mechanics of Incremental Deformation* (New York: John Wiley & Sons, 1965); and *Variational Principles in Heat Transfer* (New York: Oxford University Press, 1970).

Biot possessed a strong consciousness of the physical world that surrounded him. His keen insight enabled him to recognize the essential features of a physical phenomenon and to build them into a mathematical model without blindly including nonessentials. In addition, he had at his fingertips the tools of mathematical analysis and analytical methods of approximation, which he used skillfully to extract from the model predictions of the hitherto unpredictable.

The philosophy underlying Tony Biot's work and success is revealed in his acceptance speech on the occasion of the award of the Timoshenko Medal. This speech is published in *Applied Mechanics Reviews*, (vol. 16, no. 2, February 1963, pp. 89–90):

Let us hope for a revival of humanism and a spirit of synthesis in science. Let us also put new emphasis on engineering as a professional craft, requiring high skill, natural talent, deserving social recognition, and distinctly different from the scientific professions as such. New stirrings are appearing in this direction. I am inclined to believe that engineers and engineering schools will play an important part in restoring the unity and central viewpoint in the natural sciences. This is because modern engineering by its very nature must be synthetic.

R.L. Besplinghoff

RAYMOND L. BISPLINGHOFF

1917–1985

BY H. GUYFORD STEVER

RAYMOND L. BISPLINGHOFF, an internationally distinguished aeronautical engineer, who was renowned for his teaching, research, engineering writing, and institutional leadership in universities, government, and industry, died on March 5, 1985, of cancer. Before his death, the last of his many distinguished posts was director and senior vice-president of research for Tyco Laboratories. Raymond Bisplinghoff's personal integrity, his professional competence, energy, and thoroughness, and his sense of the important were qualities on which he built his life. He also imbued many students, colleagues, family, and friends with these same qualities.

Highlights from his numerous and varied accomplishments would certainly include Raymond's research, professional papers, and textbooks, which were and are preeminent in the fields of aeroelasticity, structures, and structural dynamics; his academic administrative work at the Massachusetts Institute of Technology (MIT) and the University of Missouri at Rolla; his career-long contribution to the U.S. military services, first as an officer in World War II and later as an adviser and leader of research programs; and his executive service at the National Aeronautics and Space Administration (NASA) in the 1960s and the National Science Foundation (NSF) in the 1970s.

The son of a flour mill proprietor, Raymond Bisplinghoff

was born on February 7, 1917, in Hamilton, Ohio, where he lived with his parents through his high school years. His stay at the University of Cincinnati, where he spent seven years earning an aeronautical engineering degree and a master's degree in physics and serving as a graduate research fellow in X-ray defraction, resulted in the beginning of a practical engineer's life for Bisplinghoff. For it was during this period that he also worked in a student cooperative program for two and one-half years at Aeronca Aircraft Corporation investigating the stress analysis, design, aerodynamics, and flight testing of aircraft.

The onset of World War II interrupted Bisplinghoff's pursuit of a Ph.D. in physics at the University of Cincinnati. He served a short stint at the U.S. Army Air Corps' Wright Field working on aircraft flutter and engine vibration. This assignment was followed by three years of service as a naval officer assigned to the Bureau of Aeronautics in Washington, D.C.

Raymond Bisplinghoff's aeronautical engineering experience was rapidly broadened during these three years with the navy. He is remembered even today by the old-timers in the aircraft industry who went to him often to exchange views on problems of aircraft structures, loads, and dynamics. During this same period of wartime service, Ray married Ruth Doherty of Cincinnati. They later had two sons, Ross and Ron.

Because teaching was one of his favorite activities, he was delighted when, following World War II, MIT gave him an appointment as an assistant professor in aeronautical engineering. He repaid this honor with sixteen years of distinguished service: two years as an assistant professor, four as an associate professor, and ten as a full professor. Ray's real contribution during his MIT stay, however, was the renewed life and vitality given to the subject of aeronautical engineering through his leadership in teaching, research, and writing and departmental management. It was also in this period that Bisplinghoff was principal coauthor (with his four students—later professors and colleagues—Holt Ashley, Robert

L. Halfman, James W. Mar, and Theodore H. H. Pian) of three exceptional textbooks: *Aeroelasticity* (Reading, Mass.: Addison-Wesley, 1955); *Principles of Aeroelasticity* (New York: John Wiley & Sons, 1961); and *Statics of Deformable Solids* (Reading, Mass.: Addison-Wesley, 1965).

While at MIT, Bisplinghoff also showed that he did not like unfinished tasks. He took a leave of absence to finish his doctoral studies and received his Ph.D. from the Swiss Federal Institute of Technology in 1957.

Bisplinghoff authored and coauthored many research papers and established himself as a preeminent expert in the fields of aircraft structures and structural dynamics. Flutter and dynamic response, especially those resulting from the gust loading of aircraft wings, were intriguing subjects during the 1950s. Bisplinghoff contributed substantially to the solution of these and other vexing problems faced by aircraft designers. During this period, he was a frequent consultant to the aircraft industry.

Certainly one of Bisplinghoff's greatest gifts to the field of aeronautics and later to the aerospace profession was his role in the education of numerous students who went on to leadership posts in industry, government, and other universities. Ray was more than their teacher, and they went on to be more than his students, becoming colleagues, lifelong friends, and, not surprisingly, his great admirers. He helped some of them in their business connections and one in particular, Lawrence Levy, with the foundation of Allied Research Associates. With one of his colleagues, H. Guyford Stever, Bisplinghoff conducted an extensive three-year research program on the effects of nuclear blasts on flying aircraft; their studies included participation in the Eniwetok Atoll bomb tests in 1951 and 1952.

In 1962 Ray Bisplinghoff broadened his engineering interests and increased his administrative responsibilities by taking a leave of absence from MIT for four years to serve as an assistant administrator of NASA. While at NASA, he led the agency's program in advanced research and technology and held a post that was key to the progress of aerospace engineering. Later, Ray became a special assistant to NASA administrator James Webb. Although he enjoyed these four years and contributed mightily to NASA's achievements, the attraction of MIT continued, and he returned to succeed Charles Stark Draper as head of the Department of Aeronautics and Astronautics.

In these early stages of the U.S. space program, MIT's "Course Sixteen" (aeronautical engineering department) was a busy place, particularly for guidance and control, a field that played an important role in developing the equipment for the Apollo moon landing project. Bisplinghoff's close ties to NASA made his leadership of the department very effective. He was personally involved in the planning efforts for many of the Apollo missions (nos. 8, 9, 10, 11, and 12). His contributions thus spanned the period that saw flights circling the moon to those that successfully landed on it. Bisplinghoff's last two years at MIT, from 1968 to 1970, were spent as dean of the School of Engineering. He subsequently left again for government service in Washington.

As deputy director of NSF from 1970 to 1974, Ray Bisplinghoff made outstanding contributions to the foundation's programs. At that time, NSF was under pressure from both the White House and Congress to strengthen its contribution to applied science and engineering. The agency was then and still is principally a sponsor of basic scientific research, but in the late 1960s and early 1970s some government leaders were beginning to recognize the early signs of a loss in the competitive strength of U.S. industries vis-à-vis their foreign counterparts. In these confusing times, NSF was asked to strengthen engineering research and its application of newly emerging science to useful technologies.

As deputy director of NSF, Ray served with director William McElroy and later with Ray's former MIT colleague Guy Stever. In this position, he took the lead in strengthening the NSF Division of Engineering (now the Directorate for Engineering) and in establishing the RANN (Research Applied to

National Needs) program. Many of the most effective of our current governmental programs to increase U.S. international competitiveness, such as the cooperative industry-academic research centers, grew out of the ideas and experiments of those days.

Another major package of applied research begun at that time was the solar and renewable energy program. NSF carried the program for several years, expanding its budget from $1 million to $50 million annually. It was later transferred to the Energy Research and Development Agency (now the Department of Energy).

In 1974 Bisplinghoff was again attracted to a top academic administrative post, the chancellorship of the University of Missouri, Rolla campus. Then, in 1977 Bisplinghoff became director and vice-president for research at Tyco Laboratories. In this position, he directed the varied research and development efforts of the laboratories, one of which was a large program in solar energy materials, an outgrowth of the work he had led at NSF. While working at Tyco, he still found time to teach a winter course in aeroelasticity at the University of Florida. Bisplinghoff retired from this post the year he died.

As he traveled along the fruitful path of his half century in engineering, Ray undertook myriad part-time jobs. One of the most significant was as chairman of the Scientific Advisory Board of the U.S. Air Force from 1979 to 1982. Yet that position was only representative of many such tasks for numerous government departments and universities.

Everywhere he served, he was richly honored. He received the Exceptional Civilian Service Medal from the U.S. Air Force, the Distinguished Service Award from NSF, the Extraordinary Service Medal from the Federal Aviation Administration, the Distinguished Service Medal from NASA, and an honorary doctorate from the University of Cincinnati. He also received numerous medals and awards for his professional engineering work, including the Godfrey L. Cabot and the Sylvanus Reed awards.

He was frequently invited to prepare distinguished addresses, including the Wright Brothers Lecture and the Theodore von Karman Lecture. In addition to membership in the National Academy of Engineering since 1965, Bisplinghoff was elected to the National Academy of Sciences and the American Academy of Arts and Sciences. He was also an honorary fellow of the Royal Aeronautical Society.

Most of all, Ray will be remembered by his many friends and colleagues for his thorough, professional engineering approach to his many jobs, a practice in which he had no superior.

Hans H. Bleich

HANS HEINRICH BLEICH

1909–1985

BY MARIO G. SALVADORI

Hans heinrich bleich died of a heart attack on February 8, 1985, at the age of seventy-five. He was born in Vienna on March 24, 1909. He studied at Vienna's Technical University, from which he obtained a civil engineering degree in 1931 and a doctor of science degree in engineering in 1934. Following his graduation, he worked in Vienna as a design engineer for A. Poor Engineers until 1939, when he moved to London and became senior design engineer for the prominent engineering firm of Braithwaite and Company. Unfortunately, there are no records in the United States of his work while in Europe.

In 1945 Dr. Bleich moved to the United States. He worked briefly as a research engineer for Chance-Vaught Aircraft in Stratford, Connecticut. He then became an associate engineer at Hardesty and Hanover, a well-known firm of bridge engineers in New York City. During his tenure with the firm, he was involved in the design of a number of important bridges and special structures.

From 1957 to the day of his death, Dr. Bleich was permanently affiliated as a consultant with Weidlinger Associates, Consulting Engineers of New York City. He participated in the design of some of the most important and innovative buildings in the United States—from high-rise office buildings to exhibition halls and special structures.

In 1967 Dr. Bleich served as a consultant to the Mount Wilson Observatory and was responsible for the support design of the observatory's new two-hundred-inch astronomical mirror at Mount Palomar. In 1967–1968, as a consultant to Parsons Brinckerhoff Quade and Douglas, Inc., he participated in the design of the Fremont Bridge in Portland, Oregon. In 1969, as a consultant to the firm of King and Gavaris, he helped design the Raritan Bridge in New Jersey.

In 1947 Dr. Bleich joined the faculty of Columbia University's School of Engineering as a lecturer and was named professor of civil engineering in 1952 and director of the Guggenheim Institute of Air Flight Structures in 1954. He retired from Columbia University in 1975 as James Renwick Professor Emeritus of Civil Engineering.

Dr. Bleich was a member of the American Society of Civil Engineers (ASCE), the American Institute of Astronautics and Aeronautics, and the American Society of Mechanical Engineers. He was also associate editor of the American Rocket Society of the American Institute of Astronautics and Aeronautics and a member of the Hull Structures Committee of the Society of Naval Architects.

Dr. Bleich was honored as a fellow of the American Society of Mechanical Engineers and as an associate fellow of the American Institute of Astronautics and Aeronautics. He also received the ASCE Laurie Prize in 1951, the ASCE J. James R. Croes Medal in 1963, the ASCE Wellington Prize in 1969, and the coveted von Karman Medal of the ASCE Applied Mechanics Section in 1973.

At the early age of fifteen, he contributed a chapter to the pioneering book on finite difference equations written by his father, Friedrich Bleich, and Ernst Melan, two world-renowned structuralists. In 1935 he wrote a book on the analysis of suspension bridges entitled *Die Berechnung verankerter Hangerbrucken*, published by J. Springer in Vienna. In 1952 he edited and completely revised his father's book *The*

Buckling Strength of Metal Structures, which is still the standard reference book on the subject.

In 1952 Bleich coauthored the ASCE manual "Design of Cylindrical Shell Roofs" and in 1960, the "Guide for the Analysis of Ship Structures," published by the U.S. Department of Commerce, Office of Technological Services. In 1968 he was a contributor to "Support and Testing of Astronomical Mirrors," published by Kitt Peak National Observatory in Arizona.

Between 1928 and 1975 Dr. Bleich published eighty-six papers and reports of the greatest importance on problems of applied mechanics. A sampling of their titles indicates the breadth of his interests: "Bending, Torsion and Buckling of Bar Composed of Thin Walls"; "The Strain Energy Expressed for Thin Cylindrical Shells"; "Response of Elasto-Plastic Structures to Transient Loads"; "Surface Waves in an Elastic Half-Space"; "Moving Step Load on the Surface on a Half Space of Granular Material"; and "Use of Nonassociated Flow Rule for Problems of Elasto-Plastic Wave Propagation." His technical reports dealt with the gamut of those applied mechanics problems that are of practical significance in the field of dynamics and, particularly, in the interactions between fluids and elastic and plastic bodies. Of special note is that in 1932 he was the first scientist to use shakedown theory.

It is hard to describe the modesty, simplicity, and courteousness of this outstanding individual. His students, to whom he dedicated unlimited time and attention, today occupy chairs in structural engineering and applied mechanics in most of the outstanding universities of our country. He was always ready to help with suggestions and to advise both his academic colleagues and his coworkers in the many engineering offices where he was a consultant. He was one of the very few outstanding research men who was also interested in and knowledgeable about the practical application of the theories he helped to develop. In short, he was a great engineer. Dr. Bleich's contributions to the work of many agencies of the U.S. government have been of the greatest importance and have been duly recognized.

His death represents a loss to the academy of one of its most valuable, widely knowledgeable, and generous members.

Hendrik W. Bode

HENDRIK WADE BODE

1905–1982

BY HARVEY BROOKS

Hendrik wade bode was widely known as one of the most articulate, thoughtful exponents of the philosophy and practice of systems engineering—the science and art of integrating technical components into a coherent system that is optimally adapted to its social function. After a career of more than forty years with Bell Telephone Laboratories, which he joined shortly after its founding in 1926, Dr. Bode retired in 1967 to become Gordon McKay Professor of Systems Engineering (on a half-time basis) in what was then the Division of Engineering and Applied Physics at Harvard. He became professor emeritus in July 1974.

He died at his home in Cambridge on June 21, 1982, at the age of seventy-six. He is survived by his wife, Barbara Poore Bode, whom he married in 1933, and by two daughters, Dr. Katharine Bode Darlington of Philadelphia and Mrs. Anne Hathaway Bode Aarnes of Washington, D.C.

Hendrik Bode was born in Madison, Wisconsin, on December 24, 1905. After attending grade school in Tempe, Arizona, and high school in Urbana, Illinois, he went on to Ohio State University, from which he received his B.A. in 1924 and his M.A. in 1926, both in mathematics. He joined Bell Labs in 1926 to work on electrical network theory and the design of electric filters. While at Bell, he also pursued graduate studies at Columbia University, receiving his Ph.D. in physics in 1935.

In 1929 he transferred to Bell's mathematical research group, which was headed by T. C. Fry and specialized in network theory and its application to long-distance communications. His extensive research in this field led eventually to the publication in 1945 of his classic book, *Network Analysis and Feedback Amplifier Design*.

During World War II, Bode participated in the development of electrical fire control devices, receiving the Presidential Certificate of Merit in 1948 for his contributions. After the war, he continued his work on military system development, which included artillery fire control and tracking systems for antiaircraft missiles and later for antiballistic missile systems. He also specialized in command-and-control communications systems.

In 1944 Bode was placed in charge of the mathematical research group; in 1952 he became director of mathematical research for Bell Labs. In 1955 he was named director of physical sciences research (including mathematics). In 1958 he became one of two vice-presidents of Bell Labs and had responsibility for military systems projects. During his career at Bell, he was granted twenty-five patents for innovations in the areas of transmission networks, transformer systems, electrical wave amplification, broadband amplifiers, and artillery computing.

Bode always felt a strong sense of unity in his career development and saw common genealogy in the technologies he worked on: from long-distance communications systems through artillery fire control to tracking systems for surface-to-air missiles. Bode's view was that a tracking system produced information, "and that's a message, and communication theory is concerned with messages and getting the correct message out of something garbled, . . . so much of the basic technology of telephone communications did turn out to be applicable, in this sense, to the problems of fire control."

During Hendrik Bode's Harvard tenure, beginning in 1967, he taught courses in communications systems and a general education course on the management and philosophy of the development of complex technologies. He synthesized the lessons he had learned from his long working life in a book published by Bell Labs in 1971 entitled: *Synergy: Technical Integration and Technological Innovation in the Bell System.* The book is an excellent exposition, in layman's terms, of the philosophy of systems engineering as it was developed, practiced, and perfected in the Bell system prior to divestiture and deregulation. Yet in retrospect, this lucidly written book exhibits not only the enormous strengths but also some of the weaknesses and vulnerabilities of this system of innovation.

Bode received many honors during his career. In 1969 he was awarded the prestigious Edison Medal of the Institute of Electrical and Electronics Engineers "for fundamental conbutions to the arts of communication, computation and control and for guidance and creative counsel in systems engineering." In addition, in 1979 he was the first recipient of the Control Heritage Award from the American Automatic Control Council.

He received the Rufus Oldenberger Award of the American Society of Mechanical Engineers in 1975. He was elected to the National Academy of Sciences in 1957 and was a charter member of the National Academy of Engineering, which was founded in December 1964. He was a fellow of the American Academy of Arts and Sciences, the Institute of Electrical and Electronics Engineers, and the American Physical Society, and he was a member of the American Mathematical Society and the Society of Industrial and Applied Mathematics.

Hendrik Bode served the National Academy of Sciences and the National Academy of Engineering in many ways during his career. From 1967 to 1971 he was a member of the Council of the National Academy of Sciences; in addition, he was the representative of the Academy's Engineering Section on the original Committee on Science and Public Policy (COSPUP), which was established under the chairmanship of George Kistiakowsky in 1965. He was also an active contributor to three widely known COSPUP studies: *Basic Research and National Goals* (1965), *Applied Science and Technological Progress* (1967), and *Technology: Processes of Assessment and Choice* (1969). These reports were the first to be prepared directly by the academy for the legislative branch—specifically, the Committee on Science and Astronautics of the U.S. House of Representatives.

Bode was a modest, private person; yet he was in great demand as a member of important government and private advisory committees. His advice was much sought after, not only on technical matters but also regarding questions of organization, management strategy, and even ethics. He was a lucid writer and expositor and was noted for his broad humanistic approach to engineering and technology.

A colleague has remarked that "he will sit for hours through a long meeting of complex discussion and heated argument without saying a word and then, in the end, in two sentences, will bring the whole argument and the whole meeting to a focus." Although an accomplished mathematician, he never used more mathematics than were necessary to make his point in an explanation, and he was able to translate complex mathematical results into simple physical pictures and analogies.

With the death of Hendrik Bode, the country and the university community lost one of the great engineering philosophers of his time.

Donald B. Broughton

DONALD B. BROUGHTON

1917–1984

BY C. G. GERHOLD
SUBMITTED BY VLADIMIR HAENSEL

THE AMAZINGLY RAPID technical progress that has characterized the last half century is the result of many separate contributions, each of which has been essential to the overall, evolving technological pattern. Donald B. Broughton, who contributed significantly to this progress, died on December 2, 1984, after a short illness. Dr. Broughton made his most important contributions while working for Universal Oil Products, Inc. (UOP) (now a division of Signal), in the capacities of chemical engineer, senior development coordinator, manager of separation process development, and senior research and development associate, and more recently in the capacity of a consultant.

The particular areas in which Broughton did his most outstanding work are the creation and development of novel separation processes. Separation technology, although little understood or appreciated by the lay public, is vital to providing the high-purity individual components that are the necessary starting materials for producing many of the goods on which our high-technology life-styles depend. These high-purity components are normally found as complex mixtures, either naturally or in synthetic products. The separation process, therefore, is essential to make them useful intermediates for the manufacture of end products.

Dr. Broughton was born in Rugby, England, on April 20,

1917. He and his family lived in Rugby and in the neighboring town of Bolton until he was seven. They came to the United States soon after, settling in Altoona, Pennsylvania, where Broughton received most of his primary school education. Later, the family moved to Philadelphia where he attended high school. In Philadelphia his scholastic attainments earned him a chemical engineering scholarship to Pennsylvania State University.

By living frugally on his $900-a-year scholarship grant and saving his earnings from summer employment, Broughton was able to finance a year of study at the Massachusetts Institute of Technology (MIT). He received his master's degree in chemical engineering from MIT in 1940. He then spent a year working as an assistant industrial chemical engineer at Rohm and Haas but decided to return to MIT, from which he received his D.Sc. in 1943.

He remained at MIT in various teaching and research positions (with the exception of a brief period of wartime service for the Navy in Washington, D.C.) until 1949. In that year, after deciding that a period of industrial work experience would enhance his expertise as a professor, Broughton accepted a temporary position with UOP, which at that time was seeking help in organizing and updating its design methods.

In 1951 UOP found itself badly in need of a process to separate and recover high-purity benzene from the products of its newly introduced platforming process. Broughton was asked to participate in this development. The assignment proved ideal for both the company and Broughton, and after the successful creation of the Udex process, he was persuaded to continue working with UOP on the development of a variety of other separation processes. Apparently, plans to return to academic life became less attractive when compared with the challenging opportunities UOP afforded to create novel solutions for industry's many pressing, unsolved problems in the recovery of pure, individual components from mixtures.

One source of Broughton's satisfaction was undoubtedly the unique nature of UOP's business—specifically the development and licensing of new processes, particularly in the petroleum refining and industrial petrochemical fields. An organization of this type also provided daily contact with a stimulating staff that included many talented and experienced engineers and scientists together with a corporate attitude that encouraged both scientific soundness and innovative approaches. UOP also assured its staff of the wide use of successful technical accomplishments.

In developing new separation techniques, Broughton relied principally on the use of mathematical models that allowed him to apply final designs to a wide variety of applications with a high degree of confidence. He was able to create these models from a minimum of data by applying established methods of physical chemistry and thermodynamics. With their help, Broughton was able to determine optimum flow arrangements and the choice of operating parameters, as well as to identify those areas requiring additional or more precise data. Pilot plant testing was usually a final step to verify and correct the parameters in his models and to uncover any unforeseen problems.

The validity of Broughton's approach is best demonstrated by the large number and variety of separation units in operation today that are based on the designs resulting from this procedure. One of these is the Parex process, introduced in 1971, for the recovery of high-purity para-xylene from petroleum products. The process is widely used throughout the world and annually produces billions of pounds of para-xylene, which is the basic intermediate for polyester fibers. Other processes in which Broughton played a vital development role are similarly successful.

Although his methodology called for a great amount of individual effort, Donald Broughton was in no sense a loner. He thoroughly enjoyed the exchange of ideas and was always willing to listen to new suggestions. His acceptance or rejection of an idea—whether his or that of someone else—depended not on the source of the suggestion, but on whether, in his judgment, it was logical.

Broughton's pioneering accomplishments in the separations field resulted in fifty sole or joint U.S. patents and at least thirty technical articles. In 1967 he received the Alpha Chi Sigma Award for Chemical Engineering Research, sponsored by the American Institute of Chemical Engineers. He was elected a fellow of the institute in 1973. In addition to these honors, he was elected to the National Academy of Engineering in 1976 and in April 1984 received the first American Chemical Society Award in Separations Science and Technology.

No less impressive than his technical accomplishments and recognition were his personal characteristics. A well-liked, dignified, and honorable man, Donald was always available to share his knowledge, experience, and ideas with others. A natural teacher, he had the unique ability to present complex concepts in a form that could be easily understood.

Broughton became a U.S. citizen in 1936 and married in 1943; his wife Natalie survives him. He had a number of interests outside of his professional and technical activities, including classical music, chess, reading, and travel.

Donald Broughton will be greatly missed by his colleagues and other friends. He will be remembered as long as the people whom he influenced by his teaching and example survive and as long as the results of his pioneering developments continue to be employed and enjoyed.

Adolf Busemann

ADOLF BUSEMANN

1901–1986

BY ROBERT T. JONES

ADOLF BUSEMANN, an eminent scientist and world leader in supersonic aerodynamics who was elected to the National Academy of Engineering in 1970, died in Boulder, Colorado, on November 3, 1986, at the age of eighty-five. At the time of his death, Dr. Busemann was a retired professor of aeronautics and space science at the University of Colorado in Boulder.

Busemann belonged to the famous German school of aerodynamicists led by Ludwig Prandtl, a group that included Theodore von Karman, Max M. Munk, and Jakob Ackeret. Busemann was the first, however, to propose the use of swept wings to overcome the problems of transonic and supersonic flight and the first to propose a drag-free system of wings subsequently known as the Busemann Biplane. His "Schock Polar," a construction he described as a "baby hedgehog," has simplified the calculations of aerodynamicists for decades.

Adolf Busemann was born in Luebeck, Germany, on April 20, 1901. He attended the Carolo Wilhelmina Technical University in Braunschweig and received his Ph.D. in engineering there in 1924. In 1930 he was accorded the status of professor (Venia Legendi) at Georgia Augusta University in Goettingen. In 1925 the Max-Planck Institute appointed him to the position of aeronautical research scientist. He subsequently held several positions in the German scientific community, and during the war years, directed research at the Braunschweig Laboratory.

In the late 1920s Italy was producing the fastest airplanes in the world and had won the famous Schneider Trophy in competition with American racers. To further development in this arena, the Italian government, under Mussolini, decided to hold an international meeting on the problems of high-speed aeronautics—the 1935 Volta Congress. The American delegation, which included Eastman N. Jacobs of the National Advisory Council on Aeronautics's Langley Laboratory and Theodore von Karman, traveled to the meeting on the luxurious *Conte de Savoia*, courtesy of the Italian government.

At this early period, the maximum speed that had been achieved, even by the Schneider Cup racers, was less than 300 miles per hour, and the idea of flying at supersonic speeds was far from the consciousness of the aeronautical community. Yet it was at this meeting that Busemann presented his first theory of the effect of sweep in reducing the drag of a wing at supersonic speed.

In his Volta Congress paper, Busemann used the so-called independence principle, which states that the air forces and pressures on a sufficiently long and narrow wing panel are independent of that component of the flight velocity in the direction of the long axis. The air forces, then, depend only on the reduced component perpendicular to the long axis. The independence principle had been used previously by Munk in a discussion of the effect of sweep on lateral stability, but no one had thought of using it to reduce the effective Mach number of the wing.

Busemann's 1935 theory was incomplete in the sense that only wings having supersonic sweep were considered; the component velocity perpendicular to the edge, although reduced, remained supersonic. In this configuration a wave drag would still exist, although the force would be directed partly inward by the inclination of the wing panels. Later, during the war, Busemann extended his theory to include subsonic sweep, placing the wing panels inside the Mach cone and thereby reducing the effective component velocity to a subsonic value. In this configuration the wave drag would disappear completely in the limiting case.

During the war years, communication with German scientists was lost, and my own somewhat belated discovery of the sweep effect, which emphasized subsonic sweep, was not immediately accepted by American aerodynamicists, including those who had attended the Volta Congress. Consequently, the first American supersonic airplane, the X–1, had no sweep. However, the National Advisory Council on Aeronautics decided to test the idea, and Robert Gilruth was able to show experimentally that the drag of a wing having forty-five degrees of sweep can be as little as one tenth that of a straight wing at Mach one.

At the end of the war, a group of American scientists traveled to Germany to learn what progress had been made in aerodynamics during the preceding years. The group included von Karman, H. S. Tsien, H. L. Dryden, and George Schairer of the Boeing Company. Schairer relates that the validity of my proposal was a principal topic of discussion during the twenty-six-hour flight to Europe.

On arrival, the group found that much research had been done on the sweep effect. When the group finally met with Busemann, von Karman asked, "What is this about wing sweep?" According to Schairer, Busemann's face lit up and he said, "Oh, you remember, I read a paper on it at the Volta Congress in 1935." Busemann went on to remind them that at a dinner following the meeting, Luigi Crocco, the prominent Italian aerodynamicist, had sketched an airplane having swept wings "and a swept propeller," labeling it "the airplane of the future."

Schairer recalls that five of the 1935 dinner guests were present at the 1945 interview, and all remembered the incident, although they had completely forgotten about the wing sweep concept during the ten-year interval. How could this have happened? Clearly, Busemann's thinking was ahead of its time. Perhaps also, as a true scientist, he had emphasized too much the limitations of his theory.

In his biplane concept, Busemann disclosed an arrangement of airfoils in which the wave system would be completely trapped between the two wings of a biplane, resulting in zero wave drag but also, unfortunately, zero lift. In principle, one could form a lifting system with no wave drag by flying the upper wing of the biplane in close proximity to a flat reflecting surface. In one experiment at the National Aeronautics and Space Administration's Ames Research Center, we enclosed the streamlines of a Busemann biplane within a tube bounded by a circular cylinder and demonstrated the absence of wave drag.

Among the most interesting and important of Busemann's ideas revealed at the end of the war was his theory of supersonic conical flow. By means of a transformation, which he attributed to Chaplygin, Busemann reduced the flow around triangular wings and around wing edges to a problem of conformal mapping in the complex plane. The conical flow theory has played an important role in subsequent studies of wing theory.

After coming to the United States in 1947, Busemann devoted considerable effort to analyze the sonic boom made by a supersonic transport. The sonic boom phenomenon was for a time not well understood, being attributed to a focusing along a caustic curve produced by the accelerated motion of the airplane. Of course, everyone knew that a supersonic plane would make waves, but who would think of the waves reaching all the way to the ground from 60,000 feet? Busemann analyzed this problem carefully and for several years sought a means to eliminate the boom. The fact that he could not find a satisfactory solution probably means that none exists.

Outwardly Adolf Busemann seemed an intense, almost ascetic figure. His scientific discussions, however, frequently relied on slightly humorous, sometimes outrageous, but very concrete analogies. Thus, writing on the occasion of Busemann's seventieth birthday, Professor Milton Van Dyke of Stanford University said:

Others of his friends will certainly praise his great contributions to fluid mechanics. I would like to recall a peripheral aspect of his genius that gives us a glimpse of how that inventive mind works. He thinks always in concrete images. Thus in extending our knowledge of fluid motion he has created a fantastical Alice in Wonderland world filled with imaginary animals, shapes, and people. Has any bestiary a more lovable animal than the "baby hedgehog"—or any utopia a shape more pleasantly named than the "apple curve"? My favorite character in all this magical kingdom is the "ingenious pipefitter," endlessly fitting his stream tubes around a body in the hope of constructing a transonic flow and then, like Sisyphus, starting over again when he fails to match the condition at infinity. I hope that these charming creatures will thrive in the literature as long as Busemann's ideas and equations themselves.

Robert W. Cairns

ROBERT W. CAIRNS

1909–1985

BY ALEXANDER H. FLAX

Robert w. cairns, former executive director of the American Chemical Society, died on January 27, 1985, of Alzheimer's disease. Dr. Cairns made substantial contributions to the technology of high explosives and propellants throughout his brilliant career, which included both government service and positions in private industry.

A native of Oberlin, Ohio, Robert Cairns received an A.B. from Oberlin College in 1930 and a Ph.D. from Johns Hopkins University in 1932; he then attended the advanced management program of the Harvard Graduate School of Business Administration. In 1934 Cairns began his thirty-seven-year career at Hercules as a research chemist, working on propellants and explosives.

He was named director of the Hercules Research Center near Wilmington, Delaware, in 1941. His successful career at Hercules continued with his appointment as director of research in 1955 and his election to the board of directors in 1960. He became vice-president of Hercules in 1967 but retired from the company in 1971 to become deputy assistant secretary for science and technology in the U.S. Department of Commerce.

Dr. Cairns also served the U.S. government on several occasions while still at Hercules. During a leave of absence from the company from 1953 to 1954, he was appointed deputy assistant secretary of defense for research and development. From time to time, Cairns also served as a consultant to various federal departments and agencies. In 1968 the presidents of the National Academy of Sciences and the National Academy of Engineering appointed him chairman of the new Joint Committee on Scientific and Technical Communication. Dr. Cairns became a member of the National Academy of Engineering (NAE) in 1969 and served as a member of the NAE Council from 1970 to 1974.

Early in his career at Hercules, Cairns investigated the fundamentals of detonation in solid explosives. These studies subsequently provided the foundation for many chemical developments in the Hercules laboratories, developments that led to numerous successful achievements in the company's military programs. These achievements, in addition to Cairns's research in the optical and photographic recording of detonations and explosive reactions, created a major breakthrough in providing improved experimental techniques for the study of extremely fast chemical reactions. The combination of knowledge and experience gained from Dr. Cairns's basic, applied research in explosives resulted in the starting point for the early stages of George Kistiakowsky's development of military explosives for the U.S. National Defense Research Committee.

Robert Cairns's early recognition of the potentialities of double base propellants for rocket applications led to the development of high-potential solventless propellants for all U.S. military rockets used in World War II. Cairns directed the role of Hercules as the sole supplier of these propellants by developing the manufacturing processes needed to produce the propellants.

A significant outgrowth of this background and experience was the practical development of a newly discovered and quite revolutionary technique for casting explosive, propellant compositions of any size. The development of this technique was a vital factor in Hercules's current role as the supplier of the final propellant stages of all present U.S. Intercontinental Ballistic Missiles (ICBMs), the propulsion stages of the Sprint, and the point-defense propellant stages of the anti-ICBM.

In 1972 Dr. Cairns was named executive director of the American Chemical Society (ACS), after having been appointed president of the society in 1968. This second appointment enabled Cairns to continue his successful career with ACS during which he eventually held all three major policy and administrative positions in the society. In addition to being named executive director, he became chairman of the board of directors in 1972.

The international aspects of chemistry were of special interest to Cairns for many years. When he became executive director of ACS in 1972, he had been active for some time in the International Union of Pure and Applied Chemistry (IUPAC), a nonprofit association of forty-five national organizations that makes recommendations for action on chemical matters of international importance and promotes cooperation among chemists of member countries. At the time of his ACS appointment, Dr. Cairns was president of IUPAC's Division of Applied Chemistry. In 1973 he was elected vice-president of IUPAC and then served as the union's president from 1975 to 1977.

In addition to his service with ACS, Dr. Cairns was a member of the American Institute of Chemical Engineers, the American Physical Society, and the Commercial Chemical Development Association. He also served as president of the Industrial Research Institute and from 1961 to 1962 was chairman of the American Section of the Society of Chemical Industry. He was president of the University of Delaware Research Foundation and a member of the honorary societies Phi Beta Kappa and Sigma Xi.

One of Dr. Cairns's most notable honors was his selection as recipient of the Perkin Medal in 1969 from the Society of Chemical Industry. Established in 1906, the Perkin Medal is the highest honor given for outstanding work in applied chemistry in the United States. The citation in part read

". . . for his leadership of group effort in the field of polymer chemistry."

In 1974 Cairns received the Industrial Research Institute Medal. This medal is given annually "for outstanding accomplishment in, or management of, industrial research which contributes broadly to the development of industry or the public welfare." Dr. Cairns was recognized primarily for his "perceptive understanding and effective leadership of industrial research and development, ranging from basic research to commercialization."

Robert Cairns was a dedicated and well-liked man. The ACS news report stated that "Cairns was a highly visible figure at ACS—his 6'7" height and head of snowy white hair were hard to miss. His gracious and friendly manner was well-known to all personnel at ACS headquarters."

The Robert Cairns family includes his wife, the former Katherine Kuhn of Columbus, Ohio; three sons, Michael John, Robert Christopher, and Stephen William Waldo; and a daughter, Lindsey Ann.

Edward T. Cleary

EDWARD JOHN CLEARY

1906–1984

BY ALEXANDER H. FLAX

EDWARD JOHN CLEARY, formerly one of the major spokesmen on water pollution control practices in the United States and the creator of the ORSANCO Robot Monitor System, a set of devices that maintains day-and-night river quality vigilance, died on March 31, 1984. A dedicated and pleasant man, Ed Cleary was instrumental in blazing new trails in the water pollution control arena and developing innovations that have been approved and implemented on an international basis.

Born in Newark, New Jersey, on June 16, 1906, Ed Cleary began his education by attending public schools. He entered Rutgers University, where he was awarded a four-year competitive-examination scholarship and a two-year graduate fellowship. He graduated in 1929 with a B.S. in general engineering. He continued his education at Rutgers, receiving an M.S. in sanitary engineering in 1933 and a Ph.D. in civil engineering in 1935.

During his undergraduate schooling, Cleary worked as a field engineer on tunnel and power plant construction projects at the Management and Engineering Corporation in Chicago (from 1929 to 1931) and at Parker and Graham, Inc., in New York City (from 1931 to 1932). While attending graduate school, Cleary worked as a research assistant at Rutgers University and then as a manager at the William J.

Howe Coal Company in New York City. After completing his master's degree, he became the executive editor of the *Engineering News-Record*, a weekly publication of the McGraw-Hill Publishing Company in New York. From 1937 to 1941 Ed Cleary was also a lecturer on public works administration at New York University's College of Engineering.

In 1949 Dr. Cleary was appointed executive director and chief engineer of the Ohio River Valley Water Sanitation Commission (ORSANCO). In these capacities, he presided over the administration of the largest regional water pollution control project ever undertaken. Eight states, in addition to the U.S. Army Corps of Engineers and the U.S. Department of the Interior, joined in this water control effort, which has succeeded in safeguarding the regional water resources of the Ohio River. The successful operation of the Ohio Valley program involved uniting the water supply needs of eleven million people and thousands of industries in constructing more than $1 billion worth of waste control facilities. In addition, the Ohio Valley facilities' international acceptance introduced Cleary's work to the international arena.

Dr. Cleary lectured on the commission's work in Latin America, England, Holland, Germany, Switzerland, and Yugoslavia. In Yugoslavia, he also conducted a seminar for public health authorities from twenty European countries. In addition, he served as a water control consultant to the Federal Republic of Germany and worked with the five-nation Rhine River Commission. In 1960 he was selected by the Economic Commission for Europe as a member of an international team to promote further collaboration in water pollution control.

At the First International Conference on Water Pollution Research in September 1962, Dr. Cleary described a unique electronic water quality monitoring system he had devised for the Ohio River. The Robot Monitor System is a unique combination of control devices that monitors river quality day and night. The system safeguards water supplies for cities, reports water characteristics to industries, and observes conditions that may affect recreational use. In addition, it issues accidental discharge alerts, identifies violations of standard pollution control laws, and serves to reduce the cost of water and waste management.

In 1963 Edward Cleary took a leave of absence from the Ohio River Valley Water Sanitation Commission to join the staff of Resources for the Future as a research associate. For fifteen months, he worked on a book that became *The ORSANCO Story: Water Quality Management in the Ohio Valley Under An Interstate Compact*; it was published by Resources for the Future in 1967. This book documented his work at ORSANCO and fully explained the Robot Monitor System.

In 1965 Cleary was elected to the board of directors of Resources for the Future. He was the first staff member to be elected to this position and served in this capacity until 1967. He then became an honorary director, although he remained both an active participant in water quality research and a familiar face at all of the board meetings until his death.

On December 31, 1971, after twenty-two years of service, Ed Cleary retired from the staff of ORSANCO, which he had served as executive director and chief engineer until 1967, when he relinquished his administrative duties to become a consultant to the commission. An excerpt from the Ohio River Valley Water Sanitation Commission Council minutes of September 15, 1971, reveals how Dr. Cleary's work was acknowledged at his retirement:

In his long tenure, since 1949, as leader and counselor in the activities of this Commission he has touched the interests of scores of industrial leaders, administrators and public officials—local, state and national— as well as multitudes of citizens in the Ohio River Valley. In so doing he has earned acclaim and unbounded respect.

After his retirement, Ed Cleary accepted a part-time appointment to the faculty of the University of Cincinnati in the Department of Environmental Health.

In addition to lecturing on the practice of environmental quality management, he served as a consultant to the National Water Commission, the International Bank for Reconstruction and Development, the White House Office on Science and Technology, the Miami Conservancy District, the Agency for International Development, the World Health Organization in Geneva, the Atomic Energy Commission, and Bechtel Incorporated's Environmental Resources Projects.

The quality of Edward Cleary's work has been recognized through the many honors bestowed upon him. He was elected to membership in Sigma Xi and Tau Beta Pi. He received the Hemispheric Award of the Inter-American Association of Sanitary Engineering (1954), the Emerson Award of the Water Pollution Control Federation (1963), the Man-of-the-Year Award of the American Public Works Association (1962), two separate Resource Division Awards of the American Water Works Association (AWWA) (1963, 1971), the LaDue Citation of the Ohio State Section of AWWA (1965), and an honorary doctorate of engineering from Rose-Hillman Institute of Technology (1972).

Cleary was also inducted into prestigious societies. He was named a member of the National Academy of Engineering in 1967; he was a diplomate in the American Academy of Environmental Engineers; and he was a member of the American Water Resources Association. He served as president of the American Public Works Association and vice-president of the Public Works Historical Society. His honorary memberships included the American Society of Civil Engineers, the American Water Works Association, the Water Pollution Control Federation, the British Institute of Sewage Purification, and the Engineering Society of Cincinnati.

At the time of Edward Cleary's retirement in 1971, a colleague at the Ohio River Valley Water Sanitation Commission stated:

We are mindful of the fact the Dr. Cleary has been the recipient of many awards and praiseworthy messages from scientific organizations, civic and industrial leaders and, especially, from his fellow engineers. We believe, however, that the richest rewards and highest praises due him reside in the silent gratitude in the hearts of the many people whose well-being has been heightened, in part at least, as a result of his monumental efforts in connection with the noble task of improving and preserving the God-given supply of water upon which life depends.

FRANK ALLEN CLEVELAND

1923–1983

ANONYMOUS

To CHRONICLE ADEQUATELY the contributions Frank Allen Cleveland has made to the nation and to his profession one immediately recognizes the necessity to talk to many people. Al, as he was known to his associates, brought to each new engineering responsibility a talent that is all too rare in otherwise accomplished engineers—he listened well. Using this ability in his field of aeronautical research and design development, he sought and made welcome the contributions of a growing host of specialists as each new system concept came into being.

In today's world of ever more extensive systems, his associates miss Al Cleveland most sorely. All remember his continually eager approach to each new challenge and the life full of accomplishments that they shared with him.

At his death on August 12, 1983, which was attributed to complications stemming from open-heart surgery, Al was sixty years old and appeared to be still ascending to the peak of his high-performance potential. He began his career by attending Stanford University where he earned an A.B. in mechanical engineering in 1943 and a master's degree in aeronautical engineering a year later. His outstanding record at Stanford was recognized by his election to Tau Beta Pi.

Although he was born in Dayton, Ohio, on January 31, 1923, Al spent a good part of his "growing up" in Madera,

California; thus it was somewhat surprising that he selected the Lewis Research Center of the National Advisory Committee for Aeronautics (now the National Aeronautics and Space Administration) as his first technical home. It is likely that the facilities and remarkable reputation of this laboratory attracted him, as did the challenge of studying and participating in the emerging development of turbine engines for aircraft. (One of his first papers dealt with the use of afterburners for turbojets in the years when even the engines themselves were novelties.)

Following approximately two years at the Lewis Research Center, Al joined Lockheed as an aerodynamicist with early assignments in the advanced design department. He immediately demonstrated his eager, almost compulsive dedication to the use of the most advanced state-of-the-art techniques, whether they applied to the products themselves or to the techniques for analyzing product capabilities.

During this period at Lockheed, Cleveland was the only aerodynamicist assigned to one of its proposal programs whose particular requirement was to provide a recoverable pilotless flying test bed for the ramjet being developed for the Bomarc missile. The ramjet concept fit well with Al's experience at Lewis, but the airframe design and the optimization of the airframe elements intrigued him even more. They gave him a chance to try out several relatively primitive analytical techniques, many of them his own, involving the use of early computers for aid in optimization.

He was undaunted by his first "computer" conclusion that his small test vehicle should have 7,000 external fuel tanks! Once his tentative programming was properly sorted out and he had survived the joshing of his associates, his conceptual contributions proved to be solid, and the test vehicle became an outstanding success. The program flew 100 test flights using approximately a dozen vehicles—all of which obtained ramjet data near Mach 3. One of the flights actually exceeded Mach 4 at approximately 100,000 feet of altitude and properly recovered itself—no small feat, considering all of these flights occurred before the end of 1951.

Al Cleveland's growing systems consciousness and conceptual acumen led to his assignment as program manager of the successful competition and following studies for the Air Force to explore nuclear power for bombardment aircraft. These studies were initially carried on in Lockheed's Burbank facilities; they were later transferred to the new division established in Marietta, Georgia. Cleveland transferred to the Georgia plant in 1956 to be the pioneering chief of advanced design, and the Air Force nuclear-powered aircraft study transferred with him.

At the Georgia plant, Al initiated the buildup of an exceptionally creative advanced aircraft design and technical team, a team that won almost every major competitive proposal effort it engaged in during the late 1950s through the 1960s. Under his stewardship, the Lockheed-Georgia Company won design, development, manufacturing, and test programs for the following:

• Utility Four-engine Jet Aircraft Program, U.S. Air Force—This program was later converted to the development of the commercial JetStar based on an original twin-engine prototype developed in Burbank.

• C-141 Logistic Transport Program—This aircraft was the first all-Georgia design. To maintain continuity and the proper technical attention, Cleveland was asked to assume responsibility as assistant chief engineer of the company and engineering program manager. By almost any exacting standards, the management of the program and the successful fulfillment of all its technical requirements attest to the excellence of Al's meticulous attention to the total system. The still growing and increasingly outstanding record of the C-141 in its service to the Air Force reinforces the conviction that Al did his part extremely well. All agree that it was his airplane.

• XV4A VTOL Hummingbird Research Program—This test vehicle demonstrated the feasibility of an augmented thrust, vertical-rising jet aircraft before the successful direct-lift Harrier was demonstrated in England.

• C-5A Heavy Logistic Transport Program—The C-5A, despite its impenetrable problems with the procurement system, was a nearly perfect technical solution for the massive collection of requirements it was supposed to meet. This airplane was also the product of Cleveland's advanced design activities. As a result of its new reincarnation for the Air Force, it will finally serve the nation at the performance level made possible by his original design.

Yet perhaps Cleveland's greatest talent, which was fully demonstrated during the Georgia period of his career and certainly recognized by many who continue in the aerospace field today, was his ability to select, inspire, and train key subordinates, many of whom have moved on to substantial careers of their own.

Based on his contributions at the Georgia plant, Al Cleveland was promoted to the corporate position of vice-president of engineering to oversee the quality of effort and enhance the creativity of all Lockheed engineers and scientists involved in corporate-wide development programs. In addition, it was his task to evaluate the total engineering temper and capability of the staff. By his own volition, he extended this responsibility to include an assessment of the contributions that the corporation and its technical executives were making in support of the educational institutions that were producing the next generation of practitioners.

All of this fit well with Al's almost constant attention to the vitality of the profession through the American Institute of Aeronautics and Astronautics (AIAA). There was hardly a time in his whole career that he did not actively support this association—with particular emphasis on its student branches. He served as chairman of the Los Angeles section of the Institute of Aeronautical Sciences (a predecessor of AIAA) in 1954. He was honored in 1970 by the invitation to deliver the Wright Brothers Lecture to AIAA members. He served as director-at-large, as chairman of the Honors and Awards Committee (spearheading a complete awards program overhaul), and as vice-president for technical activities.

These contributions resulted in his election to the national board of governors, and, in 1978, he became president of AIAA. During his tenure as president, he became even more active with the student branches (a policy determined by his own instincts rather than by the normal presidential responsibilities of the institute), and he expanded substantially the group's activities with international associations having similar goals of technical excellence.

Of the many important contributions Al Cleveland made to Lockheed while vice-president of engineering, the one that will probably have the most lasting impact was his creation of an annual awards program for those engineers throughout the corporation who had made the most notable contribution of ideas, specific tasks well done, procedures or techniques improved, or dollars saved by some technical advance. Under the program, the recipients of the awards from each of Lockheed's divisions are brought to Lockheed headquarters as a part of the corporate annual meeting and are introduced to the directors and the stockholders who attend. The effects on the individual who receives the award, the management of the division selecting him, and the corporate management and board are impressive, and they serve as a constant positive reminder to the rest of the organization of its dependence on innovative, alert engineering. Al passed away while serving as Lockheed's corporate vice-president of engineering.

Al Cleveland was elected to the National Academy of Engineering in 1980 and almost immediately began to participate in academy activities through the Aeronautics and Space Engineering Board (ASEB) of the National Research Council. He served as chairman of the Military Aviation Panel during the ASEB workshop of 1980, which addressed NASA's role in aeronautics. He was a member of ASEB from the summer of 1981 until his illness prevented him from participating further in the board's activities.

In reliving Cleveland's approach to each new task with those who were closely involved with him, one senses a universal awe of his enthusiastic immersion in the problem at hand. Yet this quality was not only a technical drive; it also included many social endeavors. He sang in his church choir and debated his divergent views of the church creed with his minister. His wife Freddie, a small-boat sailor of national caliber, involved him in racing. The yacht club has yet to find a peer for planning, scheduling, and operating a weekend racing schedule.

The universal description of his approach contains such words as complete dedication, penetration in depth, objectivity, ability to listen, fair but not precipitous judgment, initiative in giving credit where it was deserved, and an apparently infinite capability for accepting and understanding details. Impressive as this was, it was not an overbearing talent; his humor, consideration, and, above all, objective listening brought out the very best in all who had tasks to perform with him.

Al Cleveland was an engineer in the broadest sense; he showed the technical community and the world how to implement concepts that required technical talents from a multitude of disciplines. He left the aerospace world with a legacy of how to get the job done that will stand as a brilliant goal for all those who follow. People who have known and worked with Al Cleveland are grateful beyond measure for the experience.

Norman A. Copeland

NORMAN ARLAND COPELAND

1915–1984

BY ROBERT L. PIGFORD
AND SHELDON E. ISAKOFF

N ORMAN ARLAND COPELAND, a member of the board of directors and retired senior vice-president and member of the executive committee of E. I. du Pont de Nemours and Company, Inc., died on April 30, 1984, at the age of sixty-eight.

He was born on August 16, 1915, in Mercer County, Ohio, and grew up in Findlay, Ohio. He graduated from the Massachusetts Institute of Technology (MIT) in 1936 with a B.S. in mechanical engineering and did postgraduate work at the Swiss Polytechnic Institute in Zurich. Later, he studied at the University of Delaware, from which he received an M.S. in 1948 and a Ph.D. in 1949 in chemical engineering.

Dr. Copeland began his career with the Du Pont Company in 1937 as a development engineer in the Engineering Department. In the next few years, he advanced through assignments in textile fibers and neoprene synthetic rubber plants to become a senior supervisor. After a leave of absence from Du Pont to complete his education, Copeland became a senior design engineer: By 1950 he was managing engineering design for Du Pont's Film Department. He was transferred formally to the Film Department in 1951 and over the next fourteen years was a plant manager, assistant director of manufacturing, assistant director of research and development, and assistant general manager of the department.

In 1965 Norman returned to the Engineering Department as assistant chief engineer. In 1970 he was named chief engineer and from this post directed one of the largest private process design and construction engineering organizations in the world. (The Du Pont Engineering Department had five thousand employees, and there were another ten thousand people on construction contractors' payrolls.)

Under his leadership, the Engineering Department designed and built capital facilities at a cost of more than $2 billion on fifty sites in ten countries. These facilities included what at that time were the world's largest plants for the production of methanol, polyvinyl alcohol, and polyester film. Norman was also a director of the Du Pont affiliate, the Remington Arms Company.

In 1973 Dr. Copeland was named senior vice-president, a member of Du Pont's executive committee, and a director of the company. He served in those capacities until his retirement in 1977, continuing thereafter as a member of the board of directors.

In addition to his election to the National Academy of Engineering in 1977, Norman was a fellow and member of the American Institute of Chemical Engineers, a member of the American Chemical Society, and a member of the Tau Beta Pi honor society. In 1974 he was awarded the Society of Manufacturing Engineers Interprofessional Cooperation Award. In 1976 the Delaware Society of Professional Engineers named him the state's outstanding engineer. He was a registered engineer in Delaware.

Norman Copeland was a proponent of lifelong learning and maintained strong ties with a number of academic institutions. He was a member of the visiting committees for the Department of Mechanical Engineering at MIT and the Department of Chemical Engineering of Lehigh University. In 1969 he established in Du Pont's Engineering Department one of the industry's most ambitious and successful continuing education programs. The program, which is still quite active today, has provided new knowledge and skills over a wide range of engineering topics for thousands of Du Pont engineers. In addition, as a member of the University of Delaware Research Foundation, Dr. Copeland helped many new faculty members begin work in their chosen research fields.

In Wilmington, Delaware, where Du Pont has its headquarters and where Norman Copeland resided until he moved to Tequesta, Florida, in 1978, he served on the board of directors of the Wilmington Medical Center and was a strong supporter of the Boy Scouts. He was also a member of the board of directors for Community Housing, Inc., a not-for-profit organization that provides housing for moderate-income families.

Dr. Copeland was involved in the development of viscose rayon and of the technology for its manufacture, all of which preceded the commercialization of nylon and other synthetic fibers. In addition, he contributed to the development of neoprene, the first commercial synthetic rubber. During World War II, he helped improve production techniques for the large-scale manufacture of neoprene. Immediately following the war, at the request of the U.S. government, Norman was "loaned" to the U.S. Army in West Germany to assess technical aspects of the German chemical industry.

Following this assignment, he was involved in the development of the first successful polyester film and helped pioneer its use as a high-temperature dielectric and as a base for magnetic tape. He also helped develop polyvinyl fluoride film, which is used in structural building panels, and assisted in the production of polyimide film, which is applied to coat wire for high-temperature use and to insulate cable. It should also be noted that the Kapton polyimide film he helped develop has been widely used in space vehicles.

Dr. Copeland advocated a forceful and responsible approach to air and water protection. He served the National Academies of Sciences and Engineering for two years as a member of the National Research Council's (NRC) Commission on Natural Resources. Norman said, "We must be sure that what we do really improves our environment and is not just a lot of motion . . . that pollution control measures we require are justified and that the benefits gained are commensurate with the costs."

Norman Copeland was an extraordinarily successful engineer in the chemical industry at a time of rapid industrial expansion of facilities for the manufacture of today's successful polymeric materials. He combined a talent for managing the large groups of engineers who were needed for the design of plants and an understanding of the values of an approach to development based on engineering principles.

His management skills were obvious to those who worked with him because he had both the ability to do superior engineering work himself and the kind of personal qualities that attracted loyalty from the members of the organizations of which he was a part. He was a highly compassionate person of the highest integrity. He dealt fairly with individuals under his supervision and had the knack of welding the best talents of his subordinates into an integrated team effort.

Personally, Norman was a private person, a voracious reader of technical and business journals, and a student of many diverse fields including foreign languages, history, and cultures. He loved to travel and did so extensively. He became fluent in German while studying in Switzerland as a young man and maintained this fluency throughout his life. He loved to visit Germany, and he often attended German festivals in the United States. He also enjoyed reading detective novels in French and German.

Dr. Copeland was an avid sports enthusiast, with a particular fondness for golf and, to a lesser extent, shooting and fishing. He belonged to the Wilmington, Du Pont, and Tequesta country clubs and the Biderman, Jupiter Hills, and Pine Valley golf clubs. According to his son Eric, Norman described the course at Pine Valley as "a great builder of character."

He is survived by two sons, Dr. Eric S. Copeland of Wilmington, Delaware, and Dr. Terry M. Copeland of Florence, South Carolina. Norman's wife, the former Gladys Tucker of Tuscaloosa, Alabama, died in September 1982.

Stanley Corrsin

STANLEY CORRSIN

1920–1986

BY HANS W. LIEPMANN

Stanley corrsin, Theophilus Halley Smoot Professor of Engineering at the Johns Hopkins University, died of cancer on June 2, 1986. With his death the community of researchers in and practitioners of fluid physics and fluid engineering lost one of its outstanding contributors. Many of us, including myself, lost a close friend.

Dr. Corrsin was born on April 3, 1920, in Philadelphia, Pennsylvania. He obtained a B.S. from the University of Pennsylvania in 1940 and entered the California Institute of Technology as a graduate student, finishing his M.S. in 1942 and his Ph.D. in 1947.

The bulk of his research for the Ph.D. was actually finished in late 1943, but Corrsin came to Caltech at a time when a technologically unprepared United States faced the prospect of war and a modern air force had to be built in the shortest possible time. A deeper understanding of some of the fundamental problems of fluid mechanics had to be acquired by a small number of competent people to help in the design of advanced aircraft. Gifted graduate students thus were drawn immediately into research and development work, stretching their abilities and stamina to the limit.

In the five years between receiving his M.S. and Ph.D., Corrsin not only finished a thesis on the flow of a turbulent jet, which became a classic in the field, but also participated in many other research and testing projects in progress at the time, including work on what was then a secret project to develop a laminar airfoil. He also served as an instructor in aeronautics. His outstanding writing ability—he had at one time considered becoming a professional writer—was quite evident and a great help to him, even at this early stage in his career.

When Corrsin left Caltech in 1947 to become an assistant professor at the Johns Hopkins University, he was already an acknowledged expert in turbulence research. The complex, fascinating field of turbulence in all of its manifestations remained his primary interest throughout his life, just as Johns Hopkins remained his permanent academic home.

Corrsin advanced to the rank of associate professor of aeronautics in 1951 and then was named professor of mechanical engineering and chairman of the Mechanical Engineering Department in 1955. In line with changes in the departmental structure at Johns Hopkins, his affiliation changed twice: first to mechanics and materials science in 1960 and finally to chemical engineering in 1980. In 1981 he became the first Theophilus Halley Smoot Professor of Engineering and held a concurrent professorship in biomedical engineering at Johns Hopkins School of Medicine.

Corrsin contributed successfully to experimental and theoretical research. He strove for clarity of aim and precision in execution in both theory and experiment, and he was willing and able to acquire the necessary tools to deal with any physical or applied problem of interest to him. For example, Corrsin was one of the very few researchers who familiarized themselves with diagram techniques, which at one time seemed to hold promise in attempts to clarify the sequence of nonlinear coupling terms in wavenumber space. His quest for clarity and precision had one negative result: He never finished the book he planned on fluid mechanics, which was to have been based on his lecture notes. I am given to understand, however, that these notes in the hands of his pupils have contributed much to the fluid mechanics courses in several university curricula.

Short articles on dimensional analysis, the derivation of Eulers equations, and the interpretation of the viscous terms in the turbulent energy equation are further samples of Corrsin's serious concern for a correct simplicity in the teaching of fundamentals. He worked very hard and wrote easily. His hundred or so publications could easily have been doubled but for his pronounced self-criticism and urge for perfection. Corrsin's contribution to the *Handbuch der Physik* and to the *Encyclopedic Dictionary of Physics on Experimentation in Turbulence Research* is further proof of his more pedagogical interests, which culminated in a set of some twenty-five doctoral theses that were carried through under his guidance. Many of his Ph.D. students by now have made their own mark in various aspects of fluid mechanics.

Corrsin contributed a number of lasting ideas and results—for example, as his first published paper shows, he recognized the so-called intermittency in turbulence as early as 1943. The first serious experimental verification of the concept of local isotropy is credited to him. The still lively discussions concerning the validity of gradient transport in turbulent shear flows could be much improved if the participants were to take the time to read Corrsin's publications dealing with the subject.

He also contributed a number of nontrivial applications of stochastic theory to problems suggested by the turbulence field. These contributions included a study conducted with J. B. Morton of the statistical properties of the Duffing oscillator under random forcing, comparing various closure proposals for turbulence with the results from a Fokker-Planck solution.

In later years, Corrsin developed an interest in medical and biological problems and brought his expertise with fluid flow to bear on a variety of subjects such as the motion of the precorneal fluid film of the eye and maternal blood flow in the placenta. His long-standing interest and competence in aerodynamics were applied to problems of bird flight. Premedical students at Johns Hopkins had the opportunity to take his rather unusual course "Animal Motion," which offered a rare chance to learn something about real applied mechanics.

His list of fellowships and honors reflects the high esteem in which his contributions are held both here and abroad. He was a fellow of the American Physical Society, the American Society of Mechanical Engineers, and the American Academy of Arts and Sciences. He was named Docteur Honoris Causé of the University of Lyon and was elected to membership in the National Academy of Engineering in 1980. He also received the 1983 Fluid Dynamics Prize of the American Physical Society.

In a field of long standing such as fluid mechanics—a field that is crucial for a host of engineering applications, but that still contains unresolved fundamental physics problems—spectacular breakthroughs are virtually nonexistent. Progress proceeds on a wide front in larger or smaller steps. Corrsin has contributed to the fields of aeronautical, chemical, and mechanical engineering as well as to the biological and physical sciences. In some of these steps, he will be remembered as an original and productive researcher. The people who knew him personally will remember Stan as an articulate, critical, but very warm personality with an unusually pleasant sense of humor.

Corrsin is survived by his wife Barbara (née Dagett) and two children, Nancy Eliot and Stephen Davis.

LUIGI CROCCO

1909–1986

BY SEYMOUR M. BOGDONOFF

LUIGI CROCCO, former professor of the University of Rome, of Princeton University, and of the l'Ecole Centrale des Arts et Manufactures, died of a heart attack in Rome on the evening of November 19, 1986. Originally trained as an applied mathematician, Professor Crocco became one of the pioneers and leading forces in the fields of theoretical aerodynamics and rocketry and jet propulsion during a long and illustrious career in academia.

Born on February 2, 1909, in Palermo, Italy, Crocco began to conduct research during his undergraduate years at the University of Rome, where he received his B.S. in mechanical engineering in 1932 and his Ph.D. in mechanical engineering in 1936. By the time he completed his degrees, he was already heavily involved in rocketry and theoretical aerodynamics and had published several papers. (There were some who mistook these early works for publications of his well-known father, General Luigi Crocco.)

Crocco remained at the University of Rome as an assistant professor after receiving his Ph.D and became a full professor in 1939. During the 1930s, he generated a series of critical papers in theoretical aerodynamics: his derivation of the Crocco energy integral for boundary layers (1931), his vorticity theorem (1936), his definition of the Crocco point of gas dynamics (1937), and his introduction of the Crocco transformation in boundary layer theory (1939).

101

In 1949 he was invited to become a visiting professor in the Department of Aeronautical Engineering at Princeton University, and, in 1952, on the recommendation of Theodore von Karman, he accepted the Robert H. Goddard Chair of Jet Propulsion at Princeton and became the director of the Guggenheim Jet Propulsion Center, one of two such centers founded in the United States under a grant from the Guggenheim Foundation.

During his tenure at Princeton, Crocco turned his great talents to the study of the rapidly growing field of rocket propulsion. He developed his now well-known theory of combustion instability in rocket motors and remained an international leader in this field for many years. In addition to his interest in rockets, he used his expertise in mathematics and fluid physics to study complex fluid mechanical problems associated with viscous flows. He made seminal contributions to the understanding of boundary layer flows, separation, base flows, and transonic and supersonic aerodynamics. He was instrumental in developing mathematical and numerical methods to solve the fluid dynamic equations that provided the framework for many technical applications.

In the propulsion field, his contributions were made in the combined areas of fluid mechanics and combustion as applied to propulsion devices, work through which he made contributions to both liquid and solid rocket combustion. His critical contributions to the theory of rocket combustion instability were an important factor in the design of reliable thrusters of the period. He also applied propulsion theory to some of the earliest work in orbital mechanics and space flight.

During the late 1960s, Crocco's wife, Simone, became ill, prompting their return to Europe. In 1968 he became a Fulbright Professor of the Faculté des Sciences of the University of Paris. He returned briefly to Princeton in 1969, but in 1970 he settled permanently to Europe to facilitate his wife's medical treatment.

From 1970 until he retired in 1977, Crocco was a professor at l'Ecole Centrale des Arts et Manufactures in Paris. In that post, he continued his teaching and research; he also spent some time at the University of Rome, the Polytechnic Institute of Rome, and ONERA (the French counterpart of the National Aeronautics and Space Administration).

After his wife's death in 1981, he continued his research activity, visiting the United States and working closely with the theoretical aerodynamics group in Rome. He continued to enjoy theoretical work and devoted most of the later years of his life to the difficult challenge of understanding turbulence. He remained active until his sudden death at the age of seventy-seven.

Professor Crocco's stature in his field was recognized by the National Academy of Engineering, which elected him to membership in 1979. He was also a member of the Accademia Nazionale dei Lincei, the Accademia delle Scienze di Torino, the International Academy of Astronautics, l'Aerotecnica, and the Société Ingénieurs Civils de France. He was a fellow of the American Institute of Aeronautics and Astronautics (AIAA) and received the AIAA Pendray Award in 1965, the AIAA Wilde Award in 1969, and the Columbus International Prize and Gold Medal in 1973.

His ability to combine elegant mathematics and physical insights in solving practical problems in aeronautics and propulsion made him highly sought after as a consultant for industry and government in both the United States and Europe. Curtiss Wright, the Bendix Corporation, Aerojet-General, General Dynamics, Reaction Motors, Arthur D. Little, General Electric, RCA, TRW, and the National Aeronautics and Space Administration in the United States, as well as the European Space Agency, Fiat, the French Defense Ministry, and the Advisory Group for Aerospace Research and Development of the North Atlantic Treaty Organization, were among the organizations that received his assistance and counsel.

As a professor, Luigi Crocco was instrumental in developing and influencing a group of students in the United States and Europe who today occupy key positions in industry, government, and universities. The combination of these students and almost one hundred of his technical papers had an extraordinary impact on the development of the fields of aeronautics and space propulsion. In 1985 in honor of Crocco's seventy-fifth birthday, Plenum Press published a book entitled *Recent Advances in the Aero-Space Sciences*, which was edited by Corrado Casci and consisted of scientific papers by Crocco's colleagues and students.

Luigi Crocco was a European "aristocrat" in the best sense of the term. He was gently mannered and cultured, with a keen intellect and a warm handshake that made one feel special. His ability to make clear, at any level, the complex phenomena with which he worked made him one of the influential figures of a major growth period in the aerospace era.

A. EARL CULLUM, JR.

1909–1985

BY ARTHUR A. COLLINS
AND JERRY STOVER

A. EARL CULLUM, JR., a pioneer in modern communications technology, died of a heart attack on January 31, 1985, at the age of seventy-five. Cullum's work in the field of radio, television, and microwave communications helped weave the electronic network that binds the nation together. At the age of twenty-seven, he formed his own firm (A. Earl Cullum, Jr., and Associates, Consulting Engineers) and soon became a widely known and well-respected authority in the problem solving associated with radio and television broadcasting. During his lengthy career, his name became synonymous with engineering innovation.

Cullum was born in Abilene, Texas, on September 27, 1909. He moved with his family to Dallas a few years later, where he worked as a technician at radio station WFAA from 1923 to 1926 when he was a student at North Dallas High School. After high school, he enrolled in several courses in math and physics at Southern Methodist University before leaving the Lone Star State to attend the Massachusetts Institute of Technology.

Following graduation in 1931, Cullum went to work for American Airlines as an engineer in its communications research and development departments in St. Louis and Dallas. He performed a similar function a few years later (1934) for the Southwest Broadcasting Company (SBC) in Fort

Worth, but this time in the post of vice-president. After leaving the SBC's research and development operations, he formed his own company.

During World War II, Cullum was associate director of the Radio Research Laboratory at Harvard University and a consultant to the U.S. Office of Scientific Research and Development and the National Defense Research Committee. The projects he supervised were vital to national defense, and under his guidance sophisticated electronic weaponry, such as radio jammers and radar receivers, was developed. He also served as a consultant to the U.S. Strategic and Tactical Air Forces in London, England.

For his service during the war, Cullum received the Presidential Certificate of Merit in 1948. Following the war, he was appointed one of the original directors of the Joint Research and Development Committee of the Army, Navy, and Air Force in Washington. In 1948 he was also awarded a fellowship in the Institute of Electrical and Electronics Engineers.

Cullum was responsible for developing a number of important engineering practices and innovations in the broadcasting field. For example, he originated the widely used multiplication method of designing and analyzing broadcast and directional antenna systems involving more than two towers. Early on, Cullum appreciated the necessity of continuously monitoring the amplitude and phase of currents in an individual tower located within a complex array of towers designed to avoid radiation of energy in a direction that would adversely affect another station. Consequently, he developed the first coaxial sampling loop used to adjust and maintain the components of a broadcast directional system. Cullum also demonstrated that as directional antennas became more complicated, accuracy of adjustment became increasingly important, a finding that stimulated the development of unusually precise monitoring systems.

Another Cullum pioneering practice was the use of elevated ground screens to stabilize critical directional characteristics against changing ground conditions—for example, tides on the New Jersey meadows and sunflowers in Kansas. These techniques were first used at WINS-AM in New York. In his continuing efforts to improve the design of broadcast antenna systems, Cullum also originated the idea of using the area under the currents distribution curve to define accurately the radiating "moment" of an individual tower of a radiating system, thereby taking into account the effect on the current distribution of the coupling between towers.

In still another instance, he recognized the deterioration that reradiating structures, such as power-line towers or modern skyscrapers, could produce in a radiating signal, and he devised ingenious methods of detuning such structures to render them harmless. Specifically, Cullum helped to resolve problems caused by the John Hancock Tower and the Sears Tower in Chicago and assisted in obtaining the initial Federal Aviation Administration clearance for these structures.

Since its inception, the firm of A. Earl Cullum, Jr., and Associates, Consulting Engineers, has represented clients in major markets from Boston to San Diego and from Seattle to Miami, Puerto Rico, Hawaii, and Mexico. In addition to his duties with the firm, from 1960 to 1980 Cullum also served on the board of directors of the A. H. Belo Corporation—the owner of radio station WFAA, where he began his longtime romance with radio during his high school years. Cullum was nominated to membership in the National Academy of Engineering in 1970, at which time he was cited for "exceptional leadership and originality as a consulting engineer concerned with radio and television broadcasting."

Yet to examine only his efforts to advance technology would be insufficient to describe A. Earl Cullum, Jr., fully, for he was equally renowned for community and public service during the most critical periods of the Dallas–Fort Worth area development. Among his greatest accomplishments was the technical development of the first system to use microwave technology to broadcast classes from a university to an industrial facility. The system was first made opererational at Southern Methodist University (SMU), forming the basis for TAGER (The Association for Graduate Education and Research) and later for SMU's current off-campus education program.

Cullum was also an original member of the SMU Foundation for Science and Engineering and served on its executive board. He was a member of the Educational Television Foundation (KERA-TV, Dallas), the Dallas Citizens Council, the Dallas Chamber of Commerce, and the executive committees of both the St. Marks and Hockaday schools in Dallas.

Peter V. Danckwerts

PETER VICTOR DANCKWERTS

1916–1984

BY JOHN DAVIDSON

PROFESSOR PETER VICTOR DANCKWERTS, G.C., M.B.E., F.R.S., F.Eng., Shell Professor of Chemical Engineering at the University of Cambridge from 1959 to 1977, and fellow of Pembroke College, died on October 25, 1984, at the age of sixty-eight. The son of Vice Admiral V. H. Danckwerts, he was educated at Winchester and Balliol colleges, Oxford.

His war record was distinguished. As a sublieutenant in the Royal Navy Volunteer Reserve, he was awarded the George Cross in 1940 for disarming land mines that had fallen on London. The bold, imaginative approaches needed for this work—for example, lengths of string were used to extract fuses from the mines—were characteristic of his subsequent scientific endeavors. He was wounded during the invasion of Sicily and later joined the staff of Combined Operations Headquarters. In 1943 he was appointed Member of the Order of the British Empire.

Danckwerts's engineering education began after the war when he used a Commonwealth Fund (now Harkness Fund) fellowship to study chemical engineering at the Massachusetts Institute of Technology (MIT) for an M.S. This educational period at MIT (from 1946 to 1948) was a turning point in Danckwerts's career: He often spoke of the rigors of the course and the value of the MIT Practice School. While at MIT, he met T. R. C. Fox, who had just been appointed

Shell Professor of Chemical Engineering at Cambridge and was also learning the subject at that time. Fox recruited Danckwerts to become a member of Cambridge's original chemical engineering team, and it was there in the early 1950s that Danckwerts established an international reputation with a few remarkable papers.

The best known of these is his paper on continuous flow reactors, which gives basic theorems about the distribution of residence times. During the early 1950s, when Danckwerts was a junior faculty member at Cambridge, he began work on gas absorption into liquids, a topic that preoccupied him for many years and led to his 1970 book *Gas-Liquid Reactions*, a standard work on the subject.

Danckwerts's early scientific efforts were a model for what academic research should be in that minimal funds were needed and there was no necessity for the plans or proposals or grant applications that now constitute the administrative millstone we have come to associate with research. In his *Autobiographical Note*, which gives a far better impression of the man than these poor phrases, Danckwerts described his early research period as one of "academic indolence."

Yet like so many of his remarks, this is not to be taken literally: Like Englishmen before him but to a lesser extent now, he cultivated the notion of effortless achievement; only cads should be seen working. In the same style, Danckwerts professed an antipathy toward mathematics, even though his own discoveries—on residence times, gas absorption, and mixing—depended on the imaginative combination of simple mathematics and acute insight into physical and chemical realities.

His work anticipated what might be called the Bird, Stewart, and Lightfoot era of chemical engineering; he was one of the first and most outspoken critics of an education based on the assumption that all problems can be solved by striking out terms in generalized equations. Moreover, he believed that a highly mathematical education did not promote industrial innovation.

It was with industrial innovation in mind that Danckwerts left Cambridge in 1954 to work under Lord (then Sir Christopher) Hinton at the Atomic Energy Authority, but he soon returned to academic life. In 1956 he was appointed professor of chemical engineering science at Imperial College; in 1959 he returned to Cambridge as Shell Professor of Chemical Engineering. While there, he established a flourishing research school that included an active group continuing his earlier work on surface renewal at gas-liquid interfaces.

Danckwerts proved to be an effective department head at Cambridge, notwithstanding his distaste for administration: He regarded university committees as "politbureaus." Again, however, it is necessary to distinguish between off-the-cuff comments and his conduct of affairs. While affecting to despise elaborate calculations, Danckwerts ensured that the Cambridge department was the first in the United Kingdom to have its own computer—an IBM 1620. In the same way, he established a departmental electronics service. Although he did not care for the minutiae of teaching, he initiated design projects as a regular feature of the course, in line with the Institution of Chemical Engineers' requirements.

Danckwerts was active in this group and served as its president from 1965 to 1966. He formed, with a characteristically open-ended title, the Exploratory Committee, whose innovative function was to award industrial fellowships to enable faculty members to spend a year reporting on research topics that were likely to be useful to industry.

From 1958 to 1982 Danckwerts was executive editor of *Chemical Engineering Science* and during his tenure created one of the leading journals in the field. In this work, Danckwerts not only helped promote the welfare of chemical engineering, but in a modest way also contributed to the rise of one of our latter-day press barons, Robert Maxwell, who was one of the first to recognize the commercial opportunities in publishing scientific research.

In his day, Danckwerts was a great traveler. In addition to maintaining contact with the United States, he visited India,

Australia, and the Soviet Union. During the early 1960s, a Russian research student—now head of an institute—spent a year in Cambridge. Always an acute observer of humorous paradoxes, Danckwerts remarked that the visitor had said, after discussions about British government inertia, "In Russia we also have bureaucracies."

Danckwerts retained an affection for the United States and had a successful year in North Carolina in 1976, forming a link that endures—the Cambridge Chemical Engineering Department has permanently established the North Carolina State University Prize, which is given for the best student research project.

Danckwerts's election as a foreign associate of the U.S. National Academy of Engineering in 1978 greatly pleased him. It was fitting that his last honor, the year after retirement, should come from the country that had provided his formal education in the subject to which he had made such brilliant contributions.

MARCEL DASSAULT

1892–1986

BY THOMAS V. JONES

Marcel Dassault died on April 18, 1986, in Paris at the age of ninety-four. The father of French aviation and a graduate of that nation's first aeronautical engineering school, Dassault was the longtime director of Avions Marcel Dassault–Breguet Aviation, one of Europe's largest aviation companies. In that capacity, he created and produced such high-performance combat aircraft as the Mystère and delta-winged Mirage, a family of planes that today is among the most respected and widely operated fighter-bombers in the world. Dassault also made important contributions to commercial aviation with his Falcon family of executive transport jets.

From 1951 until his death, Marcel Dassault served as a member of the French Parliament. He held France's highest military award, the Grand Cross of the French Legion of Honor. He was elected a foreign associate of the National Academy of Engineering in 1976 for his "remarkable achievements in the design and development of new aircraft for military and commercial use."

Marcel Dassault's vision and extraordinary engineering talents helped to shape the first century of aviation history. He was a true pioneer whose imagination, persistence, and management of advanced aerospace technology are indelibly blended into the tricolor banner of the French nation. Despite the formidable obstacles and great personal dangers encountered in his ninety-four years, Marcel Dassault remained a man of uncommon strength and unwavering principle with a deep faith in the idea that technology and commitment can overcome almost any challenge.

Born in Paris on January 22, 1892, Dassault developed an early interest in design and scientific inquiry. At the age of nineteen, he received a degree in electrical engineering and then began to specialize in the new, little-known field of aeronautics.

In the years just prior to World War I, Dassault put his technical skills and aviation ideas to work in the service of the French Corps of Engineers. He was selected to improve the design studies of the Caudron G-3 biplane and, later, to manage its manufacture. He also developed new designs for more efficient propellers. By 1916 he was producing them, first for the Caudron G-3 and then for the Hélice Eclair, the Spad credited with giving French fliers a distinct flying advantage during World War I.

After World War I, Dassault set out to fulfill a dream that had begun in the courtyard of his primary school with his first glimpse of an airplane circling the Eiffel Tower. French aviation was about to begin in earnest, and Dassault gathered a small team of design engineers and housed them in an old furniture factory. Soon he had built up a highly successful aviation company, Avions Marcel Dassault–Breguet Aviation, to the point at which the French government nationalized his operations in 1936. In 1940 he produced the Languedoc 61, a four-engine civil transport plane. A somber shadow was cast on its maiden voyage, however: The Germans marched into Paris, and the occupation of France began.

Authorities in Nazi Germany's aviation industry quickly offered Dassault a position to design and build a fleet of aircraft in exchange for his personal freedom and protection. He defied the German high command, however, and refused their offer, spending the war years first in Vichy prisons and then at the Buchenwald concentration camp. At Buchen-

wald, he contracted diphtheria, and post-diphtheria paraly-
sis plagued him throughout the remainder of his life. When
the death camp was liberated on April 19, 1945, Dassault was
frail and weak, but his dream was as strong as ever.

With great courage and a fierce determination, Dassault
began again, his first project the design and production of
the Ouragan, Europe's first jet. Later he introduced the first
European plane to break the sound barrier, the Mystère IV,
which was followed by the Mirage III, the plane that opened
the era of Mach 2 aircraft. The Dassault Mirage, with its pure
aerodynamic shape, high performance, and uncompromising attention to detail, became the standard for modern
French combat aircraft.

The rest is legend. With the introduction of the Mirage III
in 1956, France began to meet its military aircraft requirements solely through domestic production. Today, it remains
the only European nation with an air force equipped entirely
with domestically built aircraft. In addition, Dassault's Mirage family of combat fighters remains one of France's best
export successes. By 1986 Avions Marcel Dassault–Breguet
Aviation had built six thousand aircraft for sixty-one countries.

Dassault's contributions extend far beyond military aviation. His commercial business jets are noted for both performance and reliability, and his leadership and industrial
management skills enabled Avions Marcel Dassault–Breguet
Aviation to bring France to the forefront of the European
manned spaceplane program. Always active in French poli-
tics, Dassault served his country for thirty years, as a Gaulist
deputy and as a senator for the Union des Démocrats pour
la République.

In 1967 Marcel Dassault was honored with the Grand
Cross of the French Legion of Honor, the nation's highest
military award. He was also presented with the croix de
guerre 1939–1945 for extraordinary wartime service.

In paying tribute to Marcel Dassault, we also pay tribute to
that small band of original aviation explorers whose ingenu-

ity and perseverance enabled the discovery of practical, enduring solutions to previously intractable aviation engineering difficulties. Dassault was an industrial giant, an engineer of exceptional capability, and an aviation genius. Yet most important, he was an inspiration, a resilient man whose courage and insight, genius and spirit served the engineering profession, his country, and his fellow man with extraordinary distinction.

WALTER SPAULDING DOUGLAS

1912–1985

BY THOMAS KUESEL

W ALTER SPAULDING DOUGLAS, a distinguished engineer of national and international repute, died at the age of seventy-three on March 15, 1985. He and his wife Jeannie had been living in Rhode Island in their home high on a rocky promontory jutting into his beloved ocean waters, where they had enjoyed many happy years of sailing with a host of longtime friends.

On his retirement in 1977 as chairman of the board of Parsons Brinckerhoff Quade & Douglas, the firm to which both he and his father, Walter J. Douglas, had at separate times given the family name, he moved from Plainfield, New Jersey, to his erstwhile summer home in Jamestown, Rhode Island. Douglas had remodeled the house—primarily to accommodate Jeannie's "green thumb" activities—joined the board of the local hospital and the Newport Yacht Club, and set about enjoying life with his family and indulging an interest in boating.

Walter Douglas was born on January 22, 1912, in Cranford, New Jersey. His early education culminated at Phillips Exeter Academy in 1929. He then followed his father into the civil engineering profession and received a B.A. from Dartmouth in 1933 and an M.S. from Harvard in 1935. During those early days, jobs were scarce, but Douglas secured one with the Nashville Bridge Company in Tennessee. He labored in the company's shops and drafting rooms, detailing steel, in particular, reinforcing bars—some of which he later had to carry on his shoulder in the field, causing him to grumble that he "never should have detailed them so heavy!"

In 1937 Walter Douglas obtained work with the original 1939 New York World's Fair, where he rose rapidly from assistant design engineer to engineer in charge of design. He also became the chief engineer responsible for cost forecasts and for the administrative detail associated with an organization of more than one hundred individuals in various disciplines.

It was there that he became well acquainted with various key people of the Parsons Brinckerhoff firm who were also working on parts of the fair. In 1939 Walter joined Parsons Brinckerhoff. Two years later he was called to active duty in World War II with the Navy's Construction Battalion, the Seabees. Walter Douglas served in battle areas of the Pacific, rose to the rank of lieutenant commander, and later served as acting commander of his battalion. In his future career, he drew assiduously on his wartime experiences as a commander and in construction under difficult conditions.

On his return to civilian life and Parsons Brinckerhoff, Douglas completed a series of engineering and management assignments of ever-increasing scope. Not surprisingly, several of them were of a military nature. He handled the engineering connected with the construction of several of our early postwar military air bases in France and Spain, as well as the key air force bases in Iceland and Newfoundland. These projects were followed by the design and construction of America's first underground bases—first, the so-called Underground Pentagon in the East and, later, the huge North American Air Defense (NORAD) headquarters complex deep in the Rockies.

On the international scene, in addition to his work in Europe for the firm, Douglas obtained and directed far-reaching assignments in South America. For example, in Colombia and Ecuador he accomplished nationwide comprehensive transportation planning, including the economic and financing studies necessary for its implementation.

Meanwhile, Douglas's business career with Parsons Brinckerhoff continued to progress dramatically. In 1952, at what was then a relatively early age, he had become a partner and a senior vice-president of the firm's Parsons Brinckerhoff Corporation. He soon assumed responsibility for the firm's financial administration, establishing and implementing goals for the firm that kept it advancing in size, capability, and prosperity. The company again included the name Douglas, becoming Parsons Brinckerhoff Quade & Douglas, and Walter finally assumed the positions of senior partner and chairman of the board, which he held until his retirement in 1977.

But before that retirement—in 1953—came BART! Always a profound analyst and innovator, Walter Douglas became the father of the renaissance of metropolitan mass transit. The firm's final report (essentially authored by Douglas, who was a superb writer), "Rapid Transit for the San Francisco Bay Area," became a landmark in the struggle of modern society to resolve its growing problems in moving vast numbers of its people.

The report dealt particularly with urban and suburban environments, areas that had been hampered and engulfed by the proliferation of the private automobile, the consequence of the public's love affair with it as the principal means of transportation. The seeds sown in this early work germinated and grew steadily for the next two decades; they resulted in the actual building of BART, a seventy-five-mile rapid transit system costing about $1.5 billion—a modern trailblazer in which Douglas again played a key role.

Douglas and his associates were pioneers in applying total systemwide analysis on a large scale, which specifically included the use of areawide land planning. In the resultant restructuring of metropolitan transportation, Walter led the

way for his firm and his profession in many urban and suburban areas including Atlanta, Georgia; Pittsburgh, Pennsylvania; and Caracas, Venezuela.

Nor were all these achievements without well-deserved recognition. In 1969 Walter Douglas was awarded the James
Laurie Award of the American Society of Civil Engineers
(ASCE), essentially for his outstanding work and leadership
in the field of urban transportation. In 1975 he was again
honored by ASCE, this time as one of the "Top Ten Construction Men of the Past Half Century"; in 1975 he was honored by the Newcomen Society; and in 1977 he received an
award from the National Society of Professional Engineers
for "distinguished service to the engineering profession."

In 1967 Walter Douglas was elected to the National Academy of Engineering. Later he received the first award for
"Outstanding Service" from the Building Research Board
(BRB) of the National Research Council for "distinguished
service on the Federal Construction Council."

Perhaps his most cherished award came in 1970 from his
peers in the Moles, the fraternity of tunnel and heavy construction engineers and constructors. They honored him
with their nonmember award for "outstanding achievement
in construction." Even after his retirement, there was more
recognition: In 1984 Douglas was elected to the American
Public Transit Authority Hall of Fame in Washington, D.C.

Walter Douglas was renowned in his profession as a profound as well as pragmatic engineer of integrity and courage. Although he did not try to master all the intricacies of
each technical discipline, he did maintain and enhance an
excellent working knowledge of those disciplines that were
applicable to the problems presented to him for his solution.
He earnestly believed that almost any such technical problem, however complex and forbidding it might at first appear, could be brought to a workable solution by an intense
concentration of fundamental knowledge and diligently applied analysis, accompanied by an endless perspicacity—
which he possessed in abundance.

Walter Douglas had, and constantly practiced, the ability to concentrate on a chosen subject to the exclusion of all else. This largely explains his widespread reputation for absent-mindedness and "apparent forgetfulness" and the famed trail of "lost" hats, plans, and other items scattered in his wake around the world. Incidentally, the treasured experiences of some of his associates whom he drove about in his car are almost legendary in this respect!

When a project was in trouble, Douglas's action to rectify the trouble or to fight the necessary battle was immediate and total, regardless of the cost. His courage, intelligence, and perseverance would usually bring success—to the benefit of the job itself as well as that of the firm.

Douglas moved easily among important people, many of them high public and private officials. From such associations he added to and enhanced his philosophy of operating. He once questioned a top official of a major bank about why he (the official) had so quickly changed his previous position. "Walter," said the banker, "I always keep an open mind, and I reserve to myself the right to change it—but only if something better is proven to me." Douglas adopted that philosophy and often quoted his banker friend. He insisted that practical alternatives be studied and reported, even if not specifically required by contract or client, to try to protect and provide the client and the project with all available facts and with an optimum solution.

Douglas devoted much time and effort to community service. For many years, he served as trustee and as guardian of the grounds of the Crescent Avenue Presbyterian Church in his hometown of Plainfield, New Jersey. Douglas was also a member of the board of governors, and later president, of Muhlenburg Hospital. He followed a similar course in retirement when he served as trustee of Newport Hospital in Rhode Island.

Ocean sailing was Douglas's favorite pastime, and he was an excellent seaman. He and his wife, Jeannie, often accompanied by friends, would cruise for days at a time. In this situation, he continued to apply his principle of opting for the best alternative solution—even seemingly at the last minute—much to the excitement (and later reminiscent enjoyment) of his shipmates! Walter never failed to make the best move; he was a good captain of his ship and a grand host.

We will miss him and so will the engineering profession. Walter Douglas left his mark, however; his trail, although difficult to follow, is clear for all who decide to try.

THOMAS BRADFORD DREW

1902–1985

BY SHELDON ISAKOFF

T HOMAS BRADFORD DREW, professor emeritus at the Massachusetts Institute of Technology (MIT) and former head of the Department of Chemical Engineering at Columbia University, died on May 5, 1985, at the age of eighty-three.

Professor Drew was born on February 9, 1902, in Medford, Massachusetts. He attended the Massachusetts Institute of Technology, from which he received his B.S. and M.S. in chemical engineering in 1923 and 1924, respectively.

Professor Drew began his long and distinguished academic career in 1924 as a teaching assistant at MIT. After he obtained his master's degree, he joined the faculty of Drexel Institute in Philadelphia and taught both chemistry and chemical engineering. After three years, he returned to MIT as an instructor in chemical engineering and initiated research in the fundamentals of heat transfer, a field that continued to occupy his attention throughout his lifetime and to which he made many creative and outstanding contributions.

During a six-year period at MIT, Professor Drew joined with W. H. McAdams and H. C. Hottel in pioneering efforts in heat transfer and fluid flow research. Their work culminated in their coauthorship of one of the first reviews on mathematical approaches to convective heat transfer ("Heat Transmission," *Transactions of the American Institute of Chemical Engineers* 32[1936]: 271–305).

133

In 1934 Professor Drew left the academic community for a six-year sojourn with E. I. Du Pont de Nemours and Company in Wilmington, Delaware, where he joined a small group of chemical engineers conducting research in the area of unit operations under the direction of T. H. Chilton. Their work at Du Pont proved to be quite significant: Apparently, Du Pont was the country's first industrial organization to carry out fundamental research in chemical engineering.

For Du Pont, Drew supervised research in heat, mass, and momentum transfer. In addition, he developed rational procedures for the design of chemical process equipment and manufacturing systems. Much of the data that Drew and his Du Pont colleagues generated were made available on a broad basis to chemical engineers by Drew's authoring of important segments of J. H. Perry's *Chemical Engineer's Handbook* (New York: McGraw-Hill, 1934).

Moreover, a second paper published with his coworker A. P. Colburn, "The Condensation of Mixed Vapors" (*Transactions of the American Institute of Chemical Engineers* 33[1937]: 197–215), remains one of the most incisive papers written about this highly technical area. It clarified a number of confusing misunderstandings about the subject that were prevalent at the time and is still referred to today, almost fifty years later, as a means to a better understanding of mixed vapors.

Drew left Du Pont in 1940 to begin a twenty-five-year association with Columbia University, first as a professor and then as head of the Department of Chemical Engineering, a position he held for ten years. During World War II, Professor Drew led the Columbia University research efforts associated with the Manhattan District Project.

On leave to Du Pont for two years, he was a major contributor to the design of the gaseous diffusion technique for isotope separation of the Hanford Plutonium Plant, as well as a contributor to other critical plant aspects. As the chemical engineering department head at Columbia University, he introduced some of the country's earliest courses in nuclear engineering and established a major heat transfer research facility that operated for many years under the sponsorship of the U.S. Atomic Energy Commission.

After the war, Professor Drew was a consultant to the Brookhaven National Laboratory, an association he maintained for fifteen years. During this period, he helped guide the laboratory's research program in the physical sciences; he also served as chairman of the Brookhaven Engineering Advisory Committee for eight years. During the early 1960s, he was a consultant to the Ford Foundation and worked in India to improve the quality of engineering instruction at the Birla Institute of Technology and Science. In 1965 Professor Drew returned to his first love, MIT, where he held an emeritus professorship until his death.

Drew's dedication to research and progress in the field of chemical engineering never waned. For almost thirty years (from 1954 to 1981), until shortly before his death, he served as editor of *Advances in Chemical Engineering* (New York: Academic Press), a series of volumes that featured comprehensive reviews of the many new, evolving aspects of chemical engineering during that period.

Professor Drew received many awards and honors during his long, illustrious career. He was one of the earliest recipients (1937) of the William H. Walker Award, which is presented annually by the American Institute of Chemical Engineers (AIChE) to recognize excellence in contributions to chemical engineering literature. Professor Drew was also selected by AIChE to be its Annual Institute Lecturer in 1951. His lecture, "Diffusion, What We Know and What We Don't," demonstrated his remarkable ability to apply advanced mathematics to complex physical problems and thereby derive practical engineering utility results.

In 1967 Drew was the recipient of the Max Jakob Memorial Award in Heat Transfer, given jointly by AIChE and the American Society of Mechanical Engineers. In 1983 he was designated by AIChE as one of the nation's eminent chemical engineers. Drew was also a member of Sigma Xi, Tau Beta

Pi, and Phi Lambda Upsilon honorary societies, and a fellow of AIChE, the American Association for the Advancement of Science, and the New York Academy of Sciences. He was elected to the National Academy of Engineering in 1983.

Yet Thomas Drew was far more than a remarkably talented researcher, engineer, and academician. He was a great source of advice and inspiration for his students and colleagues. He combined extraordinary technical talents with a profound sense of fairness, sincerity, personal warmth, and friendship. He had a strong sense of history, placing current events into a sound framework. He was a proud member of the Society of Cincinnati, an organization of direct male descendants of the officers who served with George Washington during the Revolutionary War.

Thomas Drew was thoroughly devoted to his wife Alice and to his three daughters, Mary Drew of Cambridge, Massachusetts; Sally Cokelet of Rochester, New York; and Wendy Cavanaugh of Manlius, New York. He will be missed very much by the many people whose lives he touched.

Paul E. Duwez

POL E. DUWEZ

1907–1984

BY MORRIS COHEN

Pol e. duwez, one of the world's foremost scientists in the field of metals and materials, died in Pasadena, California, on December 31, 1984, at the age of seventy-seven. At the time of his death, he was professor emeritus of applied physics at the California Institute of Technology (Caltech).

His contributions to the fields of education, research, and technology covered a remarkably wide range of solid-state phenomena. These phenomena included plastic deformation and wave propagation, heat transfer and transpiration cooling, powder metallurgy, stable and metastable alloy systems, high-temperature alloys and ceramic materials, magnetic and superconducting phases, and the discovery of metallic glasses by novel quenching from the liquid state.

Professor Duwez was an internationalist in his personal background as well as in his career. He was born on December 11, 1907, in Mons, Belgium, and received much of his schooling in that community. He earned a degree in metallurgical engineering at the Mons School of Mines, graduating in 1932. During that formative period, he developed strong interests in music as well as in mathematics and physics. Indeed, he started to study the cello at the age of six and remained a serious cellist throughout most of his life, with special affection for chamber music. He continued his scientific education at the University of Brussels, where he received his D.Sc. in physics in 1933.

In 1933 Dr. Duwez was also awarded a Belgian-American Foundation fellowship, which enabled him to spend the period from 1933 to 1935 as a research fellow at the California Institute of Technology. There he was privileged to work under Theodore von Karman on the mechanical behavior of solids. This personal relationship and the concomitant professional experience were destined to play a telling role in the uniqueness and scope of Pol Duwez's research achievements during the ensuing years. In 1935, at the completion of his fellowship, he returned to Belgium, but not before meeting a gracious lady, Nera Faisse, who became his bride and constant companion. Their daughter, Nadine, was born in Brussels two years later.

During the next few years, Dr. Duwez was a member of the staff of the National Foundation for Scientific Research in Mons. Before long, however, he was appointed director of the National Laboratory for Silicates and assigned the task of establishing a new facility for ceramics research. This post gave him a fine opportunity to build on his previous studies of solid-state materials. But complications of World War II soon cut short his efforts. Fortunately all of the Duwez family members managed to escape from Belgium and find their separate ways back to Pasadena in 1940.

The following year, Dr. Duwez worked as research engineer on various defense projects at Caltech. In this capacity, he was able to demonstrate von Karman's theoretical prediction regarding the propagation of plastic-deformation waves in metals as a result of impact loading. From that point on, Pol Duwez's career at Caltech was assured.

After Dr. Duwez received his U.S. citizenship in 1944, von Karman selected him to head the materials section of the newly organized Jet Propulsion Laboratory, a position he held until 1954. During that exciting decade of research in and development of high-temperature rocket materials, Dr. Duwez was also appointed to the Caltech faculty, first as associate professor in 1947 and later, in 1952, as professor of materials science. He did not retire until 1978.

As an educator, Pol Duwez's well-known creativity flourished, not only in research but also in the development of new courses in physical metallurgy and materials science. His lectures were always carefully prepared and clearly focused, conveying substance with a minimum of embellishment. He was capable of inspiring students, both in teaching and in research, and offered a rare balance of imaginative ideas while patiently allowing students the freedom to explore.

As a result, Professor Duwez and his students were often among the "firsts" on numerous fronts. They were leaders in the early investigations of titanium and molybdenum alloys for potential high-temperature applications; in the elucidation of phase relationships exhibited by refractory rare-earth oxides; and in the proliferation of the "gun technique," commonly referred to as "splat quenching," for the rapid quenching of alloys from the liquid state. The latter experimentation led to the retention of extraordinary degrees of supersaturation in solid solutions, to the formation of entirely new metastable crystalline phases, and, most significantly of all, to the discovery of metallic glasses.

Under the guidance of Pol Duwez, it was also established for the first time that amorphous alloys can be ferromagnetic and even superconducting. These findings are now considered to have been a profound scientific advance—an advance that paved the way for literally thousands of papers from laboratories around the world. Moreover, ferromagnetic metallic glasses are now in commercial production for electric transformer and device applications.

Dr. Duwez's exceptional accomplishments and experience in the materials science and engineering of materials permitted him to contribute effectively to the work of many professional and governmental committees. Among the latter, he served with distinction on the Scientific Advisory Board to the chief of staff of the U.S. Air Force, the U.S. Ordnance Advisory Board on Titanium, the U.S. Navy Advisory Committee on Molybdenum, the Subcommittee on Structural Materials of the National Advisory Committee for Aeronau-

tics, the Senior Scientists Steering Group of the U.S. Army
Ordnance Corps, the Materials Research Council of the Defense Advanced Research Projects Agency, and the NATO
Advisory Group for Aeronautical Research and Development.

Professor Duwez's 120 publications, the success of his talented students, and his extensive service on national and international committees have earned him the highest professional esteem. The honors and awards he received in this
country and abroad are indicative: the Charles B. Dudley
Award of the American Society for Testing Materials (1951);
the Champion H. Mathewson Gold Medal and the William
Hume-Rothery Award of the Metallurgical Society of the
American Institute of Mining, Metallurgical, and Petroleum
Engineers (AIME) (1964 and 1981, respectively); Edward
DeMille Campbell Lecturer of the American Society for Met-
als (1967); the Francis J. Clamer Silver Medal of the Franklin
Institute (1968); the Albert Sauveur Achievement Award of
the American Society for Metals (1973); the Belgium Priz
Gouverneur Cornez (1973); the Paul Lebeau Medal of the
French Society of High Temperature (1974); the International Prize for New Materials of the American Physical Society (1980); and the Heyn Medal of the Deutsche Gesells-
chaft für Metallkunde (1981). He was elected to the National
Academy of Sciences (1972), the American Academy of Arts
and Sciences (1976), and the National Academy of Engineering (1979).

Dr. Duwez was also a fellow of the Metallurgical Society of
AIME, the American Ceramic Society, the American Society
for Metals, and the American Association for the Advancement of Science. He was a member of the American Physical
Society, the Association of Applied Solar Energy, the Society
of Sigma Xi, and the American Association of University
Professors. Internationally renowned in his field, he was also
a member of the British Institute of Metals and the French
Society of Civil Engineers.

After Pol Duwez retired in 1978, he continued frequent

contact with both his colleagues at Caltech and with his associates worldwide until his final illness in 1984. He is survived by his wife Nera, of Pasadena; his daughter Nadine, of Paris; and a host of scientists and technologists who are the direct and indirect beneficiaries of his lifelong work.

To all of us who had the privilege of knowing him, he will be remembered as a considerate, scholarly human being of independent spirit, who preferred not to follow trends but rather to create them.

PHILLIP EISENBERG

1919–1984

BY JOHN V. WEHAUSEN

Phillip eisenberg died of cardiac arrest on December 16, 1984. For more than thirty years, he had been a leader in the application of hydrodynamics to ships and offshore structures as well as to related industrial hydrodynamic problems. He was one of the founders in 1959 of Hydronautics, Inc., a firm that, from its inception, was noted for its excellent staff and its forward-looking leadership. Phillip Eisenberg served as its president until he sold his interest in the company in April 1983.

Eisenberg was born in Detroit, Michigan, on November 6, 1919. He attended the Detroit public schools and graduated from Wayne State University with a B.S. in civil engineering in 1941. Following a further year of study at the University of Iowa's Institute of Hydraulic Research, he began his professional career as a research engineer at the U.S. Navy's David Taylor Model Basin, in Washington, D.C.

In 1944 Eisenberg received his commission as an ensign in the Navy and served on the Naval Technical Mission in Europe. Following the war, he returned to his job as a civilian at the Taylor Model Basin, becoming head of the Fluid Phenomena Branch. He interrupted his work there for further study at the California Institute of Technology, from which he received a civil engineering degree in 1948.

Upon his return to the Taylor Model Basin from the California Institute of Technology, Eisenberg continued as head of the Fluid Phenomena Branch until 1953, when he left to become head of the Mechanics Branch of the Office of Naval Research. He held this position until 1959 when he and Marshall Tulin founded Hydronautics, Inc., which was first located in a rather modest setting in Rockville, Maryland, and later moved to its present location in Laurel, Maryland.

This bare-bones description of Eisenberg's career gives virtually no sense of his importance to the field of naval hydrodynamics (a term that he introduced), an importance based on his own contributions and the influence he brought to bear on its development during his years at the Office of Naval Research and at Hydronautics, Inc. During Eisenberg's years at the Taylor Model Basin and his early years at Hydronautics (before he became so involved in its administration), there were few aspects of ship hydrodynamics to which he did not contribute.

One field, however, consistently drew Eisenberg to it and evoked his interest—cavitation and the damage resulting from it. His first publication on this subject appeared in 1947; his last, in 1978. Some of these publications are research papers and some are expository review articles. One of the latter has become a standard reference on the subject of cavitation.

Eisenberg's six years as head of the Mechanics Branch of the Office of Naval Research were fruitful in a different way. The previous years had given him an overview of the research needs of the U.S. Navy in naval hydrodynamics, and he used the influence of his new position to develop a research program that would support these vital needs. Moreover, an important legacy of these six years is the biennial symposium on naval hydrodynamics, the nineteenth of which was held in September 1984. The symposia bring together the active researchers in naval hydrodynamics from all over the world for a week of lectures and discussions. Their published proceedings form an important part of the literature of the field.

One consequence of holding a position as a research administrator can be a growing sense of frustration at seeing others doing all the interesting research work. There may also be an awareness of a dangerous tendency to use the "royal we" in speaking of this work. To avoid these pitfalls, Eisenberg and his colleague Marshall Tulin decided to form their own consulting company in 1959.

As noted earlier, Hydronautics, Inc., began rather modestly. The company's headquarters consisted of several rooms in a former residence that had been converted for business purposes. The company's experimental tank was actually a plastic backyard swimming pool. Nonetheless, the company prospered, and within five years it had become an important national resource for naval hydrodynamics research, acquiring an international reputation for the excellence of its research and engineering development. Those who have worked at Hydronautics credit this excellence to the stimulating atmosphere provided by its leadership.

Phillip Eisenberg has not lacked formal recognition of his talents and accomplishments. For his work at the Taylor Model Basin during World War II, he received the U.S. Navy Meritorious Civilian Award in 1944. He was elected president of the Society of Naval Architects and Marine Engineers in 1973 and president of the Marine Technology Society in 1976. He was a fellow in both of these societies as well as a fellow of the American Society of Mechanical Engineers, the Royal Institution of Naval Architects, and the American Association for the Advancement of Science.

In addition, Eisenberg was a Gibbs Brothers Medalist of the National Academy of Sciences in 1974 and a David W. Taylor Medalist of the Society of Naval Architects and Marine Engineers in 1971; he received the Lockheed Award for Ocean Science and Engineering of the Marine Technology Society in 1980. He was elected to membership in the National Academy of Engineering in 1974.

Eisenberg was also generous with his time, serving on visiting committees for university departments; on policy committees for the National Science Foundation, the National Research Council, and the National Academy of Engineering; and on numerous technical committees for various organizations. He was the editor of the *Journal of Ship Research* from 1961 to 1970.

These remarks would be incomplete, however, without reference to Phillip Eisenberg's personal character. He was a man of staunch integrity who set high standards of personal conduct for himself and for others. His professional standards were also high but not unrealistic. Phillip's colleagues enjoyed working with him, and he maintained a warm relationship with them. He was always a loyal and helpful friend and also a good companion. He and his wife Edith, a college classmate, were a congenial, mutually supportive couple, and it was always a pleasure to visit with them and their two daughters, Elyse and Jean, at their home.

Eisenberg's death did not come unexpectedly. His health was doubly threatened, and he had known this since early 1984. Nevertheless, he faced the not-too-hopeful future with equanimity and optimism and continued his planned work insofar as his health permitted. Although he had already lived a full and fruitful life, he was still active in public service after his retirement from Hydronautics. Phillip Eisenberg's counsel will be missed by many, but he will be missed even more as a friend.

ELMER W. ENGSTROM

1901–1984

BY WILLIAM WEBSTER

Elmer w. engstrom died at the Meadow Lakes Retirement Community in Hightstown, New Jersey, on October 30, 1984, after a long illness. Dr. Engstrom, a former president of the RCA Corporation who also headed its research laboratories in Princeton, New Jersey, played a major role in the development of color television. He retired from RCA in 1969.

Dr. Engstrom rose to the top level of one of the world's largest electronics companies from a background of research, engineering, and technical management. In his career of thirty-nine years with RCA, he directed major research and engineering programs and advanced through increasingly important executive assignments involving the manufacture and marketing as well as the technical activities of the company.

Dr. Engstrom served as president of RCA from 1961 to the end of 1965. In the ensuing two years, he was chairman of the executive committee of the board of directors and chief executive officer. He relinquished the latter title in 1968 but remained chairman of the executive committee until his retirement. During the early years of his retirement, he was a consultant to RCA and remained a member of the board of directors until 1971.

Elmer Engstrom was born in Minneapolis, Minnesota, on

August 25, 1901. He graduated from the University of Minnesota with a B.S. in electrical engineering in 1923. In later years he was awarded honorary degrees by eighteen colleges and universities.

Following his graduation from the University of Minnesota, he joined the General Electric Company in Schenectady, New York, and was assigned to engineering development work on radio transmitting and receiving equipment. When General Electric initiated commercial activity in motion picture sound equipment, he was placed in charge of the company's engineering development and apparatus design.

In 1930, when the radio and engineering activities of General Electric were transferred to RCA, Elmer Engstrom joined the corporation as division engineer in charge of the Photophone sound motion picture apparatus. Soon afterwards, he assumed engineering responsibilities for RCA's broadcast receiver development and production.

Beginning in the 1930s, Dr. Engstrom supervised RCA's television research and development program. He developed the concept of television as a complete system, introducing one of the early large-scale examples of the system's engineering concept that is now standard in major technical programs. In the postwar years, as head of RCA Laboratories, he applied the same concept in directing the development program for the all-electronic, compatible color television system.

In 1931 Dr. Engstrom directed the first test of a complete television system at RCA. The test was made in the Empire State Building, where a transmitter was installed on the eighty-fifth floor. A mechanical scanner provided a 120-line, 24-frame picture from live and film subjects. Extensive field tests were then made using the first cathode ray tube receivers. The picture clarity left much to be desired, but the equipment worked well as a system, and the tests proved that television broadcasting was possible.

In 1942, when all RCA research project activities were merged at Princeton, New Jersey, Dr. Engstrom became director of general research. In 1945 he was elected vice-president in charge of research. Under his direction the research group of the RCA Laboratories compiled a brilliant wartime record in the fields of radar, radio, shoran, sonar, airborne electronics, infrared television, and acoustics.

The end of World War II resulted in a transition to a peacetime economy. Television became a major concern of the electronics industry. A rush to establish new television stations was followed by a partial freeze as the industry and the Federal Communications Commission (FCC) settled the thorny questions of standards, first for monochrome and then for color. During the lengthy field tests, hearings, and reviews, Dr. Engstrom led RCA's technical efforts and acted as the corporation's chief spokesman. He also served as vice-chairman of the National Television System Committee, the industry committee that studied and recommended the standards eventually adopted by the FCC in 1953.

In 1955 Elmer Engstrom, then senior executive vice-president of RCA, was also placed in charge of RCA's defense activities. Spurred by the experience of the Korean War, a tremendous buildup was taking place in defense electronics. Large projects such as BMEWS (the Ballistic Missile Early Warning System) were undertaken and successfully completed by RCA.

As the principal engineering executive of RCA during the 1950s, Dr. Engstrom was responsible for the establishment in 1958 of RCA's Astro-Electronics Division, the first organization of its scope established within the electronics industry to develop space electronic systems. The very successful TIROS (Television Infrared Observation Satellite) weather-reporting satellite system was an early product of this division.

These and other contributions in the fields of both engineering and corporate management brought Dr. Engstrom a number of honors from both engineering and industrial organizations. He was one of the founding members of the National Academy of Engineering and a member of its

Council. In 1965 he presented the Charles Proteus Steinmetz Centennial Lecture at the first annual meeting of the National Academy of Engineering and received the Charles Proteus Steinmetz Centennial Medal.

In 1958 he was the recipient of the Industrial Research Institute Medal for "distinguished leadership in industrial research," and in 1962 he received the Medal of Honor of the Electronic Industries Association in recognition of his contributions to the advancement of the electronics industry. In 1966 Dr. Engstrom was presented with the Founders Award of the Institute of Electrical and Electronics Engineers "for his leadership in management and integration of research and development programs and for his foresighted application of the systems engineering concept in bringing television to the public." That same year he also received the William Proctor Prize for scientific achievement from the Scientific Research Society of America.

His foreign honors included membership in the Royal Swedish Academy of Engineering Sciences and the rank of commander in the Order of Merit of the Italian Republic. In 1965 the King of Sweden conferred on him the rank of commander of the Royal Order of Vasa.

Dr. Engstrom was the author and coauthor of numerous articles that appeared in technical publications and was a licensed professional engineer in the state of New York. He participated in the work of many major advisory groups and professional organizations during his career. Among his principal positions and memberships were chairman of the Research and Engineering Advisory Panel on Electronics; member of the Defense Science Board, Office of the Secretary of Defense; member of the Research and Development Committee of the National Security Industrial Association and chairman of its visiting committee to the Naval Research Laboratory; and member of President Nixon's Science Policy Task Force.

In 1965 Elmer Engstrom was appointed chairman of the U.S. Industrial Payroll Savings Committee by Douglas Dillon,

Secretary of the Treasury. In honor of his community activities in Princeton, New Jersey, Dr. Engstrom was given the Gerard B. Lambert Community Service Award from the Princeton Area United Community Fund and was named "Man of the Year for 1964" by the Princeton Chamber of Commerce and Civic Council.

Dr. Engstrom's great ability was to recognize, organize, and direct the proliferating talents that surrounded him. Without exception, those who worked with him had not only a high respect for his ability and integrity but also a genuine liking for the man himself. Perhaps steadfastness was his most outstanding trait.

Over the years, his personality did not change much from his days as a young engineer. Those who knew Elmer Engstrom best would tell you that. He became more experienced, of course, and more mature, but he remained quiet in mien, courteous in speech, and almost embarrassingly honest in everything he did.

He was always searching in his questioning manner and steely-eyed in his decision-making style. He had a natural reserve that was sometimes mistaken for aloofness, yet he was always quick to acknowledge the thousands of acquaintances he had made over the years, making it a point to maintain personal relationships that dated back to his days as a young engineer.

VIVIAN FITZGEORGE ESTCOURT

1897–1985

BY JAMES N. LANDIS

Vivian FITZGEORGE ESTCOURT died in San Francisco on May 11, 1985. He was one of many Stanford University engineering graduates who have attained distinction. In 1963 he was made an honorary life member of the American Society of Mechanical Engineers "for distinguished engineering leadership in plant design, operation, organization, and management of modern electric power generating facilities."

Three years later the Franklin Institute awarded him the Newcomen Gold Medal in Steam and the Newcomen Society made him an honorary life member. During his long professional life, he dedicated his highly analytic abilities to improving the quality and cost-effectiveness of steam electric plants.

His brother, a public accountant eleven years his junior, says of Mr. Estcourt, "Without the guidance of a wise father and the loving and tender care of a wonderful mother, none of us could have done what we have done." Mr. Estcourt's father was an English barrister-at-law; at the time of Vivian's birth in the Hammersmith section of London on May 31, 1897, the family also included two daughters, ages seven and three.

Vivian's early education took place at King Edward's School, a prestigious English public school in Birmingham. On his arrival in the United States in 1912, he attended Lowell High School in San Francisco, where he was a member of the Debating Society in 1913. He later entered Stanford University to study engineering and while there participated in soccer, figure skating, and hiking in the High Sierras with the younger of his sisters and her friends.

Vivian joined the U.S. Army Medical Corps, driving ambulances in France and training other drivers for the job. He was discharged on November 5, 1921, and became a U.S. citizen on December 29, 1921. Because of his army service, he did not graduate from Stanford until 1922; he finished with two bachelor of arts degrees—one in mechanical engineering and one in electrical engineering.

After graduation, he worked for seven months as a design draftsman for the Nevada Consolidated Copper Company and then joined the Pacific Gas and Electric Company (PG&E), an affiliation that was to last from 1923 to 1964. In 1923 PG&E was a hydro company that had a single small steam plant, although its steam plant capacity would eventually undergo a period of major expansion. After a short time, Mr. Estcourt became an efficiency engineer in charge of power plant betterment work, a post he retained for eight years.

Thereafter, he rose through several successive positions of responsibility and finally became manager of the Steam Generation Department. As manager he was in charge of a system of more than four million kilowatts produced by thermal power plants burning gas, oil, delayed coke, fluid coke, sulfonated tar, pitch, and acid sludge, and including the very early Vallecitos and Humboldt Bay nuclear stations, the Geysers geothermal plant, and a city business area steam heating plant.

A major responsibility he assumed early in his utility career was that of manning several steam plants during a time when the San Francisco area had almost no steam plant personnel on which to draw. For years in his operation of the plants, Mr. Estcourt required that the log sheets be made in triplicate, with one copy coming to his office for personal review. Significant verbal reports were required to be confirmed in writing. As one station-operating subordinate reports, "Estcourt ran the show . . . did not tolerate shortcomings in people . . . wanted to know everything . . . was extremely interested in personnel training . . . kept aloof . . . was very perceptive and always agreeable to making changes to aid operation no matter who might suggest them." Today, this is called hands-on management.

He wrote seven papers from 1936 to 1953 that illustrate the very wide range of his mechanical, chemical, and electrical interests. One in particular dealt with generator end-iron heating and stability when operating large generators in the underexcited region for control of system voltage, thereby extending the load range for this type of operation. Using much firsthand personal experience, he prepared two additional papers: "Manpower and Other Factors Affecting Operating Costs in Generating Stations" (ASME 53-A–95) and "Plant Management and Other Factors Affecting Maintenance Costs" (ASME 55-A–87). These two papers received the 1955 Prime Movers Award of the American Society of Mechanical Engineers for best international contribution on power plant operations.

For several years Mr. Estcourt was chairman of the Edison Electric Institute Prime Movers Equipment Availability Subcommittee. The extremely important committee work that he spearheaded consisted of collecting and analyzing power plant steam generator and turbine generator equipment availability statistics as reported by nearly all the companies that were members of the Edison Electric Institute.

Mr. Estcourt also became active in power station stack discharge research, which at that time was of great concern to public authorities and the utility industry. He was soon selected as the chairman of the Edison Electric Institute/U.S. Public Health Service Joint Steering Committee for Stack Plume Opacity Measurement and Evaluation Research.

For a period of six or more years, Mr. Estcourt devoted a

great deal of his time to encouraging graduating engineers to work in the utility industry. He wrote three papers in connection with this industry recruitment activity while serving as the American Society for Mechanical Engineers representative on the Engineers Council for Professional Development Accreditation Team for Engineering Colleges.

From 1962 through 1964 Mr. Estcourt continued his association with PG&E as a consulting engineer in thermal power production. Late in 1963 he joined the Bechtel Power Corporation as a consulting engineer. He remained with Bechtel through 1984, completing many assignments to improve plant availability, reduce capital and operating costs, and develop a means of reducing stack emissions.

The unsatisfactory performance of electrostatic precipitators in collecting ash from low-sulfur coals led him to introduce the "European Design" electrostatic precipitator in this country for high-efficiency performance with western low-sulfur coals. Mr. Estcourt recognized the need to standardize the measuring and reporting of electrical fly ash characteristics to permit the proper sizing of precipitators, and he formed and chaired an Institute of Electrical and Electronics Engineers committee to address this matter. In the field of sulfur dioxide emission control, he combined the spray dryer and baghouse concepts and was a driving force in the development and application of this dry sulfur dioxide control system, an approach that is now widely accepted. He produced four papers in his eightieth and eighty-first years.

Although Mr. Estcourt was a distinctive individual who circulated broadly, he was also a very private person and never discussed his background and experiences. In 1929 he married Helen Grant, a lovely California lady and companion. The two traveled extensively; their trips included a safari to Africa and travels to many other locales outside the United States.

Mr. Estcourt was elected to the National Academy of Engineering in 1981. He was a member of numerous other societies throughout his professional life, serving on many committees and generally ascending to the chairmanship of the committees in which his interest was greatest. He always attended conventions alone. He would sometimes surprise associates at the convention social gatherings by dancing very ably with their wives—behavior that seemed completely out of character for the man associates thought him to be: that is, someone possessing solely technical interests.

Some of his personal character traits are revealed by the statements of several individuals who worked closely with him. From a secretary of many years: "He appeared to use every moment in a disciplined way." An office technical associate noted these characteristics: "His inquisitive nature propelled him into investigating a subject of interest until he understood it fully; and he tenaciously followed through on any program until his objectives were achieved. He had little patience with ignorance or stupidity but was always ready to take an interest in and assist young, promising, eager engineers."

One of two manufacturers' representatives who dealt a lot with him said: "He was always on the look-out for a 'snow-job'; he demanded honesty and appreciated it!" The other observed: "My discussions with him were very enlightening to me. I felt he was my friend. He gave willingly of his time when questioned but answers were not expansive."

Mr. Estcourt was never able to enjoy, except in brief anticipation, the Santa Barbara home he had purchased for retirement. His last seven and a half years were spent alone in his San Francisco home, as a widower, which may account for his continuation of technical activity. In addition to being a Mason for fifty-five years, he is known to have had three other nontechnical interests, which he very rarely discussed: football, the Theosophical Society in America, and the Commonwealth Club of San Francisco. Soon after Mrs. Estcourt's death, he flew around the world, stopping at many places, including several stops in India, which his brother believes were connected with Mr. Estcourt's theosophical beliefs.

It can be said that Vivian Fitzgerald Estcourt appeared to

live his life as he wished, little affected by others, always investigating something, with the accomplishment of his objectives as his reward. He has left an enduring written record of many technical contributions to the utility industry in which he spent a long and very active professional life.

Phil M. Ferguson

PHIL MOSS FERGUSON

1899–1986

BY EARNEST F. GLOYNA
AND JOHN E. BREEN

PHIL MOSS FERGUSON, a leading pioneer in developing the basic theory of design procedures for reinforced concrete structures, died at the age of eighty-six on August 28, 1986. An outstanding civil engineering educator, Professor Ferguson was the Dean T. U. Taylor Professor Emeritus in Engineering at the University of Texas at Austin, where he taught until his retirement in 1976.

His distinguished scholarship and his leadership in developing an internationally recognized structural engineering program at the University of Texas at Austin were fittingly recognized in 1979 when the University of Texas System Board of Regents named the large structural engineering research facility at the university's Balcones Research Center the Phil Moss Ferguson Structural Engineering Laboratory. In the hundred-year history of the university, only two other buildings had ever been named for living faculty.

Phil Moss Ferguson was born on November 10, 1899, in Bartlett, Texas, a small mid-Texas town. After his high school education in Waco, he entered the Civil Engineering Department of the University of Texas at Austin, where he received his B.S. in civil engineering in 1922 and a C.E. in 1923.

His interest in structural engineering and especially in reinforced concrete resulted in his enrolling for graduate studies at the University of Wisconsin, which was then one of the

best-known American centers of plain and reinforced concrete higher studies. He received an M.S. from Wisconsin in
1924 and subsequently joined Dwight P. Robinson & Company of New York as a structural engineer. His experience in
the design of power plants and industrial buildings and in
the construction of high-rise buildings was an important influence on his teaching and research at the University of
Texas. Professor Ferguson always approached the most theoretical problems within the general framework of practicality
that was established during this design phase of his career.

For more than two decades after he joined the University
of Texas faculty in 1928, Professor Ferguson devoted his
energies principally to the teaching programs at the then
predominantly undergraduate institution. He served as
chairman of the Civil Engineering Department from 1943 to
1957 and played a leading role in establishing the department's graduate engineering programs. He supervised the
first doctoral student in civil engineering at Texas.

In contrast to many academic researchers, Phil Ferguson's
personal research and writing career did not bloom until he
had passed his fiftieth birthday. His first serious, original paper at the national level was published on three-dimensional
structural analysis in 1950. This was followed by a number
of papers exploring shear and diagonal tension in reinforced
concrete, which were recognized by the American Concrete
Institute's prestigious Wason Medals in 1954 and 1958.

Once unfettered, his research career rapidly developed,
and his writings became internationally acclaimed. Throughout this period, he attracted a number of fine students to
Austin and encouraged many of the junior faculty to seek
doctoral degrees. His international stature as a leader in
structural engineering research and his development of design procedures led to his election to the National Academy
of Engineering in 1973.

Phil Moss Ferguson was the driving force in the development of the internationally recognized structural engineering program at the University of Texas and, as a senior fac-

ulty contributor, provided leadership and stimulus for the development of the highest ranked graduate program in civil engineering in the South and Southwest. He developed a reputation as a splendid engineering teacher, and his teaching ability was recognized by a General Dynamics Award for Teaching Excellence in 1962.

Students from all over the United States and many foreign countries attended his advanced courses on the behavior and design of reinforced concrete structures and conducted research under his supervision. Many of these students have assumed leadership roles in structural engineering.

In developing the structural engineering research program, which won wide acceptance and backing from government, industry, foundations, and trade associations, Phil Ferguson provided leadership in promptly translating research data into design practice. His research accomplishments involved many fields, but most noteworthy were the series of original contributions that advanced comprehensive design recommendations for reinforced concrete structures.

Each of his research programs reflected extensive knowledge of the specific problem as well as the impact of the problem on the total design and behavioral considerations of the member in question. His keen sense of engineering design construction practice and structural behavior, which he developed as a practicing designer and nurtured with years of consulting and technical committee work, provided a breadth of view that led to many of the significant breakthroughs in modern concrete research, especially in such areas as diagonal tension, torsion, slender columns, and reinforcement development.

Professor Ferguson's famous text, *Reinforced Concrete Fundamentals*, was initially published soon after the American Concrete Institute took the first step toward allowing ultimate strength design. It has been revised three times; the fourth edition was published in 1979. The Ferguson text is a digest of available research, design aids, and philosophy. Careful inclusion of a balanced and unbiased evaluation of current design procedures, comprehensive and forceful emphasis on fundamentals, and incessant urging that tradition give way to truth and logic justified his emphasis on ultimate strength procedures.

The unusually wide acceptance of his work by the designer as well as the teacher stands as a lasting measure of his work. His texts were influential in bringing about the acceptance of the new procedures that have led to far-reaching economies. His books and papers demonstrated his creative farsightedness and deep understanding of structural engineering and technology. His research writings were recognized three times by the American Concrete Institute's Wason Medal, a distinction accorded only one other author in the institute's history, and by the Raymond C. Reese Structural Award.

No professional service gave Professor Ferguson more satisfaction than his more than forty years as a member of the American Concrete Institute Building Code Committee. He was an extremely influential member of that committee, which formulates the basic standards for design and construction of reinforced concrete structures in the United States as well as in many foreign countries.

The energies he devoted to professional and technical organizations culminated in his serving as president at the national or state level in several important societies (e.g., the American Concrete Institute, the American Society of Civil Engineers, and the Texas Society of Professional Engineers); he was also a U.S representative to several active Comité Européen du Béton commissions and headed the U.S. liaison delegation to international meetings. He was named an honorary member of both the American Concrete Institute and the American Society of Civil Engineers in recognition of his long and distinguished service to those societies. Both the University of Texas and the University of Wisconsin recognized him as a distinguished graduate.

In 1976 Phil Moss Ferguson was appointed professor emeritus at the University of Texas, signaling the end of forty-eight years on the active faculty. Although no longer involved in the active teaching and research program, his involvement and service to the university continued through his counsel to the faculty and students and his involvement in professional and technical affairs.

Declining health finally forced him to move from Austin to be closer to his son, Yale H. Ferguson, a Rutgers faculty member. These last years immediately before his death were spent in close contact with his son, his daughter-in-law Kitty, and his three grandchildren. Their loving support brought much comfort in his declining years.

Far beyond his many technical contributions, Phil Ferguson will be remembered for his spirit of uncompromising integrity, his dedication to the application of fundamental engineering principles, and his stimulation of young minds. A dedicated church member and a highly respected political conservative, Professor Ferguson was also a faculty leader in questioning the right of the state of Texas to require affirmation of belief in a Supreme Being as a condition for university employment in the 1950s. He championed the right of individuals to differ in a pluralistic, constitutional society.

A seemingly stern and demanding teacher, he inspired his students to strive for excellence but never to compromise their personal integrity or neglect their family and civic responsibilities. His passing brought forth countless students and associates, each with a story of a special encouragement or some special assistance, often financial, offered by Professor Ferguson at trying times in their careers.

He was a small, quiet, and gentle giant, who left behind him a totally changed approach to teaching, research, and graduate education in the two corners of his world that were dearest to him—his native Texas and the special world of reinforced concrete.

J. Earl Frazier

JOHN EARL FRAZIER

1902–1985

BY J. E. BURKE

J OHN EARL FRAZIER, chairman of the board and treasurer of Frazier-Simplex Inc., died on January 1, 1985, in the Washington Hospital in Washington, Pennsylvania, at the age of eighty-two. Frances, his wife of forty-seven years, died in 1983.

Earl Frazier had been associated for forty-nine years with Frazier-Simplex Inc., a company founded in 1918 by his father, Chauncey Earl Frazier. Earl Frazier had built the company into a diversified organization that provided feasibility studies, supplied equipment, designed and constructed entire plants, and consulted on virtually every aspect of the glass industry with many of the glass plants in the United States and around the world. He was elected to the National Academy of Engineering in 1978.

Earl Frazier was born in Houseville, Pennsylvania, a community near Pittsburgh, on July 4, 1902, and spent his entire life in the Pittsburgh area. He graduated from Washington High School and received a B.S. in 1922 from Washington and Jefferson College in Washington, where he concurrently served as an instructor in chemistry from 1919 to 1920. Frazier received an M.S. in chemical engineering from the Massachusetts Institute of Technology (MIT) in 1924 and a D.Sc. from the University of Brazil in 1938. He was a registered professional engineer in Pennsylvania.

For several years after graduating from MIT, Earl Frazier worked as a chemical engineer at Owens-Illinois Glass Company in Clarion, Pennsylvania. He then joined Frazier-Simplex as a fuel engineer; he became president of the company in 1945 and continued as its chief executive officer until his death. While at Frazier-Simplex, he was granted, as inventor or coinventor, fifty patents in the glass technology field. As a technical leader in his company, Earl was particularly effective in advancing the use of blanket batch charges and in promoting the use of electric glass melting rather than the standard gas firing technique.

Frazier was an ardent supporter of the American Ceramic Society (ACS)—not only of its glass division but also of the society as a whole. He was always active in the society's affairs and saw it grow enormously as the field of ceramics expanded, especially over the past couple of decades. He was a fellow of the society and served in many positions, including those of treasurer (from 1968 to 1969) and president (from 1970 to 1971). ACS awarded him its John Jeppson Medal and Award in 1976 and the Albert Victor Bleininger Award in 1969 and selected him as a distinguished life member in 1972.

He is fondly remembered by many people in the society for the delightful luncheons he gave annually in Pittsburgh at the time of the Bleininger Award presentation. Each year he would introduce all of the many attendees by name and then deliver a brief summary of their accomplishments—a prodigious feat of memory.

Earl Frazier was active in many other organizations. He was chairman of the board of trustees of the Ceramic Engineering Department at the University of Illinois and was a life member of the board of trustees of Washington and Jefferson College; he was also active at Pennsylvania State University, where the Keramos-Frazier Ceramic Library was named in his honor.

In addition, Earl Frazier was active in local community affairs. At various times he served as chairman of the board of trustees of the Washington Hospital and was president of the Washington Chamber of Commerce. He was a member of the board of trustees of the Pennsylvania Western State School, now Western Center, and served on several governing boards of other business and fraternal organizations.

Earl Frazier will be greatly missed by his many associates in the glass and ceramics professions and those in his other areas of activity as well.

KING-SUN FU

1930–1985

BY M. E. VAN VALKENBURG

KING-SUN FU, W. M. Goss Distinguished Professor of Engineering at Purdue University and pioneer and universally acclaimed leader in the field of syntactic pattern recognition, died of a sudden heart attack on April 29, 1985, in Washington, D.C. His death came while he was attending a National Research Council dinner celebrating the National Science Foundation's creation of six new engineering research centers. Professor Fu was director of one of the centers—the new Intelligent Manufacturing Center at Purdue University.

King-sun Fu was born in Nanking, China, on October 2, 1930. He received a B.S. from the National Taiwan University in 1953, an M.S. from the University of Toronto in 1955, and a Ph.D. from the University of Illinois in 1959, all in electrical engineering.

From the beginning, Professor Fu saw no conflict between basic research and its applications. He believed that if the basic research were sufficiently deep and powerful, it would solve many difficult practical problems. Conversely, he believed that important practical problems were not to be successfully solved by ad hoc methods without involving a deep theoretical foundation.

While still in Taiwan, King-sun Fu worked in industry, first at the Taiwan Power Company and later with the Chinese Broadcasting Company. After he received his doctorate, he made the difficult decision to gain further experience by joining the Boeing Airplane Company as a research engineer in 1959. The desire to teach never left him, however, and during the spring of 1960 Professor Fu taught a course at Seattle University. The following fall, he accepted an appointment at Purdue University.

Shortly after Dr. Fu's arrival at Purdue, his department head, the late Thomas F. Jones, suggested that Dr. Fu spend a semester at the Research Laboratory of Electronics at the Massachusetts Institute of Technology. That laboratory experience changed the path of his professional life because it marked the initiation of Professor Fu's interest in pattern recognition. On his return to Purdue, Dr. Fu's interests expanded to such topics as machine intelligence, image processing, computer vision, and expert system development.

Dr. Fu was known for his innovative ideas and his practical applications of them—for example, the identification and classification of crops from remotely sensed multisectorial data, the detection of irradiated chromosomes, and the computerization of a blood cell classification system. He also developed X-ray techniques for the automatic diagnosis of abnormalities of lungs, heart, liver, and pancreas. Other of his X-ray applications involved the identification and classification of fingerprints. Even more recently, Dr. Fu's methods have been applied to integrated circuit chip and metal surface inspections, which are both important to industrial automation.

At the time of his death, Professor Fu had supervised seventy-five Ph.D. students who now hold positions of leadership in industry and academia. In addition, he published more than three hundred papers and four books.

Throughout his professional career, King-sun Fu received numerous awards and much recognition. The most important of these are the American Society for Engineering Education Senior Research Award (1981), the Institute of Electrical and Electronics Engineers (IEEE) Education Medal (1982), and the Harry Goode Memorial Award from the

American Federation of Information Processing Societies (1982). King-sun Fu was elected to the National Academy of Engineering in 1976.

Dr. Fu was the founding editor of the journal *IEEE Transactions on Pattern Analysis and Machine Intelligence*. In addition, he served his profession in many other ways—for example, as vice-president for publications of the IEEE Computer Society and as the first president of the International Association for Pattern Recognition. From 1965 until his death, he held more than forty-five volunteer positions in various organizations—mostly those of the IEEE. He was also a visiting professor at Stanford University as a Guggenheim fellow and a visiting professor at the University of California at Berkeley on two different occasions.

Dr. Fu traveled widely, especially to assist his colleagues in Taiwan. He was frequently a member of American delegations to international conferences in such places as Moscow, Warsaw, Copenhagen, and Tokyo.

King-sun met his wife, Viola, while they were students at the University of Illinois. Thereafter, Viola was a constant companion throughout his lifetime of adventures. They had two sons, Francis and Thomas, and a daughter, June.

King-sun Fu never declined requests for help from his colleagues and students, whether day or night. He never asked for credit for himself. His greatness as a researcher, teacher, and person continues to shine through.

WILFRED McGREGOR HALL

1894–1986

BY CHARLES C. NOBLE

WILFRED McGREGOR HALL, one of the world's great engineers and construction managers, died in Boston on November 5, 1986, two weeks after suffering a stroke. He was ninety-two and had been professionally active almost until the time of his death. He retired as chairman of the Chas. T. Main Corporation and the Chas. T. Main Engineers, Inc., in 1985, when the corporation and its subsidiaries were sold to Parsons Corporation of Pasadena, California.

Mac Hall was born in Denver, Colorado, on June 12, 1894, and was reared in New Hampshire. He returned to Denver to attend the University of Colorado, earning his B.S. in civil engineering in 1916. This event marked the beginning of a long and distinguished career of almost seventy years in the fields of engineering and construction.

With his sheepskin packed away, Mac Hall joined Chas. T. Main, a Boston-based engineering company, as a field and research engineer in 1916. His service with Main was interrupted by World War I; he left the company in 1917 to join the U.S. Army. With the war ended, he rejoined Main in 1920. After two years, he again left to become project supervisor for various construction companies on a number of hydroelectric projects in Puerto Rico and Brazil.

In 1941 Mac Hall returned to Chas. T. Main to help the company with its World War II workload. Within two years,

179

he had been named one of Main's directors, a signal accomplishment in this closely held private firm. In 1957 he became its president; this achievement was followed in 1971 by his election as chairman of the board, a position he held until his retirement in 1985.

Mac Hall's career extended considerably beyond the length of two normal careers. He did not believe in retirement so long as his mind remained sharp and clear but held to the old tradition that a man should "die with his boots on"—which he essentially did. His record of notable engineering achievements formed a chronicle of the growth and development of the engineering field and contributed materially to the recognition and acceptance of the engineering profession's role as vital to the welfare of man and his environment.

His accomplishments in the field of physical works and their conception and realization spanned a wide spectrum of large-scale engineering projects and programs throughout the developed and developing world. Typical are the St. Lawrence and Niagara hydroelectric projects, which were the world's largest at the time and for which he had major responsibility for engineering and construction management. Of these, Robert Moses wrote to Mr. Hall that they were "a tribute to the quality of leadership in your organization and the excellence of your design and supervisory forces."

In the field of management and administration, he broadened the scope of Chas. T. Main; through innovation and the leadership and inspiration of his subordinates, he led the company to a position as one of the ten largest engineering and construction management firms in the United States. At the time of its sale to Parsons, Main employed more than 3,000 employees and was recognized worldwide as a leading design, engineering, and construction firm.

Main provided a full scope of project and construction management, as well as construction and support services. It provided these services through a multidisciplined group of professionals using the latest advances in engineering, construction, and computer technology in pursuing the clients's objectives. Under Mac Hall's stewardship, Main expanded its fields to include projects involving thermal power generation; hydroelectric power generation and a full scale of water resources; power systems transmission and distribution; industrial processes and manufacturing facilities covering pulp, paper, and forest industries, printing and publishing, chemicals, plastics and textiles, light and heavy manufacturing, and electronics and electrical equipment; total-plant energy systems; and environmental compliance, conservation, and controls.

Mac Hall drummed the firm's philosophy into his subordinates: "Do it well, on time, within budget." He engendered pride in the fact that since its incorporation, Main had served more than 3,000 clients worldwide and completed more than 14,000 assignments—a long step from one of its earliest proposals (January 28, 1893), for the design of an electric plant for the Lynn, Massachusetts, Gas and Electric Light Company.

Looking back on Mac Hall's long career, one recognizes that, in the area of engineering contributions to society, he warrants a ranking among the top individuals in the world, having earned wide recognition for his significant engineering accomplishments. Mac Hall was a fierce achiever, one of those towering giants who appears on the world scene all too infrequently. The litany of his activities and awards attests to his wide-ranging interests and prestige.

He was registered as a professional engineer in forty-two states, the District of Columbia, Puerto Rico, Turkey, and the provinces of Nova Scotia and New Brunswick. He was a fellow of the American Society of Civil Engineers; a past president of the U.S. Committee on Large Dams, the U.S. Committee on Irrigation and Drainage, and the Northeastern Chapter of the American Institute of Consulting Engineers; a director of the American Consulting Engineering Council of New England; a member of the Boston Society of Civil Engineers, the Massachusetts Society of Professional Engineers, the Society of American Military Engineers, and the Royal Society for the Encouragement of the Arts and Commerce; a past director of the Massachusetts Society for the Prevention of Blindness and the Goodwill Industries; a member of the Beavers and the Moles construction societies; and a director of the Newcomen Society of North America.

His awards were many. Among them were an honorary doctorate of engineering from Tufts University (1955), the American Society of Chemical Engineers' Outstanding Civil Engineering Achievement Award (1960), the University of Colorado Distinguished Engineering Alumnus Award (1967), the Ralph W. Horne Award from the Boston Society of Civil Engineers (1970), the George Westinghouse Gold Medal Award of the American Society of Mechanical Engineers (1971), the George Norlin Silver Medal by the University of Colorado (1972), the Newcomen Society of North America Award for Distinguished Service (1975), and the Engineer of the Year Award from the Engineers Club of Boston (1977).

In 1983 Wilfred McGregor Hall was honored by being selected for membership in the National Academy of Engineering. His election to the academy was the capstone of a long, distinguished, and honored career as a leader, an engineer, and an administrator. With his death in 1986 came the passing of the Grand Old Man of Engineering.

JOHN DICKSON HARPER

1910–1985

BY ALLEN S. RUSSELL

J OHN DICKSON HARPER, former chairman of the Aluminum Company of America (Alcoa), noted industrialist, and civic leader, died on July 26, 1985, in Pittsburgh's St. Clair Memorial Hospital of a heart ailment. He was seventy-five years old.

Mr. Harper was born in Louisville, Tennessee, on April 6, 1910. When he was fifteen years old and still in high school, he obtained a summer job running an electric truck for twelve dollars a week at Alcoa's nearby operations, where he continued to work during school vacations until he received his high school diploma. After graduation, he became a cooperative student at the University of Tennessee and alternated his schedule between classes and his job in the Alcoa plant. He also found time to be a member of the ROTC, the Pershing Rifles, and Tau Beta Pi.

In 1933, following his graduation from the university with a degree in electrical engineering, Mr. Harper went to work operating a complex powerhouse switchboard in one of Alcoa's hydroelectric plants. Two years later, he was assisting in the actual design and construction of a new generating station.

In 1943 John became assistant power manager of Alcoa's extensive Tennessee and North Carolina generating facilities. During the next eight years, he organized central load dispatching, standardized operating procedures, coordinated plant operations with the Tennessee Valley Authority, directed the development of telemetering equipment, and patented several sophisticated telemetry devices. In addition, he developed maintenance procedures for equipment and oils and administered power contracts for the facilities.

After Alcoa decided in 1951 to build a hundred-million-dollar aluminum smelter at Rockdale, Texas, Mr. Harper was given the responsibility of building and operating it. He soon found, however, that the actual building of the smelter was only one of his many construction problems. In addition to erecting a huge reduction plant in an industrially undeveloped area of Texas, Alcoa had decided to generate its power by strip-mining and burning lignite, a subbituminous coal that abounded in the area. This decision meant that while his engineers handled site preparations (getting the land ready for foundations and scooping out an 850-acre lake to store water for the smelter), Mr. Harper had to prepare area residents for a major upheaval in their landscape and their lives.

This part of the story was reported in the *Saturday Evening Post* 1955 article, "How to Get Along with Texans," by George Sessions Perry. According to Perry, Mr. Harper, wearing khakis and driving an inexpensive car, set out to win friends for Alcoa. He became acquainted with the area's ranchers, farmers, businessmen, and politicians; helped the small town of Rockdale expand to accommodate thousands of construction workers and, later, production employees; purchased property and minerals; negotiated water rights-of-way with landowners along a twelve-mile pipeline to the San Gabriel and Little rivers; and generally dispelled fears that Pittsburgh Yankees were out to ruin Texas for a profit. Later, reported Perry, when plant operations required the construction of a lake, he did not surround it with a nine-foot fence to keep the public out, but instead stocked it with bass and invited the community to enjoy it as their own.

Mr. Harper pledged to Rockdale's town council that Alcoa

would pay taxes in advance so that the town could expand such essential municipal facilities as water lines and streets. New schools also had to be built for the children who would come with the anticipated employment flood. When he learned that the weekly *Rockdale Reporter* had been campaigning for years for a municipal swimming pool, Mr. Harper arranged for Alcoa to donate the land and pay half the cost of a first-class pool installation.

Scarcely a year after ground was broken, the first potline at the Rockdale Works was producing aluminum. By early 1954 the entire smelter was in operation at a capacity of 90,000 tons a year—a figure that later expansion increased to more than 300,000 tons a year, making Rockdale Alcoa's largest smelter.

On April 24, 1954, more than seven hundred special guests, including Governor Shivers and Alcoa executives, visited the smelter for lunch and a tour that preceded an open house. The next day John Harper learned what it meant to invite all of Texas to a public inspection. He and his staff had expected ten thousand visitors at most. By nightfall, however, more than twenty thousand central Texans had poured through the plant, leaving an exhausted Alcoa staff.

In 1955 Alcoa's management decided that John Harper had fulfilled his Rockdale mission and transferred him to Pittsburgh. He was made Smelting Division general manager in 1956 and was appointed vice-president in charge of the Alcoa Smelting and Fabricating divisions in 1960. In 1962 he became, in succession, vice-president in charge of production, executive vice-president, and a director. He became president of Alcoa in 1963 and chairman of the board in 1970. He held the position of chief executive officer from 1965 until March 1, 1975. On June 19, 1975, he retired as chairman, but continued as a director. He was chairman of the executive committee from 1965 until 1978.

Ranked high among his accomplishments was the development of the Alcoa smelting process, a revolutionary, power-saving method of producing aluminum. Mr. Harper supported this project from its long, expensive development stage through its full-scale piloting at Palestine, Texas. Application of the smelting process was eventually postponed by excess capacity in the aluminum industry.

During his busy years with Alcoa, John Harper rose at 6:30 or earlier every morning, including Sundays and holidays; his tremendous drive kept him going until late at night. It was commonplace for him to work several hours in his Pittsburgh office, fly to New York in a company plane for a business luncheon or another engagement, and return to Pittsburgh by late afternoon. Typically, by dawn the next day, he could be off to Washington, an Alcoa installation on either coast, or an overseas business conference.

John Harper's leadership style in Alcoa was modeled on a practical plane. He delegated authority; expected, and got, results. He might ask advice from a dozen associates on major problems, but when it was time to act, he made the decision.

Following his retirement from Alcoa, Mr. Harper accepted the position of director and chairman of the Communications Satellite Corporation (COMSAT) and director of AEA Investors, Inc., Crutcher Resources Corporation, and Banque Paribas. The year before he passed away, he became chairman of AEA Investors, Inc.

Of all his convictions, none was more positive than his belief that no business could survive without adequate profits regardless of how prosperous it or its country might appear to be. He expressed his feelings on this point to the Dallas Management Association:

> Whatever the reasons may be, it is evident that increasing numbers of Americans seem to want the benefits of the free enterprise economic system without first putting forth the effort to earn the profits that make possible an even higher standard of living.
>
> If we are to have a public policy of prosperity without profits, this means that we must embrace a new economic and political philosophy—one in which state control and dictatorial power replace our free choice in the marketplace—and I firmly believe that this is not what Americans, including those in labor and management, really want.

The dangerous illusion of profitless prosperity feeds on ignorance, indifference, and procrastination. . . .

He called business to a broader fulfillment of its social responsibility and to deeper involvement with the society at large. To the Congress of American Industry sponsored by the National Association of Manufacturers, he said:

> A viable society in which business can prosper and grow, the kind of society all of us want, demands the intelligent exercise of public responsibility by the business community itself. . . .
>
> It makes sense to participate—with corporate money, talent, and energy—in a community project to improve conditions in the slums. In the long run, such participation will prove to be beneficial to your own business. Because, if you reduce delinquency, crime, and illiteracy, you reduce your own corporate tax load, and you convert welfare cases into productive workers.

In delivering the three 1976 Fairless Lectures, "A View of the Corporate Role in Society," at Carnegie Mellon University, he said: "I have offered as my central thesis the conviction that it is the responsibility of the corporation to deserve and keep society's trust, and that it does so by being a positive agent of change."

He also said in these lectures, "I have tried to practice the principles of management responsibility which I preach. I have devoted myself to bringing others together to work together for the common good."

John Harper was a founder and the first chairman of the Business Roundtable, chairman of the National Alliance of Businessmen, vice-chairman of the Committee for Economic Development, honorary member of the Business Council, and a senior member of the Conference Board. He was a founder and chairman of the International Primary Aluminum Institute and president of the Aluminum Association.

In addition, he was a director of the Mellon National Corporation, the Metropolitan Life Insurance Company, the Goodyear Tire and Rubber Company, and the Procter & Gamble Company. He was vice-chairman of the Committee for Constructive Consumerism, vice-chairman and a life trustee of Carnegie Mellon University, and a member of both the national executive committee of the Boy Scouts of America and the Business Committee for Arts, Inc.

Among numerous honors bestowed on Mr. Harper during his career was the Knight's Cross, Order of St. Olav, for distinguished contributions to Norwegian industry. He also held the Silver Beaver Award of the Boy Scouts of America, the American Business Press Silver Quill Award, and the Pennsylvania Society's Gold Medal for Distinguished Service. He received the 1977 Gantt Memorial Medal of the American Society of Mechanical Engineers and the first Bryce Harlow Foundation Award in 1982.

John Harper was a fellow of the American Institute of Electrical Engineers, a fellow of the American Society of Mechanical Engineers, and a life member of both the Institute of Electrical and Electronics Engineers and the American Society for Metals. He held a number of honorary degrees: doctor of engineering degrees from Lehigh University, Maryville College, and Rensselaer Polytechnic Institute; doctor of law degrees from both Carnegie Mellon University and the University of Evansville; a doctor of science degree from Clarkson College of Technology; and a doctor of commercial science from Widener College. He was elected to the National Academy of Engineering in 1971.

Mr. Harper is survived by his wife Mary Lee and her three sons of Mt. Lebanon, Pennsylvania, and Jonathan's Landing, Florida, and by his sons, John D. of Pittsburgh, Pennsylvania, and Thomas W. of Knoxville, Tennessee. He is also survived by eight grandchildren. His first wife, Samma Lucille McCrary, died in 1979. His eldest son, Rogers McCrary Harper, died in 1980.

Mr. Harper's service to the U.S. government and to the aluminum industry was long and distinguished. During his tenure as chief executive officer of the world's largest aluminum producer, he became the spokesman for the aluminum industry. He was an ardent advocate of the social responsibility of industry and an ardent promoter of private enterprise. He strengthened Alcoa's position as an industrial leader and led the company's penetration into promising and innovative market areas. A staunch believer in business and government cooperation, he was the friend and confidant of presidents of the United States.

Albert G. Holzman

ALBERT G. HOLZMAN

1921–1985

BY DONALD C. BURNHAM

ALBERT G. HOLZMAN, professor and chairman of the Department of Industrial Engineering, Engineering Management, and Operations Research at the University of Pittsburgh School of Engineering, died of a heart attack at the age of sixty-three on May 1, 1985, while attending a professional society meeting in Boston. Dr. Holzman spent his entire career—his education, his industrial experience, and his academic teaching and management years—in the field of industrial engineering.

Dr. Holzman was born in 1921 in Johnstown, Pennsylvania. He attended the University of Pittsburgh from which he received both a B.S. and an M.S. in industrial engineering and a Ph.D. in economics. After two years of experience as an industrial analyst with the Bethlehem Steel Corporation, Holzman joined the staff of the University of Pittsburgh as an assistant professor.

He moved rapidly up the academic ladder and in 1958 became a full professor in the School of Industrial Engineering. Albert Holzman retained this professorship while concurrently serving as chairman of the Industrial Engineering Department in 1965. He also served as the director of engineering operations of the NASA Technology Transfer Center from 1965 to 1972.

During the twenty years that Dr. Holzman was chairman

of the Industrial Engineering Department of the University of Pittsburgh, he organized and managed his department so well that the university became one of the outstanding industrial engineering schools in the country. Dr. Holzman not only advocated the use of traditional industrial engineering techniques and procedures, but he also brought this entire field into the new computer age at the University of Pittsburgh. In addition to promoting the use of computers in industrial engineering, he was active on a national basis in the use of operations research.

Although he was located in the heart of an industrial city, the scope of his vision extended beyond those confines, and he advocated the use of industrial engineering not only in manufacturing but also in the services area. Indeed, many of the graduates of his school went to work in hospitals and service-related industries. He believed that industrial engineering and operations research could be applied successfully in nearly every field of endeavor.

Dr. Holzman authored a number of books and scores of articles on industrial engineering and operations research. He contributed to society by marshaling the talents of engineers and scientists throughout the world in the development of the sixteen-volume *Encyclopedia of Computer Science and Technology* (New York: Marcel Dekker, 1975). Other important books he wrote were *Operations Research Support Methodology* (New York: Marcel Dekker, 1979) and *Mathematical Programming for Operations Researchers and Computer Scientists* (New York: Marcel Dekker, 1981). He also contributed to many encyclopedias on subjects such as industrial engineering, linear programming, game theory, decision making, critical path methods, nonlinear programming, and information retrieval systems design.

Dr. Holzman was a registered professional engineer in Pennsylvania and served as a consultant to numerous companies, including Westinghouse Electric Corporation, Goodyear Tire and Rubber Company, Climax Molybdenum Company, and H. B. Maynard and Company. He was a member of the board of directors of On Line Systems, Inc.

Dr. Holzman was a fellow of the Institute of Industrial Engineers and a member of the Operations Research Society of America, the Institute of Management Sciences, and the American Society for Engineering Education. He served in many high-level positions within each of these societies. He also received the Distinguished Alumnus Award in 1982 from the University of Pittsburgh Engineering Alumni Association. He was elected to the National Academy of Engineering in 1984.

Although Dr. Holzman's great achievements in the fields of industrial engineering and operations research required much devotion, he did not neglect his personal life. He placed the importance of his family and his religion above everything else. In 1945 he married Joan Michalowski, who had been a high school classmate. They had five children: three sons, Thomas G. of Atlanta, Georgia; Richard G. of Baltimore, Maryland; and David of Glenshaw, Pennsylvania; and two daughters, Judith Bajgier of Cherry Hill, New Jersey; and Jacqueline Fincher of Ann Arbor, Michigan. Joan frequently accompanied him on professional trips to South America and Europe.

Dr. Holzman was active in his church and in his local PTA. In addition to all of his personal and professional activities, he found time to play tennis weekly year-round and enjoyed playing with his dog, a Great Dane.

Together with his technical and educational achievements, Dr. Holzman made many friends among his colleagues and students. His contributions to society will continue through those who have been influenced by his work.

STANLEY GEORGE HOOKER

1907–1984

BY GERHARD NEUMANN

SIR STANLEY GEORGE HOOKER, who was recognized throughout the world as a leader in the field of aircraft gas turbine
engineering, died of cancer on May 24, 1984, in Bristol, England. Most recently, Hooker was a consultant to Rolls Royce,
Ltd., where he began his career in aviation.

During that career, Sir Stanley was known as one of the
leading British authorities in the jet engine field. He engineered a long line of outstanding aircraft gas turbines and
played a key role in developing the British aviation industry
and bringing it to a position of world prominence. No account of the growth of the industry would be complete or
accurate without paying tribute to his accomplishments.

Stanley George Hooker was born in 1907 at Sheerness,
Kent, England. In 1931 he graduated with first-class honors
in mathematics from the Imperial College of Science and
Technology. Initially, he worked on torpedo propulsion;
later, on antiaircraft rockets, which were used extensively in
World War II. In 1938 he became head of Rolls Royce's Su-
percharger and Engine Performance Section in Derby. It was
in this role that he made significant contributions to the development of the renowned Merlin engine that powered
Britain's Spitfire and Mustang fighters as well as its Lancaster
bombers.

The advent of the jet age saw Hooker at the forefront of

the pioneering technological efforts that brought revolutionary progress to the field of aircraft propulsion. In 1940 he
met Sir Frank Whittle and became interested in the work
Whittle was doing on jet propulsion. Sir Stanley followed
through on that interest by introducing Whittle to Lord
Hives, then managing director of Rolls Royce. The result was
Rolls Royce's entry into the jet engine field and the initiation
of the key role in the industry that the company occupies to
this day. Hooker was appointed chief engineer of the Bar-
noldswick Division of Rolls Royce and charged with developing the Whittle W2B jet engine.

Ronald Smelt, who conducted the flight tests of the
E 28/39 and F 9/40 aircraft that used the first Whittle jet
engines, credits Hooker as being the engineer who "indus-
trialized" Whittle's concepts and thus built up the aircraft
turbine industry in England. Smelt was also in charge of the
1946 speed runs of the Meteor aircraft powered by two Rolls
Royce Derwent V engines that established a world speed record of 603 miles per hour.

In 1950 Sir Stanley was appointed chief engineer of Bristol
Aero-Engines, Ltd., and placed in charge of the design and
development of the Proteus turboprop engine for the Bristol
Brittania civil airliner and the Olympus jet engine for the
Royal Air Force's Vulcan bomber. In 1954 he was named director of the Bristol Aeroplane Co., Ltd.; in 1959 he became
technical director of Bristol-Siddeley Engines, Ltd., which
was formed by merging Bristol Aero-Engines with Armstrong Siddeley Motors.

It was during this period that he led the design and development effort for two of the most notable engines in aviation
history: the Orpheus turbojet that was used extensively by
NATO in Fiat G.91 strike fighters and the Pegasus vertical
takeoff engine that powers Harrier aircraft. When Bristol-
Siddeley merged with Rolls Royce in 1966, Stanley Hooker
was named technical director of the Bristol Engine Division.

Sir Stanley was recognized for his achievements by his election to several of the world's more prestigious technical soci-

eties. He became a fellow of the Royal Society in 1962; he later served as its vice-president and a member of the council from 1965 to 1967. Stanley Hooker became a fellow of the American Association for the Advancement of Science in 1965 and was chosen as an honorary fellow of the Society of Engineers in 1968. Hooker was further recognized for his contributions to the British aviation industry with his appointment as Officer of the British Empire and Commander of the British Empire in 1946 and 1964, respectively. In 1981 Sir Stanley George Hooker was honored by his peers with selection as a foreign associate of the National Academy of Engineering.

Professional recognition for Sir Stanley also came in the form of several awards. The Royal Aeronautical Society awarded him the British Silver Medal (1955); the British Gold Medal (1961); and their highest award, the Gold Medal of the Royal Aeronautical Society (1967). He also received the James Clayton Prize of the Institution of Mechanical Engineers (1967) and the Churchill Gold Medal from the Society of Engineers (1968).

Sir Stanley won patents for many key technical features that became standard in high-performance jet engines. He also authored almost fifty publications, many of them on supersonic operations.

The record speaks for itself. Sir Stanley Hooker was a giant in the field of aircraft jet propulsion. In my years of running General Electric's jet engine operations, his name stood out in my mind as one of the leading forces that helped shape Rolls Royce into one of our most powerful competitors. At the same time, he held a position of honor and respect in all of our minds for the dignity and integrity with which he conducted his business affairs.

One could be proud to be part of a profession and industry that included Sir Stanley Hooker. That may be his greatest contribution, for I know that he inspired all those with whom he came into contact to work for progress and the betterment of mankind through aviation.

FREDERICK JOHNSON HOOVEN

1905–1985

BY MYRON TRIBUS

FREDERICK JOHNSON HOOVEN died suddenly on February 5, 1985. At the time of his death, he was professor of engineering at Dartmouth College's Thayer School of Engineering.

Fred was born in Dayton, Ohio, on March 5, 1905, and grew up in Dayton near the home of the Wright Brothers, whom he came to know and admire. Nearly a half century later, he used data they had obtained in their wind tunnel to design the paper airplane that won the "professional" duration-aloft category (in a field of 10,000 entrants) in the Scientific American Great International Paper Airplane Contest.

Fred Hooven loved to invent things. He held thirty-eight U.S. patents and devised numerous other inventions he never bothered to patent. He invented the first radio compass (1936), which was the initial aircraft navigation system that permitted distinction between forward and backward direction.

Hooven was particularly unhappy that his new system was removed at the last minute from the airplane of his friend Amelia Earhart and replaced with the standard system of that time. Many people believe it was this less sophisticated navigation capability that caused her to overfly her destination and become lost. Of his invention, Hooven said: "It was my own idea and it completely dominated the scene for that kind of device for a time roughly corresponding to the life of the DC-3. It's made it routine to cross the ocean, where before it was an adventure."

Other of his inventions included a bombing intervalometer (1944); an automobile ignition system; the shoran bombing computer (1948); the first heart-lung machine, which is still in use today in open-heart surgery (1952); the Harris intertype digital electronic phototypesetter (1955); and a front-end drive system for automobiles (1962).

Fred Hooven's engineering career started well before he graduated from the Massachusetts Institute of Technology (MIT) in 1927: In 1925, at DayFan Radio, he designed improved radio receivers. After his graduation from MIT, he joined the staff of General Motors (GM) and designed a brake shoe system that was installed on all GM vehicles for the next twenty-five years. After two years at GM, however, he left the company for a position at the Dayton Rubber Company, where from 1930 to 1931 he designed automobile suspension systems. He next worked in the field of aircraft performance for the U.S. Army Air Corps.

During 1931 and 1932, Hooven designed a blind aircraft landing system for the American Loth Company. Also in 1932 he independently produced the first successful high-fidelity crystal phonograph pickup. Then, as vice-president and chief engineer for Bendix's Radio Products Division from 1935 to 1937, he developed the first automatic steering system for an unmanned flight. From 1937 to 1957, Hooven was self-employed as an independent inventor, consultant, and contractor for new product research and development.

In 1957 Fred Hooven went to work for the Ford Motor Company. (A GM executive described him as a "Ford trade secret.") Yet, although he invented the front-end drive system used by GM on the Oldsmobile Toronado and Cadillac Eldorado, he could not persuade Ford to use this invention. Nevertheless, at Ford he supervised the design and development of the Falcon, Thunderbird, Fairlane, and Galaxie automobiles.

Recalling those years at Ford, Lee Iacocca writes:

The thing I remember most about Fred is that he said future cars would not be built the way cars were built then. Front-wheel-drive was the way of the future and rear-wheel-drive was antiquated. He would say, "It's silly to design cars the way we do. Why not put a power pack up front just like a horse? A horse will pull anything. Behind it you could put a fire truck, a station wagon, two people, four people, six people limousines." And of course it turned out that way, the way Fred said it would. We do have front-wheel-drive minivans today that were a glint in his eye then because he said that is the way to do efficient packaging.

Hooven left Ford in 1967 to once again become a consultant and also adjunct professor of engineering at the Thayer School of Engineering. He became a part-time professor in 1975 and remained in that capacity until his death.

Fred Hooven enjoyed engineering. In fact, he enjoyed everything he did. Hooven was interested in both model railroads and photography. He rebuilt a lens for a 35mm camera to provide extreme field depth and used it to produce a photograph of a model locomotive in front of the train station at White River Junction that was so skillfully done that it looked like an actual locomotive. (The photograph was even used on the cover of *Model Railroading* magazine.)

Hooven had fun with engineering; he built paper and balsa wood airplanes for his children and for the child he kept alive within himself. Some of these planes were propelled with carbon dioxide cartridges and were perhaps the first jet-propelled model airplanes. He also built a binary counter as a toy to amuse his grandchildren.

He liked to study whatever was new. He conversed intelligently with others about special relativity and quantum mechanics. While in his seventies, Fred Hooven continued his innovative work in the areas of prosthetic orthopedic bone replacements, music synthesizers, lightweight autos, and computerized medical diagnoses.

Fred was truly a classical engineer. He viewed the world's problems in terms of their potential solutions. His impact on students and associates was extraordinary. Fred could stretch the reach of others: He could make them broaden their horizons in terms of the problems they tackled and the ways in which they approached them. Fred Hooven was truly an inspiring teacher, colleague, and friend.

He gave of himself to others. A partial list of his public service activities includes the following: volunteer research associate in biochemistry and psychophysiology, FELS Institute for the Study of Human Development; member, Board of Education, Oakwood, Ohio; trustee, Miami Valley Hospital, Dayton, Ohio; trustee, Charles F. Kettering Foundation; founding member, Oakland University, Rochester, Michigan; member, visiting committee, MIT; member, Commerce Technical Advisory Board, Panel on Electric Automobile and Air Pollution; and reviewer for the UFO Sighting Committee.

Fred Hooven wrote numerous articles that were designed to demonstrate the historic significance of various inventions. He reviewed in detail the data from the Wright Brothers' wind tunnel, proving by computer simulation that their original design was unstable. He commented: "A bicycle is also unstable. They were bicycle makers so they could fly it."

Those of us who were fortunate enough to know him will remember him as a wise man—one of those fully developed human beings whom we are sometimes privileged to encounter during a lifetime. Fred Hooven was warm, sympathetic, and kindly. He would often take the other side of an argument just to make someone think a little harder. He would confront other people and their ideas in such a way as to make them go home and rethink their position—yet never in such a way as to make them love him less.

Fred Hooven was devoted to his wife Martha, with whom he had three sons and a daughter. I miss him deeply.

Olaf A. Hougen

OLAF ANDREAS HOUGEN

1893–1986

BY CHALMER KIRKBRIDE

OLAF ANDREAS HOUGEN, professor emeritus of the University of Wisconsin, died January 7, 1986, at the age of ninety-two. He had been associated almost continuously with the Chemical Engineering Department at that school from 1916 until his retirement in 1963 and indirectly thereafter for twenty years. He made major contributions to the development and growth of the "modern" (1925–1945) concept of chemical engineering.

Professor Hougen's ancestry is traceable to fifteenth-century Norway. All four of his grandparents emigrated from Norway in the 1800s and homesteaded in Iowa and Dakota.

Olaf Hougen was born in Manitowoc, Wisconsin, on October 4, 1893, the eldest of six children. His family lived in Decorah, Iowa, from 1897 to 1907 and then moved to Tacoma, Washington. He entered the University of Washington in Seattle in 1911, at the age of eighteen. In those days, there were no courses in unit operations, material and energy balances, heat and mass transfer, engineering thermodynamics, or process design. Studying mathematics beyond calculus was discouraged. There were no textbooks in chemical engineering except those of a descriptive nature dealing with industrially applied chemistry. In addition, throughout his college years, Olaf—and most other students—were required

207

to find employment to finance their education. Hougen recorded that the entire cost of his college education was $1,689.92, of which he earned $1,044.80, or about sixty percent.

Upon graduation in 1915, there was no professional employment available to him. In the fall of 1916, however, he began his long association with the University of Wisconsin. Later, during his first year of graduate studies, on April 6, 1917, war was declared on Germany. In May 1918 Hougen was drafted, inducted at Camp Grant, and left for military training at Camp Wheeler, Georgia. Shortly thereafter, he was singled out for chemical warfare service and assigned to Saltville, Virginia, in June 1918.

There, in the "salt capital" of the Confederacy, his assignment was to prepare sodium cyanide through the newly invented Bucher process, which involved the interaction of nitrogen with a pelletized mixture of sodium carbonate, coke, and iron oxide at high temperatures. The desired product was recovered by extraction with liquid ammonia. Hougen nearly lost his life during this assignment by accidentally inhaling the cyanide when removing accumulations of solids from an evaporator.

Following an honorable discharge from the army, he returned to Madison, Wisconsin, married Olga Berg, and moved to Niagara Falls for employment with Carborundum Company. Here his duties included studying the properties of refractories for use in high-temperature environments.

In September 1920 he became an assistant professor at the University of Wisconsin at the modest salary of $150 a month. Despite the fact that advanced degrees in fields such as chemical engineering were considered unnecessary at Wisconsin, Hougen worked during the summer months on his doctoral thesis. The project that constituted his thesis work had been initiated at the request of the American Gas Association; its objective was the development of the theory of gas absorption in spray and packed towers. The work was conducted by Hougen and a graduate student named Kenneth M. Watson.

With the exception of two summers devoted to his thesis work, when Hougen was not in classes he spent most of his time working in industry. He found such employment to be necessary for financial reasons. In retrospect, he seems to have been fortunate in this experience in that it led him to emphasize industrial applications in his subsequent work.

The decade from 1925 to 1935 was the era in which the greatest advances were made in the field of chemical engineering. These advances occurred most particularly in the development of the principles of material and energy balances. During this period, Kenneth Watson suggested to Hougen that the two of them collaborate to develop a text on the subject. Their product, *Industrial Chemical Calculations*, was published by John Wiley in 1936.

In 1938 Hougen advanced to the rank of full professor at Wisconsin, a step that marked the turning point in his career. Thus, twelve years after receiving his doctorate, years that had been full of frustration and lack of support, his talent and energies were finally released. With tenure established and the prospect of talented graduate students with whom he could work, he was finally able to devote time to experimental and theoretical studies. The focal point of his research became the extension of studies that he had begun in 1925 and to which Alan Colburn had contributed most significantly in 1929.

World War II also had a profound effect on Hougen's career in that it postponed research activities everywhere. Luckily, Kenneth Watson returned to Wisconsin in 1942 and worked with Hougen on a number of endeavors, including advances in chemical engineering theory and practice, teaching, and research, as well as plant design, construction, and operations. They also initiated an ambitious program on applied kinetics and industrial reaction rates. In 1942 the American Chemical Society, under Hougen's chairmanship, sponsored a symposium on the subject.

It was during this time that the text *Industrial Chemical Calculations* was revised and extended, giving place to *Material and Energy Balances* as the first part of another work, *Chemical*

Process Principles. In addition, Hougen devoted a great deal of time to the National Defense Research Committee and the War Production Board on matters related to the war effort. He also responded to a request from the Advisory Committee on Industry of the Royal Norwegian Ministry of Supply that he prepare reports on progress in the world silicate industries.

Following the Chicago kinetics symposium, the University of Wisconsin Research Committee allotted an annual sum of ten thousand dollars for a ten-year period to conduct research on the principles of industrial reaction rates, kinetics, and catalysis. The research sponsored by this support paved the way for further research on thermodynamics and applied kinetics and ultimately led to the books *Thermodynamics* and *Kinetics,* which were coauthored by Hougen and Kenneth Watson. The former was later revised in collaboration with Roland Ragatz.

Especially satisfying and enjoyable to Hougen were his two Fulbright professorships, one in 1951 to Norges Tekniske Hogskole in Trondheim, Norway, and the other to Japan in 1957. His influence in the two countries resulted in significant changes in teaching methodology, as attested to by teachers and practitioners, alike. Returning from Japan by way of Taiwan, India, and Thailand afforded Hougen the opportunity to provide public lectures, to visit those countries' universities, and to meet faculty and students. As he had hoped, such exposure served to encourage many students from these countries to pursue chemical engineering studies at Wisconsin. From 1961 to 1963, he was science attaché to the Scandinavian countries and lived in Stockholm, Sweden.

Olaf Hougen retired in 1963 but continued to be actively involved in numerous public service and literary projects. One project from which he derived much satisfaction was the preparation of an historical account of the University of Wisconsin's Department of Chemical Engineering. Also highly prized by Hougen was his receipt of the Royal Order of St.

Olav, First Class, which was conferred by King Haakon in 1969 in appreciation for his service to Norway. He was elected to the National Academy of Engineering in 1974.

Olaf was a lifelong member of the Lutheran Church and contributed both substance and time to its activities. His wife Olga died in 1976. His remaining years were spent in a retirement home in Madison, Wisconsin.

Olaf Hougen's life was one of selfless dedication to his family, his profession, his students and associates, and the many and varied social and professional groups with which he was affiliated. His was a life showing great self-restraint and a vitality that found expression in his professional work, in his public service, and in love for his fellow man. Much of his genius lay in his ability and desire to identify talent in others and to create an environment in which that talent could flourish and bear fruit.

Although it may, indeed, be said that he contributed to major changes in the practice and teaching of chemical engineering during a period of forty years, it is the magnificent inventory of goodness that has accumulated in the lives of those with whom he lived and worked that is Olaf Hougen's chief contribution.

HERBERT E. HUDSON, JR.

1910–1983

BY RICHARD HAZEN

Herbert e. hudson, jr., principal engineer and chairman of the board of Water and Air Research, Inc., died on September 13, 1983. Born in Chicago on September 21, 1910, he attended Chicago public schools, Crane Technical High School, and the Northwestern Military and Naval Academy at Lake Geneva, Wisconsin. He entered the University of Illinois at Urbana in 1927 and graduated in 1931 with a B.S. in civil engineering (he pursued the sanitary engineering study option). He and Annabelle Woods were married May 28, 1932.

Better than any school for his future career, however, were Hudson's ten years as an assistant to J. R. Baylis, director of the Chicago Experimental Filtration Plant. For many years, Chicago counted on ever longer and deeper intakes from Lake Michigan to provide good water. By 1930, however, the need for filtration could not be ignored. Baylis was unusually competent and thorough. With Hudson doing much of the legwork, the two missed few aspects of water conditions in Lake Michigan and of the best way to treat them.

Between 1941 and 1942 Hudson worked on the design of the South Filtration Plant (at 320 megagallons per day [mgd], the largest in the world) and thereafter became a research associate in the chemistry department at the University of Illinois, working on the removal of chemical warfare

213

agents from water and on the development of needed analytical methods.

In 1944 Hudson entered the U.S. Army, serving first in the Sanitary Corps and then in the U.S. Army Corps of Engineers. He continued his studies on the removal of chemical agents from water at the Medical Research Laboratory at Edgewood Arsenal in Maryland. Later, at the Engineering Research and Development Laboratory, Fort Belvoir, Virginia, he worked on the development of diatomite filters for field use by troops. His final assignment—to the Engineer Section, Combined Intelligence Objectives Subcommittee—took him to England, France, and Germany to gather information on German field-water-purification processes. He remained in the U.S. Army Reserves until 1958, when he retired with the rank of major.

Returning to Chicago, Hudson worked a short time for the Chicago Department of Public Works before being named head of the Engineering Subdivision of the Illinois State Water Survey in Urbana. From 1946 to 1955 he was in charge of the collection of statewide data on ground, surface, and atmospheric water resources, as well as the analysis and publication of official reports on water resources. The experience brought him a broad base of information on water resources in the Midwest, information that included both their development and shortcomings. It also gave him substantial knowledge and understanding of geology and ground-water developments, which he put to good use after leaving the Water Survey.

In 1955 Herbert Hudson joined the engineering firm of Hazen and Sawyer in Detroit. He subsequently took charge of the design of a 200-mgd addition to Detroit's Springwells plant; the project also involved the specification of the details of treatment processes and selection of major equipment. In addition, he provided the technical layout of a 160-mgd plant for Wayne County, south of Detroit. (The plant was subsequently taken over by Detroit and expanded to a capacity of 240 mgd.)

In handling the work at Detroit, Hudson looked to the universities for two sanitary engineers to spend the summer visiting the major water plants in the West, looking for good and bad features, comparing performance, and so forth. At the same time, Hudson persuaded the water system manager at the Wyandotte, Michigan, water plant to compare the performance of conventional constant rate filters with declining rate filters, in which the flow through the bed was reduced as the filters became dirty. The test, which took nearly a year to complete, demonstrated that the declining rate filters produced better-quality water and cost less to build. This same process was later adopted for the two plants in Detroit and subsequently by the Hazen and Sawyer firm and other firms throughout the country.

Hudson came to New York in 1957. He became a partner in Hazen and Sawyer and was named to head the firm's water treatment activities. He designed new water treatment plants at Luke, Maryland; Poughkeepsie and Tuxedo Park, New York; Point Pleasant Beach, New Jersey; Greensboro, North Carolina; Danville, Virginia; North Chicago, Illinois; and in both Cali and Bogotá, Colombia. He traveled to Libya twice to advise Exxon on water prospects. In addition to these responsibilities, he participated in the preparation of a report to the U.S. Army Corps of Engineers evaluating the water resources in the northeast United States following the 1960 drought. He also wrote reports on the operation of water plants at Elizabethtown, New Jersey; Bay City, Michigan; Washington, D.C.; and Bogotá and Cali, Colombia.

In 1971 Hudson resigned from Hazen and Sawyer to become president of Water and Air Research, Inc., in Gainesville, Florida. Aside from managing the firm, Hudson conducted and guided hydrological and ecological evaluations, provided guidance on the design and operation of numerous water treatment plants, and acted as a consultant to the World Bank, Pan American Health Organization, National Housing Board of Brazil, and Panama Canal Company. He was also an adjunct professor of environmental engineering sciences at the University of Florida from 1971 until his death.

Herbert Hudson was an active member of many technical societies, but his particular interest was the American Water Works Association. He held a number of posts: director, chairman of the Committee on Education, chairman and secretary of the Illinois Section, and chairman of the Water Resources and Water Purification Division. He was also an honorary member of the association. He was elected to the National Academy of Engineering in 1978 and was both a member and president of the American Academy of Environmental Engineers, as well as a fellow of the American Society of Civil Engineers.

A regular attendant and speaker at societal meetings, Hudson authored numerous papers. Four outstanding works are Chapter 5, "Rapid Mixing and Flocculation," in *Water Treatment Plant Design* (New York: American Water Works Association, 1969); Chapter 7a in *Water Quality and Treatment* (New York: McGraw-Hill, 1971); *A Handbook of Applied Hydrology*, coauthored with Richard Hazen (New York: McGraw-Hill, 1964); and *Water Clarification Processes: Practical Design and Evaluation* (New York: Van Nostrand-Reinhold Co., 1981).

Unlike most engineers with important technical responsibilities, Herbert found time for other pursuits. He read a great deal, enjoyed music, dabbled in photography and art, and enjoyed talking with people from all walks of life in the United States and elsewhere. He was also a humorist; addressing a technical meeting, he would meet his critics with a smile and often disarm them with a joke.

Herbert Hudson is survived by his wife Annabelle and his two sons, Ken and Herbert. According to his son Herbert, "his work was his life." The accomplishments and influence of Herbert Hudson in promoting the health and welfare of millions of people by providing safe water supplies attest to his status as an engineer who has made a major contribution to society.

JEROME CLARKE HUNSAKER

1886–1984

BY ARTHUR E. RAYMOND

J EROME CLARKE HUNSAKER, who became widely known, ad-mired, and influential as a result of his lifelong contributions to the field of aviation, died at his Boston home on September 10, 1984, at the age of ninety-eight. Jerry will long be remembered as a gentle, friendly man, as well as a superb teacher, engineer, and administrator. He was modest, urbane, clear-headed, and at experienced ease with almost all the important phases of his field, which encompassed research and the design, manufacture, and operation of airplanes, seaplanes, and rigid and nonrigid airships.

He was born in Creston, Iowa, in 1886 and was educated in the public schools of Detroit and Saginaw. He graduated from the U.S. Naval Academy at the head of his class in 1908, five years after the Wright brothers' first flight, which occurred when he was at the impressionable age of seventeen. After a year of sea duty, he was ordered to the Massachusetts Institute of Technology (MIT), where his interest in aeronautics became a passion, and he began a study of wind tunnels as a means of obtaining the basic data needed for successful flight.

He then journeyed to Paris and, with the help of his wife, the former Alice Avery, and Eiffel's assistants, he translated Eiffel's pioneering work in the testing of airplane models. When he returned to MIT in 1914, Jerome Hunsaker constructed a forty-mile-per-hour tunnel and inaugurated the institute's first graduate course in aeronautical engineering. In 1916 he was awarded a D.Sc. for wind tunnel research on aerodynamical stability.

During his life, his interest in and knowledge about wind tunnels grew and broadened to cover other research tools. He was appointed by the president as chairman of the National Advisory Committee for Aeronautics (NACA), with its many laboratories; he remained there for sixteen years. His final major achievement, which was attained in 1967, was the supervision and construction of the Navy Supersonic Laboratory at MIT to study aircraft and missile designs involving speeds as high as two thousand miles per hour (a long way from his original forty-mile-per-hour tunnel).

In 1916 the Navy placed him in charge of the Aircraft Division of its Bureau of Construction and Repair, and he was soon responsible for the design, construction, and procurement of all naval aircraft. In 1918 Jerome Hunsaker was assigned responsibility for two special engineering projects— to build a Zeppelin and to build a flying boat to cross the Atlantic. The latter became known as the NC (Navy Curtiss) project, and four units were built. Three units began flights from Newfoundland in May 1919; two were wrecked near the Azores, but the NC-4, under Commander A. C. Read, continued on to Lisbon and Plymouth, the first crossing of the Atlantic by an aircraft of any type. The Zeppelin project resulted in the completion of the *Shenandoah*, the first rigid dirigible to employ helium as a lifting gas.

In 1921 Dr. Hunsaker was transferred to the newly organized Navy Bureau of Aeronautics, where he had an opportunity to realize practical results from the great accumulation of research and experimental data that had been obtained during the war. In 1923 he was detailed as assistant naval attaché at London, Paris, The Hague, Rome, and Berlin, remaining on duty until 1926, when he resigned to join the research staff of Bell Telephone Laboratories in New York as assistant vice-president. While there, he developed wire and radio communication services for civil aviation.

In 1928 Dr. Hunsaker became vice-president of the Goodyear-Zeppelin Corporation, which had been formed to build the Akron and Macon airships for the navy. Following the completion of the airships, he returned to MIT as head of the Department of Mechanical Engineering and, later, the Department of Aeronautical Engineering. He retained the latter position until his retirement in 1952 at the age of sixty-eight, but held the title of lecturer for another five years. Until he was well into his eighties, he maintained an office at MIT, to which he walked from his home on Beacon Hill—a distance of nearly two miles.

His years at NACA, forerunner of NASA, were particularly important because of the standing and scope of that organization. NACA was an unparalleled asset to the country with its laboratories (Langley, Ames, and Lewis), experienced staff, and broad research program that became the original core of NASA, essential to the completion of the Apollo Program on schedule.

Dr. Hunsaker was elected to the National Academy of Sciences (NAS) in 1935 and was very active in academy affairs. In 1967 he was also elected to the National Academy of Engineering (NAE). Because his election came so near the end of his most energetic years, however, his interest in and activities with NAE never matched his involvement in NAS.

Jerome Hunsaker was the first president of the Institute of the Aeronautical Sciences, which later merged with the American Rocket Society to become the American Institute of Aeronautics and Astronautics (AIAA). In fact, Hunsaker teamed with Lester Gardner to become a major force in its formation in 1932. He became an honorary fellow of that organization and also of the Royal Aeronautical Society and the Imperial College of Science and Technology of Great Britain. He was also an honorary member of the American Society of Mechanical Engineers and the Institute of Mechanical Engineers of Great Britain. In addition to his memberships in NAS and NAE, he was a member of the Society of Automotive Engineers, the Society of Naval Architects and Marine Engineers, and the American Philosophical Society.

His list of awards is long and impressive: Navy Cross (1919); Franklin Medal (1942); Medal for Merit (1946); Honorary Commander of the Most Excellent Order of the British Empire (1948); Legion of Honor (1949); Wright Trophy (1951); Godfrey L. Cabot Trophy (1953); Langley Medal (1955); Elder Statesman of Aviation, National Aeronautic Association (1955); Water-based Aviation Award, Institute of the Aeronautical Sciences (1957); NACA Distinguished Service Award (1957); Gold Medal of the Royal Aeronautical Society (1957); U.S. Navy Award for Distinguished Public Service (1958); and the Julius Adams Stratton Prize (1967).

He found time among his other activities to publish more than 130 papers—only a few of them jointly—and to supervise NACA's yearly annual reports (nos. thirty-three through forty-two). The section on aeronautics in the original *Marks' Standard Handbook for Mechanical Engineers* of 1916 bears his name.

A partial summary of his papers shows the breadth of his interests. The list begins with several papers on wind tunnels, but then moves on to such other subject matter as gas-tight airplane fabric, casein glue use in laminated construction, duralumin aluminum alloys, venturi airspeed meters, spruce airplane compression struts, similitude theory of aerial propellers, airplane rubber shock absorbers, airplane radiators, cavitation research, and a number of papers on static and dynamic stability. There were many papers written on dirigibles, including the blimp type that was used for patrols. Others dealt with biplanes, triplanes, dihedral wings, safety, communications, and, of course, the education and training of engineers, including curriculum surveys.

As time went on, his subjects broadened even further into titles such as "Forty Years of Aeronautical Research" and "A

Half Century of Aeronautical Development," as well as a number of biographical memoirs. His last memoir, written in 1967, is a biographical memoir and tribute to Hugh Dryden, his longtime right hand at NACA.

In addition to his professional life as a scientist, Hunsaker showed a keen interest and competence in business and public affairs. He was a director of Shell Oil Company, Goodyear Tire and Rubber Company, McGraw-Hill Publishing Company, Inc., and Tracerlab, Inc. He was also a regent of the Smithsonian Institution and a life trustee of the Boston Museum of Science.

Countless numbers of his MIT students in mechanical and aeronautical engineering from 1933 to 1952 have made their mark in the world. Most feel a tremendous debt of gratitude to Jerry Hunsaker as their teacher, mentor, and friend.

Tamaki Ippoumatsu

TAMAKI IPPONMATSU

1901–1985

BY WALKER L. CISLER

TAMAKI IPPONMATSU, internationally recognized and highly respected for his long-standing pioneering work in the field of nuclear energy for power production, died on January 24, 1985, at the age of eighty-three. At the time of his death, he was adviser general of the Japan Atomic Power Company. His contributions to the very successful use of nuclear energy in Japan are acknowledged internationally.

Tamaki Ipponmatsu was born on April 29, 1901, in Hiroshima-ken, Japan. He received a B.S. in electrical engineering in 1925 from the Kyoto Imperial University and a Ph.D. in engineering from the Osaka Imperial University in 1945.

Dr. Ipponmatsu was one of the key leaders in the development of the electric power industry after World War II. In 1947 he became managing director of the second largest utility company in Japan, the Kansai Electric Power Company. Ten years later, as a result of recognition of his work in the nuclear energy field, he was appointed vice-president of the Japan Atomic Power Company. He was promoted to president in 1962, and in 1970 he became chairman, a position he held for seven years. Dr. Ipponmatsu then became executive councillor and finally advisor general from 1981 until his death in 1985.

Although his main interest in later years was nuclear energy, his broad contributions to the electrical engineering field resulted in many prestigious appointments: president of the Institute of Electrical Engineers of Japan; executive secretary and adviser to the Japan Committee for Economic Development; director of the Muto Institute of Structural Mechanics; and director of the Japan Motive Power Association.

His special contributions to engineering were recognized in Japan when he was awarded the Blue Ribbon Medal of Japan (1959) and the Second Class Order of the Rising Sun (1977). He was also honored by Great Britain in 1977 when he was named Commander of the Order of the British Empire. He was elected a foreign associate of the U.S. National Academy of Engineering in 1978.

Dr. Ipponmatsu was a pioneer in the field of nuclear engineering because he was one of the first to recognize the importance of evaluating all aspects of the nuclear fuel cycle: uranium procurement, uranium enrichment, spent fuel reprocessing, and—a very important area—the problems of satisfactory waste disposal. Through his early emphasis on these aspects of the cycle, Dr. Ipponmatsu was instrumental in focusing international attention on nuclear energy as a viable remedy for the world's energy problems.

A number of his achievements in the nuclear energy field are clearly documented in his numerous publications, which include "Problems on Nuclear Power," in the *Journal of the Japan Society of Mechanical Engineers* (vol. 75, no. 647, November 1972 [Tokyo]) and "IAEA Conference on Environmental Aspects of Nuclear Power Stations" (New York: August 1970). Dr. Ipponmatsu also authored two books: *Overall Energy Planning of Power and Fuel* (Kyoto: Denki Shoin, May 1948) and *A Story of Tokai Nuclear Power Station* (Tokyo: Tokyo Keizai Press, September 1971).

Despite his active technical and engineering life, Tamaki Ipponmatsu also found time to devote to cultural and civic matters. He was particularly active in promoting the use of nuclear power in Japan, and his efforts led to the wide public acceptance of its use. As a result of those efforts, to a considerable extent, nuclear power is now economically producing a significant part of the energy requirements of Japan.

In a country such as Japan, which is deficient in energy resources, the acceptance of nuclear power has meant much to its phenomenal economic growth. Japan and the world of nuclear power will greatly miss Tamaki Ipponmatsu.

GEORGE WILLIAM KESSLER

1908–1983

BY WALTER BACHMAN

GEORGE WILLIAM KESSLER retired in 1973 as vice-president for engineering and technology of the Babcock and Wilcox Company, where for many years he was a leader in advancing the art and science of steam generation in marine and stationary power plants of both the conventional and nuclear types. He died on July 25, 1983, in Winter Park, Florida.

George Kessler was born on March 1, 1908, in St. Louis, Missouri, the son of William Henry and Blanche M. (Pougher) Kessler. He graduated from the University of Illinois in 1930 with a B.S. in mechanical engineering. During his years at the university, he was a member of various honorary societies.

After graduation, Mr. Kessler was employed by Babcock and Wilcox as a student engineer and in 1932 was assigned to the company's Analytical Engineering Department in New York. He was transferred to the Marine Department in 1933 and became its head in 1938. During this period the United States was beginning to revitalize its naval and merchant fleets. From 1938 until his retirement, George Kessler was associated with every major advance in marine steam generation; in many cases, he initiated these advances.

He contributed significantly to the boiler designs that resulted in the highly efficient U.S. naval and merchant marine fleets that were indispensable to victory in World War II.

After the war, he was a leading contributor to the design of nuclear steam generators and new types of marine boilers of all kinds.

In 1946, when the nation's utilities were embarking on a vast expansion program, Kessler was transferred to the Babcock and Wilcox Stationary Department. Named to positions of increasing importance and responsibility, he made major contributions to the highly efficient steam generating plants, both conventional and nuclear, that have been so important to the economic development of the United States. During this period, he continued his interest in the marine field and actively participated in the development of boiler designs for the experimental naval destroyer programs and the early nuclear submarines, the *Nautilus* and the *Sea Wolf*. His influence on power plant design extended to a number of Western European countries and Japan.

He was appointed assistant chief engineer in 1953 and chief engineer in 1954. He was named vice-president of Babcock and Wilcox in 1961.

George Kessler was the holder of many patents. He also presented many technical papers and was the author of the chapter on boilers in the *Marks' Standard Handbook for Mechanical Engineers*. His paper on furnace explosions and their prevention, which was published in 1961, gave him wide recognition as an authority on boiler control and safety. As a result, he served on a number of technical and research committees, including those of the Society of Naval Architects and Marine Engineers, the American Society of Mechanical Engineers, the Shipbuilders Council of America, the American Standards Association, the National Academy of Sciences, the Metals Properties Council of the Engineering Foundation, and the Welding Research Council.

In 1964 he was made a fellow of the American Society of Mechanical Engineers; he was elected to membership in the National Academy of Engineering in 1969. He was also a member of the American Society of Naval Engineers, the Society of Naval Architects and Marine Engineers, the Propeller Club, the Franklin Institute, and the honorary societies Tau Beta Pi, Phi Eta Sigma, Sigma Tau, and Pi Tau Sigma.

On July 28, 1951, Kessler married Alice Maxwell, who died January 26, 1973. The couple is survived by two children, Judith Kessler Green and Dr. William Clarkson Kessler, and several grandchildren.

Edward W. Kimbark

EDWARD WILSON KIMBARK

1902–1982

BY EUGENE C. STARR

Edward Wilson Kimbark, an internationally known electrical engineer, author, and educator, died February 8, 1982, at the age of seventy-nine. Although he had formally retired in 1976, at the time of his death he was serving as a part-time consulting engineer with the Bonneville Power Administration in Portland, Oregon.

Dr. Kimbark was born in Chicago on September 21, 1902. He earned a B.S. in electrical engineering in 1924 from Northwestern University in Evanston, Illinois, and an M.S. and Ph.D., also in electrical engineering, in 1933 and 1937 from the Massachusetts Institute of Technology (MIT).

His noteworthy accomplishments extended over forty years. From 1963 until his retirement, Dr. Kimbark was employed by the Bonneville Power Administration in the Pacific Northwest. There he developed and guided the use of a large network analyzer that was used to plan for system power flow and stability. As head of the Bonneville's Systems Analysis Unit, he and his staff developed the fundamental performance requirements of many stability controls that are still in use today. These controls included those used to regulate series capacitator switching, dynamic braking, direct current (DC) line power boosting, generator dropping, load rejection, and single-pole switching.

In 1976, based on the studies of Dr. Kimbark and his unit, a modulation control was added to the Pacific Intertie high-voltage DC line that allowed the damping of a chronic regional power oscillation. Owing to the upgraded transfer capabilities of the parallel high-voltage alternating current intertie that were provided by this control, substantial economic benefits were felt throughout the western region.

During the last years of his life, Dr. Kimbark investigated the wider uses of single-pole switching. In recognition of his work, he received the Institute of Electrical and Electronics Engineers' (IEEE) Best Paper Award (1975). Other awards included the U.S. Department of the Interior's Gold Medal for Distinguished Service (1974) and IEEE's Habirshaw Award (1980) for the "advancement of electric power transmission through innovative research, classic textbooks, and inspirational teaching."

Dr. Kimbark's earlier career included positions in academia and industry. He was professor of electrical engineering at MIT from 1939 to 1950; assistant professor of electrical engineering at the Polytechnic Institute of Brooklyn from 1937 to 1939; a teacher of electrical engineering and graduate subjects at MIT from 1933 to 1937; assistant curator of the Division of Power at the Museum of Science and Industry in Chicago from 1929 to 1932; an instructor in electrical engineering at the University of California from 1927 to 1929; and, from 1925 to 1927, a substation operator and assistant in the testing laboratory of the Public Service Company of Northern Illinois, in Evanston, Illinois.

From 1950 until 1955, he was professor of electrical engineering at the Instituto Tecnológico de Aeronáutica at São Paulo, Brazil, where he taught classes using his fluent Portuguese. On his return to the United States, Dr. Kimbark served as the dean of engineering at Seattle University in Seattle, Washington, from 1955 to 1962. He was instrumental in securing accreditation of the school by the Engineering Council for Professional Development in 1962.

Dr. Kimbark was widely recognized as a leader in the advancement of power system practices. His three books on power system stability, which were completed in 1948, 1950, and 1956, and his volume on direct current transmission, completed in 1971, continue to be basic power system references. He also wrote or coauthored three other notable publications, in addition to definitive papers in his field. Dr. Kimbark's principal fields of interest were electric power transmission, including high-voltage DC transmission; symmetrical components and the related transformation of variables; single-pole switching; subsynchronous resonance; and power system stability.

Dr. Kimbark was elected to the National Academy of Engineering in 1979. He was a fellow and life member of IEEE and its Power Engineering Society. He was also a member of the Conférence Internationale des Grands Réseaux Électriques à Haute Tension, the National Society of Professional Engineers, and the American Society for Engineering Education. In addition, he belonged to the Eta Kappa Nu and Sigma Xi fraternities and the Phi Beta Kappa honorary society.

Dr. Kimbark and his wife Iris, who survives him, shared an avid interest in cultural affairs. As a matter of fact, at the time of his death, he was active as chairman of the Chamber Music Society of Oregon.

His cheerful personality and graciously helpful attitude endeared him to his students, associates, and many friends.

THURSTON E. LARSON

1910–1984

BY RICHARD S. ENGELBRECHT
AND WILLIAM C. ACKERMANN

D<small>R. THURSTON E. LARSON</small>, noted engineer and leader in water quality research, died on March 21, 1984, in Urbana, Illinois. He left behind a rich heritage of published research findings, major contributions to the field of water technology, and a research foundation.

Thurston Larson was born in Chicago, Illinois, on March 3, 1910. He earned a B.S. in chemical engineering in 1932 and a Ph.D. in sanitary chemistry in 1937 from the University of Illinois. He was a registered professional engineer in Illinois.

Dr. Larson's principal work was carried out for the Illinois State Water Survey, where he began his career as an assistant chemist in 1932. By 1937 he had risen to the position of chemist; he became head of the Chemistry Section in 1948. In 1956 he was appointed assistant chief of the Water Survey, a position he held until his retirement in 1977.

After retiring, he was awarded the title of assistant chief emeritus. Yet Dr. Larson's "first love" was research, and although he held an administrative position at the Water Survey after 1948, until he retired he continued to be active in bench-level research and to develop new water quality studies. As an administrator, he was instrumental in identifying and developing new programs for assessing the quality of the Illinois ground water and surface waters, programs that not only depicted temporal changes in mineral constituents but also identified potential water quality problems.

From 1962 onward, Dr. Larson was also professor of environmental engineering in the Department of Civil Engineering at the University of Illinois. In that capacity he significantly enriched the department's graduate program in environmental engineering by presenting seminars, advising graduate students on research problems involving water chemistry, and serving on thesis committees.

Dr. Larson made numerous outstanding contributions to environmental engineering through his research in the areas of water quality assessment and control. He was one of the first to recognize the problems associated with the corrosion of water pipes and, as a result, was a pioneer in corrosion research. In fact, he was the first to recognize the measurement of nondestructive corrosion by polarization resistance. His research on the tuberculation phenomenon associated with the corrosion of metal pipes is particularly noteworthy. Thurston Larson also developed a method and apparatus that have been widely adopted in industry for the accurate and sensitive measurement of steam purity. Three of the four patents that he held were related to this measurement.

Dr. Larson's research interest was not limited to corrosion, however, but instead spanned several areas involving water quality considerations. He was active in developing analytical methods for improved sensitivity in measuring chemical constituents in water. He was also recognized for his research in water treatment processes—in particular, water softening processes—and in the use and measurement of various disinfectants that are applied to treat water supplies. His long and productive periods of active research are duly reported through his scholarly publications in technical literature.

Although he was an internationally recognized researcher, Dr. Larson was also a practitioner. Those responsible for water supply utilities and others in the water technology field frequently sought his advice in analyzing and solving water quality problems. From the beginning of his professional career, he maintained a deep interest in the operation and management of water treatment and distribution systems. As a result, he was well aware of the problems, both technical and managerial, that confronted the operators and managers of water supply utilities.

This awareness resulted in his establishing the Annual Water Works Management Short Course in 1952. This program, which has been held annually at the University of Illinois Allerton Park Conference Center since 1952, was the first of its kind. Dr. Larson served as its general chairman for many years.

Thurston Larson was perhaps most prominent as a professional leader in the American Water Works Association (AWWA). Within AWWA's Illinois Section, he chaired numerous committees and held many offices, both before and after being elected chairman of the section in 1959. At the national level, he was on the board of directors and for many years was chairman of the association's research committee. He represented AWWA on the Standard Methods for the Examination of Water and Wastewater Committee; during his tenure, the committee published the tenth, eleventh, and twelfth editions of *Standard Methods for the Examination of Water and Wastewater*.

In 1970 Dr. Larson was elected national president of AWWA. He was instrumental in establishing the AWWA Research Foundation and served on its board of trustees for many years; the foundation continues to have an active and prominent role in sponsoring water quality research. AWWA honored Dr. Larson with a number of awards—the Goodell Prize (1957), the George Warren Fuller Award (1961), the Diven Medal for outstanding service (1966), the Research Award (1972), and an honorary membership award (1974).

Thurston Larson was also prominent in the affairs of the American Chemical Society (ACS) and its Division of Environmental Chemistry (formerly the Division of Water, Air, and Waste Chemistry); he was chairman of the division for a number of years. In addition, he represented ACS on the

U.S. Public Health Service Drinking Water Standards Advisory Committee. In 1971 he received a citation from ACS's board of directors for his role as chairman of the twenty-six-member task force that developed the report, "Cleaning Our Environment—A Chemical Basis for Action." This report, which was translated into Arabic and Japanese, had a very positive impact during the environmental movement of the early 1970s.

Dr. Larson actively participated in the affairs of numerous other professional organizations through committee assignments and his publications. He was a fellow of the American Association for the Advancement of Science and the American Institute of Chemists, a diplomate of the American Academy of Environmental Engineers, and a member of the National Association of Corrosion Engineers, the Water Pollution Control Federation, the International Water Supply Association, the International Association on Water Pollution Research and Control, and the United Kingdom's Institution of Water Engineers and Scientists.

He was elected to the National Academy of Engineering in 1978 for his leadership in water supply research and those of his contributions to the field of environmental engineering that were related to water quality criteria and standards. Among his many activities was his participation as a member of various committees of the National Research Council. Dr. Larson was a member of the Subcommittee on Water Supplies of the Committee on Sanitary Engineering and the Environment from 1958 to 1964; chairman of the Panel on Public Water Supplies of the Committee on Water Quality Criteria in 1972; a member of the Committee on Nitrate Accumulation in 1971; a member of the Subcommittee on Special Ions of the Safe Drinking Water Committee from 1976 to 1977; and a member of the Committee on the Potomac River from 1976 to 1977.

Dr. Larson also actively participated in committees of the U.S. Public Health Service (USPHS) and the U.S. Environmental Protection Agency (EPA). From 1960 to 1966, he was a member of the USPHS Environmental Science and Engineering Study Section; he was chairman of the section from 1963 through 1966. He was a member of the EPA Advisory Committee on Drinking Water Standards in 1973. In addition, he frequently served as a consultant on special matters to these two agencies and to the U.S. Army Environmental Hygiene Agency.

Dr. Larson married Veda E. Taylor in 1938. He is survived by his wife and two sons—Byron of Taipei, Taiwan, and Bruce of New York City.

Thurston Larson was widely admired—not only by his professional associates but also by a wide circle of practitioners in the water supply industry, people who recognized his leadership in achieving the high level of water quality this country continues to enjoy. He was blessed with a congenial personality, which led to his being liked, as well as admired.

Harold B. Law

HAROLD B. LAW

1911–1984

BY HUMBOLDT W. LEVERENZ

Harold b. law, the inventor and developer of methods and structures for making video devices that are now used worldwide, especially for television, died on April 6, 1984, at the age seventy-two. He retired from RCA in 1976 as director of its Electronic Components, Materials, and Display Device Laboratory. In his retirement, he devoted himself to farming his acreage near Hopewell, New Jersey, and took agricultural courses to enhance his proficiency. He died suddenly in the "saddle" of his tractor.

Law conceived and applied the method of using light to simulate electronic beams for printing phosphor screens in color picture tubes for television and computers and for multicolor displays used in many other devices. An earlier achievement was his method for making the delicate glass/ mesh target required for image orthicon camera tubes; the method included a technique for making very fine high-transmission metal meshes from a ruled glass master.

Harold Law was an active, quiet, kindly man, who delighted in helping those he knew and in benefiting countless others through his inventions. Whether seated or afoot, he always looked as though he was thinking—mainly because he *was* thinking.

He was born on September 7, 1911, in the small town of Douds in southeast Iowa, where his father taught school and

243

had a small farm. The family moved to Kent, Ohio, around 1914, but Law returned during the summers to his grandfather's farm, where he enjoyed doing the chores.

In high school he applied himself to school subjects, manual arts, band, and sports, as well as such extracurricular activities as building and flying gliders. After some gliding practice, he persuaded a local airplane pilot to teach him to fly a power plane—lessons that included a solo flight—in one morning.

Law financed his undergraduate years at Kent State University by working six hours a night; he graduated in 1934 with a B.S. in liberal arts and another in education. After teaching mathematics for a year in Maple Heights, Ohio, he entered graduate school at Ohio State University and received his M.S. in physics in 1936. He again taught mathematics, this time for two years, and then returned to Ohio State, receiving his Ph.D. in physics in 1941.

During his graduate work, Harold read an article about RCA's research on electron multipliers, and he attempted to duplicate some of the reported results. After he graduated, he applied for a position in RCA's research division in Camden, New Jersey, and began work there in June 1941. He was assigned to a group that was trying to make more sensitive electron emitter surfaces and to use electron multipliers in camera tubes. He found that he liked designing, fabricating, and testing experimental electron devices because, as he said, "it suited my do-it-yourself nature."

When RCA consolidated its research in new buildings near Princeton, New Jersey, in 1942, the newly married Law moved there and became part of a group whose task was to develop the image orthicon tube invented by Albert Rose. Rose guided the overall effort; Law worked on the secondary-electron-emitting target (a very thin sheet of special glass mounted a few microns from a very fine mesh metal screen); and Paul K. Weimer worked on the electron multiplier and the electron optics of the scanning beam.

Ideally, the image orthicon could have a thousand times

the sensitivity of the iconoscope, but the techniques and materials needed to make the tube with the required precision were not available. Law attacked the target problems with his hands-on, "mind-on" vigor and serendipity. Out of his efforts evolved the technique of using a fine diamond point to rule grooves on a glass plate. This step was followed by evaporating platinum to a thin film over the plate and then rubbing off the surface film. The platinum left in the grooves was electroplated with copper and pulled out intact; it was then welded to a frame and heated to about 500°C, at which point the screen was pulled flat by internal cohesion, as manifested by surface tension.

Rose stated: "This remains the classic way of making fine mesh (1,000 lines/inch) screens, highly transparent (80% open area), and highly uniform." Yet the heating-to-tauten technique was so unusual that the patent examiner said that it could not work because it was well known that metal expands when heated. Law took heating equipment, frame, and mesh to the Appeals Board in Washington to demonstrate the efficacy of the procedure.

Harold Law also made the thin, uniform glass emitter target by heating it to temperatures high enough for cohesion to pull it flat. After the Law-Rose-Weimer team achieved practical image orthicons, they attended the first public demonstration by RCA in which it was shown that the tube could give a television picture of a young woman's face illuminated by the light from a single match. The image orthicon was the acme of the photoemitter-type camera tubes and was in commercial use for many years.

After World War II, major efforts were initiated to develop color television. The approach advocated by RCA was to provide a compatible color system—that is, one whose pictures could be seen in color on new color sets and in monochrome on existing black-and-white sets. The RCA concept was deemed to be impossible by many because it needed pioneering inventions of systems, circuits, devices, and the methods for making them. RCA engineers devised many potential solutions from which the few practical ones had to be chosen, developed, and demonstrated under time pressures that had been imposed during hearings held by the Federal Communications Commission, which favored standardizing a noncompatible color system.

A key part of the "sought-for" compatible color television was a device to reproduce the color picture, a solution that was then unknown. In September 1949, a special meeting was called at RCA Laboratories, which was attended by Harold Law and other selected members of the technical staff. Those present were invited to participate in a three-month "crash program" to demonstrate the feasibility of a color picture tube. Overall organization and coordination of the effort were assigned to Edward W. Herold.

Law welcomed the challenge and recalled some experiments he had done "on the side" to make color phosphor screens in patterns by using a photographic process. He chose to use a form of three-electron-beam, three-phosphor-element color kinescope invented by Alfred C. Schroeder. In Schroeder's device the beams went through holes in a mask, each beam striking one array of phosphor dots emitting one color.

In mulling over and experimenting with means to deposit the hundreds of thousands of phosphor dots in exactly the right spots, Law conceived the idea of using a light source placed at the deflection center of one electron beam. The light source would shine through the mask apertures and strike a transparent plate coated with a photosensitive binder containing one of the phosphors, affixing the phosphor dots in those locations. The process would be repeated for the other two beams and colors.

Law's invention, with flat masks and flat phosphor screens, was used to show the feasibility of the color kinescope within the three-month deadline, and the RCA compatible color system eventually prevailed. An extension of Law's technique, using curved masks and depositing the phosphor dots on the curved inside end of the kinescope, was announced by N. F. Fyler, W. E. Rowee, and C. W. Cain in 1954. The method is still used to produce color picture tubes worldwide.

As might be expected, Law's important invention was contested, and the patent was not issued until 1968. The turning point in the lengthy litigation came when Edward Herold gave cogent supporting testimony from his records as coordinator of the crash program and subsequent developments.

Harold Law was elected to membership in the National Academy of Engineering in 1979, having previously been named a fellow of the Institute of Electrical and Electronics Engineers (IEEE) in 1955, a fellow of the Society of Information Display in 1971, and a fellow of the Technical Staff of RCA Laboratories. He was a also member of the American Physical Society and Sigma Xi. He received the Television Broadcasters Association Award (1946); the IEEE Zworykin Television Prize (1955); the Consumer Electronics Scientist of the Year Award (1966); the IEEE Lamme Medal (1975); and the Frances Rice Darne Memorial Award (1975). From Kent State University, he received the Outstanding Graduate Citation (1959) and an honorary D.Sc. (1984). RCA gave him five awards.

His thirteen publications include "The Image Orthicon—A Sensitive TV Pickup Tube" (with A. Rose and P. K. Weimer), in *Institute of Radio Engineers Proceedings*, (vol. 34, July 1946); "A Technique for the Making and Mounting of Fine-Mesh Screens" in *Review of Scientific Instruments* (vol. 19, December 1948); and "The Shadow-Mask Color Picture Tube: How it Began" in *IEEE Transactions on Electron Devices* (vol. ED–23, July 1976). Two of his "inventions," the method of making fine-mesh screens and photographic methods of making electron-sensitive mosaic screens, are particularly outstanding among his thirty-eight U.S. patents.

Harold Law met his wife Ruth (née Workman), a gifted mathematics teacher, through his sister, Mabel. He is survived by Ruth; their married daughters, Linda Krantz, Sara Schlenker, and Kathy Orloski; six grandchildren; and his sister, now Mabel Winters. He once told Ruth that he enjoyed his work with RCA as much as his work on the farm. About the farm, he said, "Living on this place is as near to heaven as you can get."

George M. Low

GEORGE MICHAEL LOW

1926–1984

BY JAMES C. FLETCHER

GEORGE MICHAEL LOW, a long-term pioneer in the nation's space program and a key figure in the success of the Apollo lunar landing, died of cancer at age fifty-eight on July 17, 1984. During the previous eight years, George Low was president of Rensselaer Polytechnic Institute and, in addition to developing the institute into one of the nation's finest, played a leading role in formulating the nation's science and technology policy.

In fact, in recent years, whenever strong leadership was needed to resolve a new problem or to pursue a new opportunity in any branch of science or technology, George Low's name was always at the top of the list. His contributions covered a broad span of disciplines: aviation, education, manufacturing technology, research, space automation—almost anything on the "cutting edge" of technology.

George Low was born in a small town just outside of Vienna, Austria, in 1926. His family emigrated to America when George was only fourteen, by which time his obsession with engineering and technical matters was already well established. After graduating from high school in only two years, he entered Rensselaer Polytechnic Institute in Troy, New York, but was drafted into the army at the age of eighteen.

During his army service, he became a naturalized citizen

(in 1945) and received his pilot's license. He was discharged in 1946 and returned to Rensselaer, earning a B.S. (1948) and an M.S. (1950) in aeronautical engineering. While at Rensselaer he married Mary R. McNamara, of Troy, New York, a wonderful lady who supported George fully in all his later endeavors.

In 1949 George Low joined NASA's predecessor organization, the National Advisory Committee for Aeronautics (NACA), and began work as a research scientist at Lewis Research Laboratory in Cleveland, Ohio. He remained there until 1958, publishing many reports on his research. He soon demonstrated leadership qualities at the Lewis lab in several capacities, the last of which was chief of the Special Projects Branch, a position he held until NASA was formed in 1958. At that time he was brought to Washington as chief of manned space flight for the newly formed agency.

In his new capacity, he helped prepare the material for President John F. Kennedy that led to the president's announcement in 1961 that the country would embark on a program to land men on the moon before the end of the decade. As the new Apollo program got under way in 1964, the Manned Spacecraft Center (now called the Johnson Space Center) was established in Houston, Texas, and George Low was appointed deputy director. In this capacity, he had overall responsibility for the Gemini and Apollo spacecraft development, as well as for future program development and flight and astronaut operations—in fact, for all activities related to manned space.

In April 1967, after the disastrous Apollo fire that killed three astronauts, NASA administrator James Webb agreed that Low should work fulltime on Apollo spacecraft development as manager of the Apollo spacecraft program. In this capacity, Low worked a grueling ninety-hour week for more than a year and a half. In 1968 he declared that the Apollo spacecraft was flight-worthy and persuaded deputy administrator Thomas Paine to move the first flight to the moon ahead of schedule to December 1968, thus leading to the historic *Apollo 8* flight around the moon during the Christmas season with astronauts Frank Borman, Bill Andrews, and Jim Lovell aboard.

The moon landing soon followed on July 20, 1969, with Neil Armstrong setting the first human foot on the moon—a step that completed the program that George Low had recommended and President Kennedy had approved eight years previously. A plaque in the Smithsonian Air and Space Museum placed less than a month after his death attests to this fact.

In December 1969 Low was again summoned to Washington, this time by President Richard Nixon, to become deputy administrator of NASA. He served in that capacity until all the Apollo flights were completed, including the Sky Lab and the Apollo-Soyuz programs. The latter had been initiated by President Nixon and Premier Brezhnev during the historic summit conference of 1972. (At the suggestion of Dr. Henry Kissinger, however, Low had been sent on several secret missions to the Soviet Union to determine with absolute certainty that the program was feasible, both technically and politically, before the president agreed to place it on the agenda for the summit conference.) The entire program, from start to finish, was completed in three years—another near miracle, especially considering the requirement of joint development by two countries with completely different cultures and political systems.

At the conclusion of the Apollo program and after twenty-seven years of government service—not withstanding NASA's embarkation, under his leadership, on the new space shuttle program—Low began to consider the many offers he received of positions outside the federal government. The choice was easy. Even during his NASA days, he had enjoyed being with young people, and his vision of the future included the education of the next generation of leaders in the world of technology—the follow-on, so to speak, of the Apollo heritage. Thus, when he was invited in 1976 to become the fourteenth president of his old alma mater, Rensselaer Polytechnic Institute (RPI), he accepted readily and began his second career.

RPI had always had an exceptional student body, most of which was drawn from the top five to ten percent of students taking college admission tests. Low proceeded to broaden its earlier reputation as a first-class undergraduate school to that of a national research university and a pioneer in several areas of new technology. This program involved a number of activities on Low's part, many of which required new skills that had not been apparent during NASA days—for example, raising money. Low's mastering of such skills was soon evident as new buildings were constructed, an industrial park was developed, prestigious faculty were added, and RPI established new programs in manufacturing technology, computer graphics, and integrated electronics that were among the first in the nation.

Recognizing that the national visibility of RPI depended partly on his own contributions, George began to accept assignments on the national level that he felt were sufficiently important to require leadership from someone of his stature. Perhaps the assignment with greatest visibility was his chairing of the commission established under the National Research Council to examine in detail the operation and maintenance procedures of the Federal Aviation Administration after the disastrous DC-10 crash in Chicago in 1979.

Within the National Academies of Science and Engineering, his contribution was most outstanding in his role, in 1981, as the first chairman of COSEPUP (Committee on Science, Engineering, and Public Policy). Studies ranging from a broad consideration of security restrictions on university research to the technical competitiveness of U.S. industry were conducted under COSEPUP's jurisdiction; all such studies involved the nation's top scientists and engineers. National policy in science and engineering has, to a large extent, been derived from the studies sponsored by COSEPUP, which Low chaired.

George Low had many talents and used them well to serve

the nation and to educate future world leaders. His writing and speaking skills were well known and were used effectively in managerial positions, in many of his published speeches, and in his numerous committee assignments (and, occasionally, as an outlet for his quiet humor, as the author of this tribute can testify).

Another talent was his keen sense of institutional mechanisms and how they aided or hindered whatever program he might be implementing at the time. This ability was especially apparent at NASA headquarters in dealing with the White House and Congress, but it was also noticeable in his public speaking engagements at RPI and in his dealings with the governor and the state legislature of New York.

He was a relentless program manager with an enormous capacity for absorbing details—to the wonder of everyone who worked for him. At one point, during the period following the Apollo fire, he said, "I probably know as much about toggle switches as anyone else does in the world." Toggle switches had been one of the flaws in the Apollo spacecraft. As a program manager, he had little tolerance for sloppy work, excuses for errors, or general incompetence. One did not remain for long on Low's team if any of these characteristics was apparent. On the other hand, he never failed to praise those who did measure up. In fact, many of Low's protégés are now in charge of significant portions of the NASA program and active in other parts of government. It is to be expected that more recent graduates of RPI will be equally successful.

George Low rarely commented on his many accomplishments, but once when asked, he stated: "A career isn't a plan, it's a series of opportunities." For him, that statement was, indeed, true. He could have remained a skilled, successful researcher and enjoyed it, or he could have been an exacting designer-engineer. Yet the combination of his talents and his capacity for hard work when the occasion required it pushed him into more and more responsible positions—a progression that ended only with his death—as president of RPI, chairman of COSEPUP, and a director of the General Electric Company.

His clearsighted perception of future trends led him to a firm, positive belief in progress and, although his vision was always on "the future," his contributions, both at NASA and at RPI, were practical, well thought out, and completed in "the present." His interest in the future was reflected in an interest in youth, not only at NASA and RPI but also in his devotion to his five children, Mark, Diane, David, John, and Nancy.

Low received many honors, medals, and honorary degrees throughout his career, beginning, perhaps, in 1963 with the Arthur Flemming Award for the ten outstanding young men in government and continuing with the National Academy of Engineering's Founders Award in 1978—the highest award given by the academy. On July 20, 1984, the fifteenth anniversary of the landing on the moon and three days after George Low's passing, President Reagan announced that Low would receive the Medal of Freedom, the nation's highest award to a civilian.

George Low was impressive as an associate, awesome as a boss, but kindly and gentle as a friend. As the president said on July 20, "We're grateful for what George Low has done and the ideals he stood for, and we'll miss him very much."

Hans A. Mauch.

HANS ADOLPH MAUCH

1906–1984

BY EUGENE MURPHY

A MAJOR CONTRIBUTOR TO rehabilitation engineering, a distinguished engineer in several other areas, and a strong personality, Hans Adolph Mauch repeatedly predicted he would live to be a hundred years old. Tall, tough, and an advocate of vigorous exercise, at age seventy-seven he worked long hours. Instead of quiet relaxation, he and his wife undertook such major adventures as a trip around the world, including some days and nights on the Trans-Siberian Express in 1983.

He seemed in excellent health when he went to his laboratory as usual the morning of January 13, 1984. Yet, suddenly, he collapsed from a massive stroke. After lingering a week in intensive care, he died on January 20, 1984.

Fortunately, the S-N-S, his well-known hydraulic artificial knee designed to control both swing and stance phases of walking for above-knee amputees, was a well-established product here and abroad (more than 12,000 had been sold). Voluntarily, Mauch had progressively lengthened the warranty period to two years on this ingenious, complex, yet dependable mechanism.

He had also made plans for three of his associates to attend regional meetings of the American Orthotic and Prosthetic Association in April 1984 to introduce new variants of the knee that might broaden the possibilities for prescription and especially to announce the availability of the long-awaited Mauch multifunction hydraulic ankle joint. He had deliberately planned that the presentations by these younger men would emphasize the point that the future of Mauch Laboratories did not depend solely on his own health. Indeed, Mrs. Mauch (long a director of the company) has since taken over the presidency, employees have been purchasing stock, and the recently expanded plant building has been equipped with modern machinery that includes three computer-controlled machine tools.

Hans Mauch was born in Stuttgart-Bad Cannstatt, Germany, on March 6, 1906. He was educated in mechanical, electrical, and electronic engineering at the technical universities of Stuttgart and Berlin. He received the advanced degree of Diplom Ingenieur at Berlin in 1929, where he was in the top two percent of his class.

One of his professors was Georg Schlesinger, who had contributed so much to German work in prosthetics during World War I, work that included writing a third of the classic German text *Erstazglieder und Arbeitshilfen*. Yet the contact appeared to have no immediate influence on Mauch's interests. He began his studies for the doctorate in engineering, but dropped them when he found that his choice of a thesis subject had been preempted by another dissertation at a different university.

He took a position with E. Zwietusch & Company in Berlin in 1930 and worked until 1935 on methods for the control of pneumatic conveyors, which were then widely used not only in department stores and hospitals but also to carry mail in large cylinders from one post office to another in many cities. He was in charge of research and development efforts involving automatic conveyors and sorters; these efforts included the development of a method by which each cylinder would carry an easily changed, predetermined code that, despite unpredictable rotation and high velocity, could be read automatically and signaled ahead to set switches that would divert the capsule to its correct destination.

Mauch was employed as a civilian engineer in the German

Air Ministry from 1935 to 1939. He left to establish his own consulting engineering office in Berlin, which he headed until the end of World War II. He developed testing equipment and aviation and automotive engines and accessories; he also acted as a consultant to the German Air Ministry, where he was later placed in charge of the terminal development of the V-1 buzz bomb, the first guided missile. He knew, and sometimes differed with, many of the top German engineers of the period, including Wernher von Braun.

Mauch's third major consulting activity was original research and development in the fields of aviation medicine and prosthetic devices. In this bioengineering sector, Hans Mauch cooperated closely with Ulrich K. Henschke, a radiologist with a Ph.D. in physics. Head of the Aeromedical Institute in Munich, Dr. Henschke worked on a variety of physiological problems.

After World War II, the U.S. Air Force assembled many top German scientists and engineers at Heidelberg. There, Henschke and Mauch collaborated on an important chapter, "How Man Controls," of a two-volume work, *German Aviation Medicine—World War II*. This chapter was a pioneering effort in what later became known as the fields of cybernetics and human factors engineering. Henschke and Mauch also assembled an extensive bibliography of German work on artificial limbs, designed a metal artificial leg that was intended for mass production of components and easy assembly to an individually fitted socket, and constructed a series of models illustrating various concepts for stabilizing the knee joint of an above-knee prosthesis.

In March 1946 the U.S. Army surgeon general sent a team to Europe to survey artificial limbs. In addition to important information on various devices and procedures including the suction socket leg and cineplastic surgery to control arms, the team brought back the Henschke-Mauch bibliography and the concepts they developed involving knee control. Subsequently, Henschke and Mauch went to Dayton, Ohio, late in 1946, to work as civilian employees at the Aeromedical Laboratory of the Wright Air Force Development Center. Yet, they were able to devote only a small portion of their efforts to prosthetics. Later, Mauch and several others worked evenings and weekends in the basement of his small home with support by the Veterans Administration through its National Academy of Sciences' contract.

Hans Mauch became a naturalized U.S. citizen in June 1955. He left the Aeromedical Laboratory in 1957 to set up his own organization, which was incorporated in 1959 as Mauch Laboratories, Inc. The company engaged in research, development, and manufacturing in the biomedical engineering field.

Except for a classified project to develop a novel space suit for the Air Force and NASA, which the company performed from 1959 to 1964, all of Mauch's work until the mid-1970s was devoted to rehabilitation projects sponsored by the Veterans Administration in coordination, through various National Research Council committees, with projects of other agencies. In recent years, after termination of his VA contracts, further improvements in the company's devices were made by Mauch as proprietary developments.

After exhaustive development and evaluation efforts that culminated in a nationwide clinical trial, the original Henschke-Mauch Model A semivoluntary stance-and-swing hydraulic leg for above-knee amputees was shortened, refined, and renamed the S-N-S. A simpler Model B to control only the swing phase was produced briefly in 1963; it has been refined and is currently sold as Model S. Several other companies produced swing-phase units under the Mauch patent, which was assigned to the VA and licensed to others without royalties after training at Mauch Laboratories.

The Mauch swing control provides programmed resistance that automatically varies with knee angle and walking speed, plus the possibility of independent adjustment of resistances to flexion and extension. The stance phase control always allows extension, but automatically imposes a high (but adjustable) resistance to knee flexion *except* after a brief application of a hyperextension moment, normally after the heel leaves the ground.

The rigid locking of the device is normally undesirable (the residual limb could be injured after stumbling), but it can be obtained voluntarily if desired—for example, for prolonged standing or for driving an automobile with flexed knee. Conversely, very low resistance to flexion can also be ensured for bicycling. These knee control features are superior to other brakes and locks that have been disclosed in literature and patent applications here and abroad for well over a century.

The S-N-S is the sole survivor of many years of effort by numerous capable engineers and interdisciplinary teams supported by substantial government projects. The genius, persistence, and vision of Hans Mauch are demonstrated by his eventual success with the S-N-S, the recent acceptance of the hydraulic ankle, and his yearning to attain a truly voluntary yet subconscious control of swing-and-stance phase movement.

Although this memoir focuses on Mauch's contributions to hydraulic lower limb prostheses, he made thoughtful, ingenious contributions in many fields, including aviation and aviation medicine, space suits, and the human factors aspects of displays and controls. Mauch was the inventor or coinventor of more than eighty patented inventions in nine countries and the author or coauthor of numerous papers and reports. Under VA contract, he developed several types of personal reading machines for the blind, another area he and Dr. Henschke had explored in Heidelberg. His audible-output Stereotoner direct-translation reading aid, which was smaller, lighter, and lower in price than the widely known tactile-output Optacon, reached limited commercial production.

Hans Mauch was elected to the National Academy of Engineering in 1973. He served on its General Engineering Peer Group from 1976 to 1978, and he consistently attended the academy's annual meetings. He also served for a quarter of a century on many National Research Council committees and working groups in prosthetics. He was a consultant to the U.S. Air Force and to the U.S. Department of Health, Education, and Welfare.

In 1944 he received the Knight Cross to the Merit Cross from the German Air Ministry, the highest nonpolitical decoration for civilians. The U.S. Air Force awarded him the Outstanding Civil Service Commendation in 1956 and the Outstanding Inventor Award in 1960.

Hans Mauch married Austrian-born Tatjana Schmid in 1948. She also came to the United States to work for the U.S. Air Force. They had three daughters.

A brilliant, well-educated, cultured man, Mauch was a creative inventor and developer, a valuable member of committees and councils, and a delightful friend. Sometimes a naive suggestion to him would bring the rebuff, "We already thought of that in Heidelberg!" or he would produce an old notebook containing a similar sketch and the record of the notion's failure. Nevertheless, he would explore suggestions carefully and accept good ideas or data. Another able engineer once observed, "The trouble with Mauch is that he's a perfectionist!" Well, what's so bad about that, especially when his work was offered to the consumer at such a surprisingly reasonable cost?

Robert C. McMaster

ROBERT CHARLES McMASTER

1913–1986

BY ROBERT I. JAFFEE

ROBERT CHARLES MCMASTER, one of the pioneers of non-destructive testing, died of cardiac shock at his home in Delaware, Ohio, on July 6, 1986. Dr. McMaster, who was seventy-three when he died, was Regents Professor Emeritus of Welding Engineering and Electrical Engineering at Ohio State University (OSU).

He was elected to the National Academy of Engineering in 1970. He retired from OSU in 1977 and spent the last nine years of his life in a typically proactive, Bob McMaster style: involved in countless projects, including continued consulting, editing the second edition of his monumental *Nondestructive Testing Handbook*, and attending to his family to whom he was devoted.

McMaster received a B.S. in 1936 in electrical engineering from Carnegie Mellon University in Pittsburgh, Pennsylvania; an M.S. in 1938 in electrical engineering from California Institute of Technology (Caltech) in Pasadena, California; and a Ph.D., magna cum laude, in electrical engineering and physics in 1944, also from Caltech. At Caltech, McMaster supervised welding and X-ray radiography, his first encounter with the field of nondestructive testing (NDT). His Ph.D. research involved the effects of light on power transmission lines. His teachers included Nobel Laureates Carl D. Anderson, Robert A. Millikan, and Enrico Fermi.

267

Bob McMaster's first job after finishing his Ph.D. was with Battelle Memorial Institute's Columbus Laboratories, where he cut quite a swath as supervisor of electrical engineering from 1945 to 1954. It was during this period that Bob McMaster became one of the nation's first television weathermen. From 1950 to 1964 he broadcast twice a day at WBNS-TV in Columbus, providing for his watchers a virtual education in weather forecasting that included the "why" as well as the "what" in the local weather picture.

His Battelle days included important work on the use of sonic and ultrasonic wave-assisted oil well drilling and power tools, a topic he continued at OSU. This experience culminated in the licensing of industry to produce high-power-level prezoelectric transducers for metal working and hand tools. McMaster continued his work on NDT, applying the xerox copying process developed by Battelle for Haloid Company, which later became Xerox Corporation, to radiography in the xeroradiography units being marketed by Xerox. Xeroradiography is now widely used in medicine for early cancer detection.

McMaster joined Ohio State University in 1955. He began as a professor of welding engineering and later became Regents Professor of Welding and Electrical Engineering. He taught courses in NDT and welding to both graduate and undergraduate students. Bob McMaster turned out to be a superb teacher. His booming lecture voice and carefully printed blackboard will never be forgotten by his students, to whom he was known as "Doc." His courses in welding and NDT principles and analysis were also perhaps the best English and mathematics courses his students ever had. A report with grammatical errors would be returned with a suitably pithy comment scrawled in the margin for correction before it would be accepted.

Of McMaster's more than three hundred publications and nineteen patents, perhaps the most significant to his field and to society as a whole is the *Nondestructive Testing Handbook* that he edited for the American Society for Nondestructive

Testing. The two-volume first edition appeared in 1959; McMaster finished the second edition in 1986, before his untimely death. His achievement in compiling, and often rewriting, the contributions to this work is staggering.

The manuscript of the first edition totaled 2,700 typed pages, contained 1,250 illustrations, and stood twenty-six inches high when stacked. The award-winning publication was so comprehensive, far reaching, and definitive that it is still widely used twenty-seven years after its publication and has been translated into many languages including French, Spanish, Russian, and Chinese.

McMaster received many honors during his lifetime. He was a life member of the American Society for Nondestructive Testing (ASNT), the American Society for Testing Materials (ASTM), the American Welding Society, the American Society for Metals, and the Institute of Electrical and Electronics Engineers; he was also a member of the American Society for Engineering Education and Sigma Xi. He presented the ASNT Mehl Lecture in 1950 and the ASTM Edgar Marburg Lecture on nondestructive testing in 1952. For the American Welding Society, McMaster presented the Educational Lecture in 1962 and the Adams Honor Lecture in 1965.

In 1970 he was appointed national lecturer of the Midwest region of Sigma Xi. He received the National Reliability Award (1966), the Carnegie Mellon Merit Award (1971), the Ohioana Citation for distinguished service in engineering and research (1971), the American Welding Society Charles H. Jennings Memorial Award (1975), and the OSU Meritorious Service Citation (1980).

From his primary society, the American Society of Nondestructive Testing, McMaster received many honors and awards. He was ASNT president from 1952 to 1953 and received the ASNT Fellow Award (1973), the Coolidge Honor Award (1957), the DeForest Award (1959), the Tutorial Citation (1973), and the Gold Medal (1977). He was awarded honorary membership in 1960.

McMaster's work on NDT was of great timeliness because it coincided with the development of fracture mechanics during the early 1950s, a period marked by catastrophic failures of turbine and generator rotors and rocket motor casings. The juxtaposition of the development of NDT and fracture mechanics appears to be more than coincidental.

Prior to an understanding of fracture mechanics and the development of finite element stress analysis, NDT was used primarily for radiographic inspection. Fracture mechanics required accurate knowledge of flaw size and location relative to the static dynamic stresses that are applied to large, critical components. McMaster's work on advanced NDT techniques, including ultrasonic and eddy-current methods, was vital to the new fracture mechanics technology that was created during the 1950s to analyze failures and predict the life of components.

McMaster had a sophisticated view of NDT in the total context of science and engineering and of the importance of NDT to society. His later publications dealt more and more with management responsibilities and ethical philosophy in the application of NDT. He saw NDT as a broad family of technologies that extended human powers of perception beyond the inspection of industrial materials to many fields, including noninvasive medical diagnostics, geophysical sensing, meteorological environmental monitoring, and radiometric probing of space. His humane vision of the NDT profession is one of his many legacies.

McMaster is survived by his wife, Laura Gerould McMaster; his sons, L. Roy McMaster and James A. McMaster; his daughter, Lois McMaster Bujold; his sister, Mrs. Max T. Rogers; and seven grandchildren. Roy is an investment counselor, Jim works in chemical plant research and development, and Lois writes books on science fiction. Laura McMaster recently closed the house on the left bank of the Scioto River, where they lived happily for seventeen years. Bob and Laura McMaster were members of the Liberty Presbyterian Church in Delaware, Ohio, the churchyard in which he was buried on July 9, 1986.

Bob McMaster leaves behind a living legacy of hundreds of people with whom he came in contact, students and professional colleagues, to continue his work in nondestructive testing.

Theodore J. Nagel

THEODORE J. NAGEL

1913–1986

BY JOHN E. DOLAN

THEODORE J. NAGEL, an internationally recognized authority on the planning, operation, and reliability of electric power systems, died January 14, 1986, in Tucson, Arizona, after an extended illness. He was seventy-two.

At the time of his retirement in 1982, Nagel had spent forty-three years with the American Electric Power (AEP) Service Corporation, rising through the company's ranks from assistant engineer to senior executive vice-president and assistant to the chairman. He played a large role in making the seven-state American Electric Power System what it is today—a major force and leader in this nation's electric utility industry.

In his forty-three years with AEP as an engineer, system planner, and executive, seventeen were spent as the engineering executive responsible for the development of future planning programs. Today, that system, with its 22.8 million kilowatts of generating capacity and more than 21,700 miles of high-voltage transmission lines, is his legacy.

Ted was born on December 20, 1913, in Andes, New York. He received his B.A. in 1936, his B.S. in electrical engineering in 1937, and his M.S. in electrical engineering in 1938, all from Columbia University.

He was first employed by the AEP Service Corporation in 1939 as an assistant engineer. After four years of service with the U.S. Navy during World War II, he returned as a senior engineer in 1946. He was promoted to head of the System Planning and Engineering Section of the former System Planning and Operation Department in 1954, rising to head of the newly formed System Planning and Analytical Division in 1959 and to deputy chief engineer and chief planning engineer in 1966. He was named vice-president of system planning in 1967, senior vice-president of system planning in 1973, executive vice-president of system planning in 1974, and senior executive vice-president and assistant to the chairman in 1976. He was also a director of the AEP Service Corporation and of two AEP System operating companies—Appalachian Power Company and Wheeling Electric Company.

Nagel joined the U.S. Navy in 1942 as an ensign, served mainly in the European theater, and was discharged as a lieutenant commander in 1946. During his service in Europe, he met and later married his wife, Dee. They became the parents of a son, Philip, and a daughter, Pamela.

Together with Nagel's impressive work history, his service on various industry and government technical and advisory committees established his credentials as an expert on power supply planning and reliability. When the Great Blackout of 1965 struck the Northeast, Nagel was not in his New York office but at an AEP System management meeting in Roanoke, Virginia, approximately four hundred miles away. The blackout disrupted electrical service to thirty million customers over an eighty-thousand-square-mile area.

Nagel was summoned to Washington by Joseph P. Swidler, chairman of the Federal Power Commission. His initial assignment was to assist in the commission's inquiry into the blackout, which was to be conducted by its Advisory Committee on Reliability of Electric Bulk Power Supply, and eventually to prepare its report to the president. The product of his research while a member of this committee was released as Volume 2 of *Prevention of Power Failures*. The document ultimately led to the industry's reliability coordination effort in both the United States and Canada. Later, when a similar but less severe failure hit the Pennsylvania-New Jersey-Maryland area, Nagel was called upon again—and again he responded effectively.

Owing to his solid reputation in advisory committee work, Nagel was invited to participate in all three of the National Power Surveys conducted by the Federal Power Commission. During the first, he served as a member of the Transmission and Interconnection Special Technical Committee; for the second, he was a member of the East Central Regional Advisory Committee; in the third, he participated as a member of the Energy Distribution Research Task Force.

Nagel was also instrumental in the formation of the East Central Area Reliability Coordination Agreement Group (ECAR), the first of nine such regional groups to be organized across the country. He served as chairman of its Coordinating Review Committee from 1970 to 1976. In addition, he was chairman of the Technical Advisory Committee of the North American Electric Reliability Council (NERC) for two years. The council's membership is composed of all nine regional groups. Nagel was also the NERC Engineering Committee's representative on foreign activities.

In addition, he was a member of the Conférence Internationale des Grands Réseaux Electriques à Haute Tension, the international organization devoted to the planning, development, and operation of large high-voltage electric systems. In 1982 he was named international chairman of its System Planning and Development Committee.

Nagel was elected a member of the National Academy of Engineering in 1973 and served on its Committee on Power Plant Siting. A longtime member of the Institute of Electrical and Electronics Engineers (IEEE), he was elected a life fellow of that body in 1979. IEEE's Power Engineering Society honored Nagel and his former AEP colleague Howard C. Barnes by presenting them with its William M. Habirshaw Award in 1979. This award, which is given annually in recognition of "outstanding contributions to the field of electrical transmission and distribution," was presented to Nagel because of his work in the planning—and Barnes' work in the engineering—of the nation's first 765,000-volt transmission system. The network was conceived in the 1960s during research work conducted by AEP at its extra-high-voltage transmission laboratory in Apple Grove, West Virginia. Construction of the first sixty-six-mile section of this 765,000-volt system was begun in 1967, and service began in 1969. The final ninety-six-mile link in the network was not placed in operation, however, until September 1986. This addition increased the system's total length to 2,022 circuit miles.

Nagel was a member of three professional honorary fraternities: Tau Beta Pi (engineering), Eta Kappa Nu (electrical engineering), and Sigma Xi (science research). He was the author or coauthor of more than twenty professional papers.

A final honor was bestowed on Nagel at the time of his retirement: the AEP System named its newest extra-high-voltage transmission station for him—the Nagel Station near Kingsport, Tennessee.

Ted Nagel was a man of substance, character, and intellect. He was a devoted husband, a good father, and, in his work, a dedicated engineer. Perhaps the most appropriate tribute to this quiet, soft-spoken man are the words on the bronze plaque that stands in the Nagel Station yard in the hills of northeastern Tennessee: "Theodore J. Nagel, distinguished engineer and planner who devoted 43 years to the American Electric Power System."

Ted, you planned it all very well.

Herbert M. Parker

HERBERT M. PARKER

1910–1984

BY MERRIL EISENBUD

Herbert m. parker, who played an important role in organizing the radiological safety programs in the United States during and after World War II and who achieved worldwide recognition for his contribution to the excellent safety record of the nuclear industry, died at the age of seventy-three on March 5, 1984.

Mr. Parker was born in Accrington, England, on April 13, 1910. He received an M.S. in physics from the University of Manchester in 1931 and began his career as a medical physicist at the Christie Hospital and Holt Radium Institute in Manchester. While there, he shared in the development of the Paterson-Parker method of determining the size of the radiation dose to cancerous tissue from radium therapy. This method was a major development in radiotherapy, which is still used more than half a century after it was first published.

In 1938 Parker was invited to join the staff of the Swedish Hospital in Seattle, where he was placed in charge of radiological physics at the Tumor Institute. He became associated with Simeon T. Cantril, a radiologist at the institute who, together with Parker, was to play a prominent role in the wartime atomic energy program. In 1942 Parker joined the University of Chicago's "Metallurgical Laboratories," the assembly site for the nucleus of the Manhattan Project. In 1943 he moved to Oak Ridge, where he established the radiological safety program for the first of the major U.S. atomic energy research and production centers.

This program was no small undertaking. Before World War II, U.S. researchers' experience with radioactive substances was extremely limited. Only slightly more than one kilogram of radium had been extracted from the earth's crust, but the processing and use of that small amount of radium, mainly in luminizing compounds, had already caused the deaths of more than one hundred persons. Additional injuries and deaths had been caused by overexposure to the X-rays used in medical practice. With this limited base of experience, Parker and his small group of associates faced the prospect that the material to be processed by the Manhattan Project would be the radioactive equivalent of hundreds of tons of radium!

Fortunately, information from earlier misadventures with radium and X-rays provided a starting point for dealing with the new problems that had to be faced. The use of this meager information to design procedures that safeguarded atomic energy workers and the public from the effects of ionizing radiation was one of the truly remarkable and unheralded technological achievements of the Manhattan Project. New instrumentation had to be developed, people trained, and procedures instituted that would protect human lives and also permit the expeditious achievement of the program's goals.

Herbert Parker played a key role in establishing the basic philosophy of radiation protection and in developing the information and skills that were needed to implement it. He was a leader in introducing units and quantities into radiation protection that are relevant to the absorption of energy in tissue. He invented the rep (forerunner of the rad, the term in current use) as a practical energy absorption dose unit. He modified the rep by factors that accounted for differences in biological effects to produce the rem, a unit that allowed doses from different kinds of radiations to be summed. The rem, which can be considered a unit of risk, is still in use.

After he established the basic radiation protection program at Oak Ridge, Parker was transferred in 1944 to a new industrial complex at Hanford. Here, E. I. du Pont de Nemours and Company, Inc., had been charged with the design, construction, and operation of facilities to produce and separate plutonium. To process and separate plutonium in large quantities from highly radioactive reactor fuel, as well as to machine and fabricate plutonium metal, it would be necessary to operate the world's first large nuclear reactors. Parker was sent to Hanford to organize and direct the facility's program of radiological protection.

At Hanford, Herbert Parker not only organized a model radiological protection program, but he also initiated research to develop new instrumentation and to obtain information on the dispersion of radioactive materials in the environment—information that was required for improved radiation protection. He participated in classic investigations of diffusion in the atmosphere, soils, and water (e.g., the Columbia River).

Herbert Parker actively supported early studies of the environmental and biomedical aspects of radioactive particles containing fission products and plutonium. He was also among the first scientists to undertake quantitative assessments of the effects of reactor accidents, presenting a landmark paper on the subject at the first United Nations Conference on the Peaceful Uses of Atomic Energy in 1955.

In 1947, when the operation of Hanford was transferred from Du Pont to General Electric, Parker became manager of operational and research activities in radiological sciences. Appointed manager of Hanford Laboratories when it was formed in 1956, he led the development efforts that produced a research facility capable of addressing the complex technical, engineering, and scientific problems of the nuclear energy field. He held this position until 1965, when responsibility for the operation of the labs was transferred from General Electric to Battelle Memorial Institute and the facility was renamed the Pacific Northwest Laboratory.

Mr. Parker remained with Battelle until his death, serving

at various times as consultant to the director and as an associate director. He was also a distinguished consultant to many other organizations, including the American College of Pathology and the Advisory Committee on Reactor Safeguards of the U.S. Nuclear Regulatory Commission.

Herbert Parker was widely respected by his peers with whom he joined in the work of a number of professional groups. He was elected to the National Academy of Engineering in 1978. He was a member of the National Council on Radiation Protection and Measurements, and he served as chairman of its Scientific Committee on Basic Radiation Protection Criteria. He was also a member of the American Nuclear Society, where he served on the board of directors. He was a fellow of the American Physical Society and of the British Institute of Physics, and he served on numerous scientific and technical committees, freely contributing his ideas and knowledge.

Parker was certified as a health physicist by the American Board of Health Physics and as a radiological physicist by the American Board of Radiology. He received the Distinguished Achievement Award of the Health Physics Society and the Janeway Medal of the American Radium Society.

Herbert Parker had many fine personal qualities in addition to his intellectual capabilities. He was a handsome man of commanding appearance, and he had an extraordinary ability to surround himself with talented people. He was noted for his dry British humor and outstanding speaking ability. Herbert and his wife Margaret lived comfortably on the banks of the Columbia River, where they propagated prize irises, of which he was very proud. He is survived by his wife and four children, Henry, John, Elizabeth, and Linda.

His many colleagues throughout the world are grateful for his accomplishments and for the privilege of having been his associates and friends. The extraordinary safety record of the atomic energy industry in the United States and elsewhere is the result, to a large degree, of the fundamental pioneering work of Herbert Parker.

J. M. Pettit

JOSEPH MAYO PETTIT

1916–1986

BY WILLIAM KAYS,
OSWALD VILLARD, JR., AND
WILLIAM RAMBO

JOSEPH MAYO PETTIT, professor emeritus of electrical engineering and president of the Georgia Institute of Technology, died on September 15, 1986, in Atlanta after an eleven-month battle with cancer. Pettit was dean of the Stanford School of Engineering from 1958 until 1972, when he went to Georgia Tech as president.

Born in Rochester, Minnesota, on July 15, 1916, Joe was the son of Joseph Asahel and Florence (Anderson) Pettit. His father was a Portland, Oregon, surgeon and his mother a registered nurse. He was named in part for the physician who delivered him, Dr. Joseph Mayo, a friend of the Pettits and a member of the Rochester family that founded the Mayo Clinic.

He received his B.S. in 1938 from the University of California at Berkeley. Transferring to Stanford that year, he was awarded an M.S. in electrical engineering in 1940 and a Ph.D. in 1942. He married Florence Rowell West in 1940; he is survived by her and by a son, Joseph B., of Santa Barbara, California; by two daughters, Mrs. Marjorie Wilbur and Mrs. Marilyn Backlund, both of Palo Alto, California; and by three grandchildren.

From 1942 to 1945 Pettit served with the National Defense Research Committee's Radio Research Laboratory at Harvard University. The staff of this laboratory, which was devoted to radar countermeasures, eventually numbered approximately a thousand. Pettit became the assistant executive engineer. In 1944 he was a technical observer with the U.S. Air Force (USAF), serving in Indochina. In recognition of this service, he received the Presidential Certificate of Merit. In 1945 he served as associate technical director of a USAF branch laboratory in Malvern, England.

From 1945 to 1947 Pettit was a supervising engineer at the Airborne Instruments Laboratory in New York City. In 1947 he returned to Stanford as an associate professor of electrical engineering; he was named a full professor in 1954. He authored or coauthored three engineering textbooks published by McGraw-Hill and was a major contributor to a two-volume compendium of the results of the Harvard laboratory's wartime research.

In 1958, after a year as associate dean under Fred Terman, Joe succeeded to the post of dean of engineering. This was at the beginning of the "Sputnik" era, and he was quick to see the opportunities for growth, as well as the opportunity to lead a good but provincial engineering school into national prominence. Under Terman's leadership, the Electrical Engineering Department had already made that move, but the rest of the school had a long way to go.

The next thirteen years were, indeed, an extraordinary period. The university, with Fred Terman as provost during the first eight years, became a national force, and the School of Engineering under Pettit led the way. The departmental structure was expanded from five to ten departments. The departments added were Material Science and Engineering, Applied Mechanics, Operations Research, Chemical Engineering, and Engineering Economic Systems. Funds for expansion became available, and Pettit was able to secure major grants from both the National Science Foundation and the Ford Foundation to make this expansion possible. Major new buildings, including the McCullough Building for electrical engineering and the newly formed Center for Materials Research, the Durand Building for the Aeronautics and Astronautics Department and the Space Sciences Program, and the Skilling Classroom Building, were all built during this period.

At the same time, the school's sponsored research program expanded several-fold, and, although the program in electrical engineering continued to be the largest, all of the departments participated in an unprecedented expansion. During this period, the School of Engineering emerged as one of the major graduate engineering schools in the country, while the undergraduate program continued to offer an educational experience that encompassed the liberal arts—a more wide-ranging program than could be found at most other engineering schools.

How far the school had come under Pettit's leadership became evident in 1965, when the results of the first national survey of graduate engineering programs were published as the Carter Report. Every department had become one of the leaders in the country. By the end of the 1960s, Stanford was the leading producer of Ph.D.s in engineering in the United States. All of this expansion required a much larger faculty. As dean, Joe Pettit played a major role in recruiting the faculty that was really the key to the subsequent success of the school. Whole new areas of research were initiated by appointing people with established reputations, while more rigorous criteria were enforced in the appointment of junior faculty.

Pettit was an early member of the newly formed National Academy of Engineering, and by the end of his tenure, Stanford was exceeded only by the Massachusetts Institute of Technology in the number of National Academy of Engineering members on its faculty.

Educational innovation was of greatest interest to Joe Pettit, and he was undoubtedly the foremost national pioneer in the development of televised instruction as an adjunct to the graduate program. He introduced a radically flexible undergraduate academic program, and his use of student ratings of instructors, although not a new idea, was nevertheless introduced and developed to new levels.

His interest in education led him to be very active in the

American Society for Engineering Education, and his activities culminated in his being elected president of that institution. From that point on, he was universally recognized as one of the two or three national leaders in engineering education.

By 1971, however, he was ready for a change, and the call came from Georgia Tech. The move to this institution brought a succession of challenges that Pettit met with enthusiasm. His basic ideas were firm and clearly enunciated in his inaugural address: recruiting and retaining outstanding faculty, strengthening the graduate program, and upgrading facilities, with quality always the goal.

His colleagues have remarked on his overriding insistence on quality. Their consistent support was enlisted by his ready acknowledgment of the achievements of individuals and groups, by his leadership, and by his steady availability for consultation and advice. The success that attended his planning was also no doubt contagious.

During Pettit's fourteen-year tenure as president of Georgia Tech, both undergraduate and graduate enrollment increased by forty percent. The female student enrollment alone increased fivefold to more than twenty-three hundred by 1986. The link between an effective graduate program and suitable research opportunities had been firmly established in Joe's Stanford experience. With his strong encouragement, research expenditures increased more than eight hundred percent, to more than $100 million in 1985 and 1986.

The additions and improvements in facilities ranged from new student residences and academic buildings to the bookstore and athletic areas. They included a research building on the Tech campus, designed to facilitate interactions with Atlanta's plans for expansion as a major technology center. The improvements also reached into the state as a whole in accordance with a long-standing institutional mission.

Looking toward the 1986 centennial year observance, Pettit initiated a five-year, $100 million centennial campaign in

1983. It was to have been completed in 1988. The goal was in fact met in June 1986, prompting him to remark, "What we have set out to do we have accomplished, like good Georgia Tech engineers—within budget and ahead of schedule." It is perhaps illustrative of the full range of Joe Pettit's interests and administration that, in its centennial year observance, the institute established in his honor an endowed chair, a graduate fellowship program, and an athletic scholarship.

Although he felt secure in his plans and actions in the academic domain, his background was not always as complete as he might have liked for dealing with some other matters coming before a university president. Joe was apt to remark, not always humorously, about such miscellaneous matters as his involvements with the state government or about the problems of finding a football coach acceptable to all constituencies.

The Pettits at times expressed the hope of returning to the Stanford community, possibly upon Joe's retirement in 1987. It is fortunate for a great many that the Georgia Tech years, the crowning period in a remarkable career, have left a visible wealth of accomplishments with values that will be appreciated for years to come.

HYMAN GEORGE RICKOVER

1900–1986

BY JOHN W. SIMPSON

Admiral hyman george rickover, the man responsible for the creation of the nuclear navy of the United States, died July 8, 1986, at the age of eighty-six. Rickover retired from the U.S. Navy in 1982, after sixty-three years of active duty.

Hyman Rickover was born January 27, 1900, in the village of Makow, about fifty miles north of Warsaw, in what was then a part of Czarist Russia. When he was six, he came with his mother and sister to the United States to join his father.

When Rickover started grammar school, he knew only a few words of English, but avid reading of magazines brought to him by his mother soon improved his knowledge of the language. While attending high school in Chicago, where his family settled, he held a full-time job delivering Western Union telegrams. During the period he delivered telegrams, he became acquainted with Congressman Adolph Sabath. Through the intervention of a family friend, Sabath, himself an immigrant, appointed Rickover to the U.S. Naval Academy.

Rickover entered the U.S. Naval Academy at Annapolis in 1918 and in 1922 graduated 107th in a class that started with 896 students. Upon graduation, he began his career as an officer in the navy and after routine assignments to various ships, he was sent to the Navy Postgraduate School in Annapolis in 1929. He went on to Columbia University, where he earned an M.S. in electrical engineering. It was at Columbia that he met Ruth D. Masters, who was there pursuing a graduate degree in international law. They were married in 1931 and had one son, Robert.

In 1937 he was selected for "Engineering Duty Only" (EDO). In 1939 the navy assigned Rickover to the Electrical Section of the Bureau of Ships, with responsibility for the design and procurement of all of the major electrical equipment needed for U.S. Navy ships during World War II.

Although Hyman Rickover is better known for his nuclear-related activities, he also made a major contribution to the navy's success during World War II. It became apparent from the experiences of the British that a ship's electrical equipment often did not operate properly during or after being subjected to the explosions that were encountered in the course of battle. Our later experience in the Pacific showed that a lack of fireproofing was another major problem.

Rickover drove industry and the navy to develop a complete new line of electrical equipment that was not only markedly superior in performance to all previous equipment but that was also essentially fireproof and continued to perform under the severe shock of explosions during combat. The data obtained by the navy technical mission to Japan after the war determined that the lack of these improvements was a major factor in the outcomes of many of the naval battles that occurred in the Pacific.

As the war was ending, Rickover had a short tour of duty on Okinawa; after the war, he served as inspector general of the 19th Mothball Fleet. Although he made a success of overseeing the mothballing of ships that was occurring now that the war had ended, Rickover saw what he believed was a much more important challenge.

In 1946 a project was begun at the Clinton Laboratory (now the Oak Ridge National Laboratory) to develop a nuclear electric generating plant. The navy decided to send eight men to this project, including three civilians and one senior and four junior naval officers. Realizing the potential that nuclear energy held for the navy, Rickover applied. Although he was not initially selected, through the intercession of his wartime boss Admiral Earle Mills, Rickover was finally sent to Oak Ridge.

Before going to Oak Ridge, Rickover spent time in Washington studying all of the available information on the possible use of atomic energy for naval propulsion. He also talked to everyone who had anything to offer. At Oak Ridge, he and the other naval officers had offices in the same small building with the Daniels Pile group, but they did not take part in the actual development and design effort.

The Pile group's objective was the construction of a high-temperature, gas-cooled, beryllium-moderated reactor for generating central station electricity. Rickover and his officers were busy not only monitoring what the Daniels Pile group was doing but also assisting that group with much outside organization and studying every aspect of the work at Oak Ridge to determine its applicability to naval propulsion. In addition, they later visited the other facilities under the Manhattan District.

In 1947 the Atomic Energy Commission (AEC) was formed, and all responsibility for nuclear energy was transferred to that organization. Toward the end of 1947, it became apparent that there was insufficient information available for the construction of the reactor. Nevertheless, while the Daniels group was working on a final report, Rickover unofficially persuaded them to do a conceptual design of a water-cooled reactor for a submarine. Almost single-handedly, Rickover then persuaded Admiral Nimitz and the secretary of the navy that a nuclear submarine should be built. After enlisting the help of the Military Liaison Committee, he persuaded AEC to formalize the naval reactor study and succeeded in being appointed head of both the navy and AEC naval reactor groups. The naval group was transferred bodily into AEC in 1949.

Getting the authorization to develop a nuclear submarine

was, in itself, a major accomplishment. The reputation Rickover had gained in the industry during World War II for getting things done was of great help in persuading contractors to become involved in his nuclear work, even though he had lukewarm or no support in most areas of the government. By late 1948 the research on a pressurized water reactor was centered in the Argonne National Laboratory, and Westinghouse had been given a contract to do the engineering and construction of a nuclear submarine prototype and the necessary research, development, and design for the *Nautilus*. At the same time, General Electric was given a contract of the same scope for a liquid metal-cooled submarine power plant. With these objectives reached, the nuclear submarine program was under way in earnest.

Because the prototype for the *Nautilus* propulsion plant was the world's first high-temperature nuclear reactor, a host of reactor physics problems had to be solved. Not only were the basic data that were needed for the reactor design unavailable, the reactor design methods also had to be developed. In addition, there were no available engineering data on the performance of metals in high-temperature and high-pressure water; neither had a steam propulsion plant ever been designed for operation in a modern submarine. The necessity for deep submergence compounded the problems. New design methods had to be created, and new materials such as zirconium and hafnium had to be developed.

During this same period, the parallel development of a liquid metal reactor propulsion plant was being undertaken by General Electric under Rickover's guidance. This program led to the construction of the *Sea Wolf*.

During the summer of 1953, just as the *Nautilus* prototype was being successfully tested, the navy cancelled the requirement for a nuclear carrier. But Rickover was undeterred. He was able to persuade the Atomic Energy Commission to begin a program for the development and construction of a central station electric generating plant. He saw this not only as an opportunity to transfer technology to industry but also as a way of continuing the development of larger reactors that might solve some of the problems of reactors of the size that would later be required for carriers.

On January 17, 1955, the signal "Underway on nuclear power" was flashed from the *Nautilus*, marking a dramatic moment in naval history. The invention of the steamboat had led only after many years to commercial steamships and even later to a steam-driven navy.

Prior to that time the *Nautilus* submarines had really only been diesel surface ships that could submerge for brief periods and travel at slow speeds. The new *Nautilus* revolutionized naval warfare immediately. From the day she was put to sea, she was the most important naval vessel in the world, with the capability of inflicting great damage on an entire enemy fleet. This capacity was demonstrated in maneuvers many times.

Yet many new technical problems remained to be solved. Shippingport was the first large reactor with a containment. Uranium oxide was developed as the fuel for the slightly enriched reactor, and a new zirconium alloy, Zircalloy II, was developed for the fuel cladding. A new control system had to be developed. The long life required of the nuclear core brought out many problems in the reactor physics area. Compatibility with a utility system had to be ensured.

Despite these problems, Shippingport, the first U.S. nuclear electricity generating plant, was synchronized with the Duquesne Light Company system in December 1957, just four and a half years after the start of the project. The building of Shippingport was the step that made central station nuclear power possible.

Until his retirement in 1982, Rickover was responsible for the propulsion plants of all ships in the nuclear navy. His contribution was not confined to design, however; it also included the selection and training of personnel. The people who were involved in the nuclear submarine program, both in industry and in the navy, today are spread throughout most of the important places in the nuclear industry as well as in the government.

In addition, there is little doubt that his attention to detail and his insistence on quality, rigorous maintenance, safety, and the reduction of radiation exposure all worked together to make our nuclear ships superior. In addition, the transfer of technology that was begun with *Nautilus* and Shippingport was a major factor in the preeminence of the United States in the nuclear power field. This transfer must be regarded as another of Rickover's important contributions.

Rickover was strongly backed by many influential members of Congress. He was skilled at keeping these men knowledgeable about what he was doing by taking them on visits to the various project areas and by providing demonstrations. Yet probably the major reason he received such strong backing was that he was succeeding at a time when major successes were rare in this country. The confidence that the Joint Committee on Atomic Energy had in Rickover was a key factor in the passage of the Atomic Energy Act of 1954, a most important piece of legislation that has been little changed even now.

Rickover took great interest in high school and college education during most of his professional life. He emphasized the need for rigorous preparation in mathematics and the sciences. When the Naval Academy undertook a profound overhaul of its program, it sought his counsel, among others, and followed his advice in offering a wide diversity of fields of concentration in place of the former standard curriculum for all.

The actual research, development, and design of the nuclear plants Rickover had caused to be built were performed largely by contractors. These activities, however, were conducted under the careful eye of Rickover's staff, who approved almost every design detail. All of the major technical decisions were approved personally by the admiral. The essential element of this aspect of nuclear development was Rickover himself. The people doing the actual work could have been replaced by others, but there was only one Rickover. Without him, there might have been a nuclear navy and industry in time, but they would have been delayed many years, perhaps decades.

Rickover received many honors and awards during his career. Most notable were the Distinguished Service Medal with Gold Star (1946) and the Legion of Merit with Gold Star (1952); the Most Excellent Order of the British Empire (1946); the Egleston Medal Award of Columbia Engineering School's Alumni Association (1955); the American Society of Mechanical Engineers' George Westinghouse Gold Medal (1955); the Cristoforo Columbo Gold Medal (1957); the Michael I. Pupin 100th Anniversary Medal (1958); the Congressional Gold Medal (1959); the Institute of Electrical and Electronics Engineers' Golden Omega Award (1959); the Atomic Energy Commission's Enrico Fermi Award (1965); the National Electrical Manufacturers Association's Prometheus Award (1965); the Presidential Medal of Freedom (1980); and numerous honorary degrees. He was elected to the National Academy of Engineering in 1967. He was also the author of several books. In 1974 he married Eleanor Ann Bednowicz, a navy nurse.

It cannot be stressed too strongly that Rickover was the sine qua non of all the developments with which he was associated.

GERARD ADDISON ROHLICH

1910–1983

BY EARNEST F. GLOYNA

GERARD ADDISON ROHLICH, an outstanding educator and environmental engineer, died suddenly of a heart attack on September 16, 1983, at the age of seventy-three. At the time of his death, Dr. Rohlich held dual positions as professor of civil engineering and professor of the Lyndon Baines Johnson School of Public Affairs at the University of Texas at Austin.

The world is a better place in which to live because of the efforts of Gerard A. Rohlich. The contributions he made in providing safe drinking water supplies, abating water pollution, and improving the general environment have been varied and numerous. His career spanned four decades of teaching, research, administration, scientific and professional activities, and public service.

Dr. Rohlich applied the principles of the biological, chemical, and physical sciences and of engineering to the solution of real-world problems. An excellent teacher, Dr. Rohlich helped to mold the careers of other engineers and scientists. He also left his mark on the engineering profession and on society through his distinguished contributions and unselfish public service.

Gerard Rohlich was born on July 8, 1910, in Brooklyn, New York. His engineering career was launched when he served as an engineering assistant in New York City's Bureau of Sewers while concurrently studying civil engineering in 1934. He enrolled at the University of Wisconsin in Madison and earned a second undergraduate degree in civil engineering in 1936 and an M.S. in 1937. His illustrious academic career began as an instructor at the Carnegie Institute of Technology. He returned to the University of Wisconsin in 1939 and earned his Ph.D. in sanitary engineering in 1940. In 1941 Dr. Rohlich joined the faculty of Pennsylvania State University as an assistant professor and advanced in rank to associate professor.

His teaching career was interrupted briefly while he served as senior sanitary engineer for the War Department's Office of Engineering from 1943 to 1944 and as chief project engineer with the Elastic Stop Nut Corporation of America in 1945. In 1946 he returned to the University of Wisconsin as professor of civil engineering to begin a tenure on the faculty that would last until 1971.

While at the University of Wisconsin, Gerard Rohlich became one of the first individuals in the United States to evaluate the variables that affect the activated sludge process for the treatment of municipal and industrial wastewaters. Many of the findings of this early research have been reconfirmed in more sophisticated laboratory-controlled bench-scale experimentation.

His pioneering work in the use of oxidation-reduction potential measurements to control biological systems was also considered by many to be a significant contribution. However, his fundamental work on eutrophication of lakes and streams and the application of these findings to the control of eutrophication in natural waters are landmark achievements that established his preeminence in the areas of ecology and environmental conservation.

Highlights of his career at the University of Wisconsin include his directorship of the Water Resource Center and the Institute for Environmental Studies. He also served as associate dean of the Graduate School; participated as a member of the governor's Water Resources Committee, which drafted the Wisconsin Water Resources Act; and served on the Wisconsin Natural Research Board, a position in which he had a significant impact on the aquatic environment in the state of Wisconsin. For his continued contributions in this area, Dr. Rohlich was recognized as Wisconsin's Water Man of the Year by the National Water Works Association in 1969.

In 1972 Gerry Rohlich went to the University of Texas at Austin to assume the dual positions of C. W. Cook Professor of Environmental Engineering and professor in the Lyndon Baines Johnson School of Public Affairs. At Texas, he became more involved in formulating public policy and in public service. While continuing his research and his role in the education of future engineers and scientists, Gerry was also able to influence future civic leaders and policymakers then enrolled in the School of Public Affairs, providing individuals responsible for establishing public policy with an appreciation of natural ecosystems.

A personal source of pride to Gerry Rohlich was his election to the National Academy of Engineering in 1970 for his contributions to improving man's environment and for his work teaching engineers about environmental control. Some of Dr. Rohlich's later public service activities and contributions to the profession included his chairing the National Research Council Committee on Water Quality Criteria and the Committee on Safe Drinking Water. The reports of these committees are significant documents that have become valuable resource materials for engineers and scientists. He also chaired the National Research Council Committee on the Potomac Estuary Study.

In addition, Dr. Rohlich undertook the monumental assignment as chairman of the National Research Council Committee on Eutrophication. The findings of this committee, in addition to the results of his extensive research into eutrophication, were documented in published reports that are currently used worldwide as source material. He also served on the National Research Council Environmental Studies Board. At the time of his death, Gerry chaired the Environmental Engineering Panel of the Science Advisory Board of the U.S. Environmental Protection Agency.

Many honors were bestowed on Gerry Rohlich by his peer groups. He received an honorary and life membership in the Water Pollution Control Federation; he was one of the Walker Ames lecturers at the University of Washington; he held an honorary membership in the Brazilian Section of AIDIS (Inter-American Association of Sanitary Engineering); and he was a fellow of the American Society of Civil Engineers.

His awards included the Harrison Prescott Eddy Medal for Noteworthy Research, the Benjamin Smith Reynolds Medal for Excellence in Teaching at the University of Wisconsin, the Karl Emil Hilgard Prize of the American Society of Civil Engineers for research in hydraulic engineering, the George Warren Fuller Award of the American Water Works Association, and the Gordon Maskew Fair Award presented by the American Academy of Environmental Engineers for his achievements, leadership, and contributions to the total environmental effort.

Gerry Rohlich enjoyed the respect, admiration, and friendship of the students he guided and the faculty with whom he collaborated in research and teaching. In addition, he quickly garnered the respect of everyone else with whom he came in contact during his lifetime. He was a well-known, well-respected figure in the Department of Civil Engineering at the University of Texas at Austin. Through those persons now involved in government, private industry, and academia who passed within his sphere, Dr. Rolich's technical expertise, ethics, and philosophies are continuing to have a major impact on the environmental quality of the world in which we live.

Gerry Rohlich devoted a substantial amount of his time to public service, advising and assisting local, state, and federal agencies and governments throughout the world on engineering problems related to the control and enhancement of the environment. His dedication to developing and implementing solutions to the problem of maintaining and improving the quality of man's environment was sincere and substantial.

GEORGE JOHN SCHROEPFER

1906–1984

BY JOSEPH T. LING

GEORGE JOHN SCHROEPFER, a pioneering leader in the design and management of wastewater treatment and disposal systems and professor emeritus of sanitary engineering in the Department of Civil and Mineral Engineering at the University of Minnesota, died in Minneapolis on March 11, 1984.

George Schroepfer was born in St. Paul, Minnesota, on September 7, 1906. He graduated in March 1928 with a B.S. in civil engineering from the University of Minnesota. An M.S. followed in June 1930, and a professional civil engineering degree was awarded in June 1932. Schroepfer began studies for a Ph.D., but he was soon sidetracked by an exceptional opportunity and the challenge to play a key role in the development of major (capital costs of $16 million in 1933) new sewage treatment facilities for the Minneapolis/St. Paul metropolitan region.

In November 1933 he accepted the position as assistant chief engineer for the Minneapolis/St. Paul Sanitary District (now the Metropolitan Waste Control Commission) and was assigned responsibility for the design and construction of these new facilities. In June 1938 he was appointed chief engineer and superintendent of the Sanitary District.

These official duties notwithstanding, George Schroepfer maintained an active involvement with the University of Minnesota and with sanitary engineering education. In September 1945 he accepted an appointment as professor of sanitary engineering in the Civil Engineering Department of the University of Minnesota. Research laboratories were quickly established, and graduate students from around the world arrived to study under Professor Schroepfer's direction. In addition, the University of Minnesota quickly became recognized as a leader in sanitary engineering research education.

Recognition of the exceptional academic and professional talents of George Schroepfer came early. As a senior-year undergraduate student, he was admitted to the national honor societies of Chi Epsilon and Tau Beta Pi and received the American Society of Civil Engineers (ASCE) Northwestern Section Senior Student Award. In 1932 he was admitted to Sigma Xi. Ten years later, George Schroepfer was elected president of the Water Pollution Control Federation; in 1943 he became president of the Northwest Section of ASCE.

He was a consultant to the National War Production Board from 1942 to 1945 and in the postwar years was in great demand as a consultant to companies both in the United States and abroad. His services were especially sought by developing countries and by such agencies as the Pan American Health Organization, the World Bank, the Inter-American Development Bank, and the U.S. Agency for International Development.

Professor Schroepfer devoted much of his effort to technical and professional societies and received a number of medals and awards in recognition of his contributions. Included among his honors are the Rudolf Hering Medal of the American Society of Civil Engineers (1945) and the George Warren Fuller Award of the American Water Works Association (1957).

Beginning in 1947 with the William D. Hatfield Award, he received almost every award and medal of the Water Pollution Control Federation, including the Arthur Sidney Bedell Award in 1955; the Harrison Prescott Eddy Medal (1956); the Radebaugh Award of Central States Water Pollution

Control Association, a constituent association (1965); the Charles Alvin Emerson Medal (1968); the Thomas R. Camp Medal (1970); the Gordon Maskew Fair Medal (1976); and the William J. Orchard Medal (1977). In 1983 the Central States Water Pollution Control Association established the George J. Schroepfer Award to honor exceptional contributions of members to the field of water pollution control, and Professor Schroepfer was the first recipient of this award.

The Brazilian Section of the Inter-American Association of Sanitary Engineers, the Water Pollution Control Federation, and ASCE all elected Professor Schroepfer an honorary member. These and other such awards, a long list of publications and consulting reports, and his memberships, both regular and honorary, in many professional organizations, are eloquent testimonials to a most distinguished and productive professional career. In 1981 George Schroepfer was elected a member of the U.S. National Academy of Engineering, the highest professional recognition accorded an engineer by his or her peers and an honor reserved for a very select few in the world engineering community.

Throughout his active professional career, Professor Schroepfer made many outstanding contributions to the field of environmental (sanitary) engineering, ranging from scientific research to professional practice. Particularly noteworthy was his pioneering research work on the anaerobic contact process for treating wastewaters having a high concentration of organic matter. His technical publications in the areas of economics, financing, and charges for wastewater collection and treatment systems were unique; he truly "bridged the gap" between research and practice.

The sanitary engineer, through the introduction of safe public drinking water supplies and wastewater treatment facilities, has done more during the past 150 years to raise life expectancy worldwide than any other professional. George Schroepfer was aware of these contributions and was also profoundly concerned that a large part of the world still suffered from a lack of these basic needs. He can take comfort from the fact that the many students who came to learn from him, who came from all corners of the globe, are now themselves pursuing the same objectives and thus multiplying his effectiveness.

I became acquainted with Professor Schroepfer in 1948, when I became his first Ph.D. student at the University of Minnesota. Those who were privileged to know George Schroepfer quickly recognized a man of resolution, determination, and independence; a commanding figure and natural leader—attributes that certainly helped him toward success in his long professional career. Less immediately visible were his deep and abiding humanitarian concern for others and the wit and charm with which he endeared himself to his colleagues, especially his students.

Undoubtedly, George Schroepfer will be missed. Recently, those who were associated with him resolved collectively to equip a conference center, in the newly constructed Civil and Mineral Engineering Building at the University of Minnesota, to be named in Professor Schroepfer's honor. This represents one small way to remember this outstanding man, his good work, and his influence.

D. B. Sinclair

DONALD BELLAMY SINCLAIR

1910–1985

BY GORDON S. BROWN

Donald bellamy sinclair, chairman emeritus of GenRad Inc., died on August 24, 1985, following a brief illness. Dr. Sinclair was one of our nation's early pioneers in the development and manufacture of today's widely used electrical measuring instruments and automated test systems. He was also a dedicated public servant—a man who left his mark on a large number of professional, civic, and cultural activities.

Dr. Sinclair's professional career spanned more than four decades, thirty-nine years of which were spent with GenRad Inc. He joined the company as an engineer in July 1936, when it was known worldwide as the General Radio Company. At that time the company was privately owned and engaged primarily in the bench-top scientific laboratory business. Don held numerous engineering and management positions with GenRad Inc., including those of chief engineer from 1950 to 1960 and president from 1963 to 1973. Dr. Sinclair was chairman of the board when he retired in 1974.

During his tenure, the technical focus of the company shifted to those activities in which it would become best known as a leader in the development and manufacture of modern electronic test systems for use in electrical and semiconductor manufacturing, field service, and engineering design applications. This success was primarily a result of Don-

ald Sinclair's vision, his professional skill, and his ability to
lead. Always uppermost in his mind was the welfare of his
colleagues, whom he viewed as team players and not mere
employees. His goal was to enhance their productivity, creativity, and stature.

Dr. Sinclair was born in Winnipeg, Manitoba, on May 23,
1910, and became an American citizen in 1943. As a teenager, he was a radio ham and operated a high-power spark
transmitter from the attic of his parents' home. From 1926
to 1929, while an undergraduate at the University of Manitoba, he was a radio operator for Western Canada Airways.

In 1930 he transferred to the Massachusetts Institute of
Technology (MIT). As an undergraduate in MIT's cooperative course in electrical engineering, he spent his cooperative
school terms with the New York Telephone Company, the
Bell Telephone Laboratories, and the Western Electric Company. After receiving a B.S. in 1931, Don worked first as a
research assistant and later as a research associate at MIT. In
1935 he was awarded a D.Sc. and shortly thereafter joined
the staff of the General Radio Company.

One of Dr. Sinclair's early achievements with the General
Radio Company was his development of a state-of-the-art,
wide-tuning-range, high-frequency radio receiver that had a
field strength measurement application covering the band
from one hundred to three thousand MHz. This important
development occurred at a time when the U.S. military had
a critical need for wide-range receivers with radar countermeasure applications.

In July 1941 the General Radio Company received orders
from the Radiation Laboratory at MIT for a number of airborne intercept equipment prototypes that were based on
Sinclair's receiver. These prototypes became the first U.S. radar intercept receivers built for use by the military. His work
then led quickly to the development of the receiver designated by the Signal Corps as the SCR-587 and by the U.S.
Navy as the ARC-1 receiver.

Early in 1942 the Radio Research Laboratory (RRL) was

established at Harvard University. Under the direction of Professor F. E. Terman of Stanford University, its mission was the development of radar countermeasures. As a consequence of Dr. Sinclair's earlier work on broadband receivers, General Radio permitted him to split his time between its Cambridge Laboratory and RRL. At RRL, he was one of the leaders in organizing, managing, and providing technical direction for the overall program. He was also appointed technical director of the RRL Search Receiver Group.

The book *The History of U.S. Electronic Warfare* by Alfred Price, published by the Association of Old Crows, provides an excellent overview of Sinclair's role in this important phase of World War II. It specifically describes his work regarding the equipping and testing of aircraft for Ferret missions, and it also details his initial flight experiences as the RRL representative on the first operational flights to Europe of the Ferret test airplane.

This aircraft was used for nighttime excursions into the hostile territory of the Mediterranean theater to determine the location, coverage, characteristics, and tactics of enemy ground and airborne radar. The reports of these excursions yielded information vital to the development of successful U.S. countermeasure operations in both the European and Pacific theaters. Based on the successful missions of the Ferret, Don Sinclair was awarded the President's Certificate of Merit by President Truman in 1945.

Of lasting significance is his genuine concern for the quality of life of his fellow citizens and his willingness to accept major roles in numerous public service programs. He worked for better schools, better theaters, and better churches. In addition, he promoted better cooperation between nation and nation, state and scientist, and scientist and scientist.

Symbolic of these activities was his participation on the school committee of his hometown of Concord, Massachusetts. During his seven-year tenure, one year of which included serving as chairman, the town grew rapidly. It was

Don Sinclair who guided the study of the town's demographics and then presented the voters with a sound projection of the anticipated increase in numbers of pupils. He recognized that a much stronger program in the basics of the curriculum was required, that teachers with quite different skills needed to be recruited, that teacher compensation had to increase significantly, and that without a broad base of public support, which he helped achieve, the school committee could not accomplish these community goals.

At the university level, Don Sinclair was a member of the Corporation Visiting Committee for the Electrical Engineering Department at MIT and the Visiting Committee at Carnegie Mellon University in Pittsburgh, Pennsylvania, and he served on the Advisory Board of Northeastern University and Wentworth Institute, in Boston, Massachusetts.

Dr. Sinclair was elected to membership in the National Academy of Engineering (NAE) in 1965, and in 1968 he was named a member of the NAE Aerospace Board. He also served on the NAE International Activities Committee. He was a fellow of the Institute of Radio Engineers and became director in 1945; he was elected president of the institute in 1952. He was also a fellow of the American Institute of Electrical Engineers and one of the leaders whose joint efforts resulted in forming today's Institute of Electrical and Electronics Engineers.

In 1958 and 1959 Don Sinclair was a participant on two of the first occasions that American and Western engineers were invited to address both the Soviet and Hungarian academies of sciences on the subjects of microwave electronics, microwave circuits, antennas, and electrical circuits. These were among the first reciprocal visits by American scientists as part of a cultural exchange with scientists from behind the Iron Curtain after World War II.

Don Sinclair was overseer of the Boston Symphony Orchestra; a trustee of the Wang Center for the Performing Arts; chairman of the Fiscal Affairs Committee of King's Chapel, Boston; and a corporation member of the Morgan

Memorial, Inc., of Boston and Emerson Hospital in Concord. He also served as director of the National Shawmut Bank of Boston, the Shawmut Association, Inc., and the Liberty Mutual Insurance Company of Boston.

His legacy evolved primarily from his ability to evaluate issues quickly, compromise justly between immediate popular beliefs and long-term good convictions, and process his own convictions and creativity through the consensus of his fellow workers. He maintained extremely high ethical standards —demanding no less from himself than from others. He was also a prolific contributor and a person who quickly gained the respect and friendship of many.

As a tribute to his enduring contributions to education and his profession, the GenRad Foundation established, in December 1985, the GenRad Visiting Professorship at MIT. The holder of this chair is known as the Donald B. Sinclair Visiting Professor of Electrical Engineering (or of Computer Science, as appropriate). The status "visiting professor" testifies to Don's belief that universities could benefit greatly by being able to bring to their faculties, even for short periods, leaders who worked at the cutting edge of new fields.

He was a great man. For fifty-three years, he enjoyed the love and devoted support of his charming wife Willona. She survives him along with their four children: Douglas C. of Pittsford, New York; Robert A. of Arlington, Massachusetts; D. Fraser of Petersham, Massachusetts; and Heather S. Moulton of Cambridge, Massachusetts. There are also three grandchildren.

Alfred D. Starbird

ALFRED DODD STARBIRD

1912–1983

BY JOHN S. FOSTER

ALFRED DODD STARBIRD, retired army lieutenant general and authority on nuclear weaponry and military communications systems, died of cancer on July 28, 1983. Throughout his career of public service, which spanned nearly fifty years, Dodd Starbird exemplified the ideal of a leader with his highly developed management and leadership skills and his devotion to duty.

Dodd Starbird's achievements as an athlete, soldier, engineer, and government adviser are well documented. Yet, it is his expertise as a manager, a skill often overlooked in standard biographies, that distinguished him from many other military and civilian leaders. He was in many respects the ultimate manager—one who possessed the ability to organize and control the most complex projects and, equally important, to elicit the best from those who worked with him.

His leadership skills were forged at the U.S. Military Academy at West Point. Upon graduation from West Point in 1933, Dodd Starbird was commissioned as a second lieutenant in the U.S. Army Corps of Engineers. In 1937 he received an M.S. in civil engineering from Princeton University. This engineering background enabled him to analyze difficult situations and to formulate carefully considered solutions. Similarly, his prowess as an athlete—he was a member of the U.S. pentathlon team that won a gold medal in the

1936 Olympic games—afforded him the stamina he would need during long, grueling hours spent on critical national security projects.

During World War II, Dodd Starbird proved to be an able combat officer. He served on temporary duty with the First Division Staff of the U.S. Army during its landings in North Africa and with the Fifth Corps during its landings and early operations in Normandy. He commanded a Third Army engineer combat group from January through June 1945, and then returned to the War Department General Staff.

It was during the postwar years, however, that Dodd Starbird's managerial skills were expanded. In 1949, for example, he played a key role in Sandstone, the first technically significant nuclear test at Eniwetok Atoll. After various assignments in the Pacific and Europe and two years in the Office of the Chief of Engineers, General Starbird was named director of military applications of the Atomic Energy Commission, a position he held from 1955 to 1961. His leadership helped accelerate atomic weapons development, which then introduced a new American nuclear deterrent capability.

Those who worked with Dodd Starbird in his various roles during the 1950s characterized him as a careful, precise person who worked extremely hard to understand all aspects of a problem. Said one former colleague: "He was a great manager because he not only understood what the scientific and technical people were trying to do, but he also thought up practical ways to help."

Under Dodd Starbird's supervision, outstanding progress was made in transferring nuclear fission and fusion development from research to military applications. Yet of equal importance was his work in developing Atomic Energy Commission positions on U.S. disarmament proposals to control nuclear weaponry.

Dodd Starbird's effectiveness was reflected in the way he went about his job. He examined each problem in painstaking detail, with the result that he understood all of the key issues thoroughly before making a decision. This made it possible for program managers to do their jobs with the utmost effectiveness. A strong "people" manager, the general took a personal interest in those who worked for him and strove to gain their understanding and support for the task at hand. He was neither overly critical nor did he engage in second-guessing. Instead, he secured sufficient information to provide constructive solutions for even the most highly sensitive projects.

Above all, Dodd Starbird was a tireless worker. With a spirit of equanimity and good humor, he developed massive advisory reports on many complex technical and political issues, most of which were requested on extremely short notice. Moreover, despite his total dedication to national security, he still found time to go skiing with his wife, Evelyn Wallington Starbird, and their three children, as well as to pursue one of his favorite pastimes, long-distance running.

In 1961 the general was placed in command of the U.S. Army North Pacific Division supervising a large construction project in Portland, Oregon. In the fall of that year, the Soviets resumed nuclear atmospheric testing, and the Department of Defense called on General Starbird to leave his position at the North Pacific Division to plan, mobilize, and command the Joint Task Force Eight for Operation Dominic, the final nuclear tests in the Pacific.

He accepted without hesitation and accomplished the necessary preparations in an unprecedentedly short time to ensure that the 1962 atmospheric testing program was successful. The task force's work had barely ended in 1962 when Dodd Starbird was appointed director of the Defense Communications Agency, which oversaw all of the command-and-control operations for the Department of Defense.

During the Vietnam War, General Starbird served as director of the Defense Communications Planning Group, a cover name for the organization that pioneered the development and deployment of the "McNamara Barrier" program. This program used aerial and unattended ground sensors to detect Viet Cong troop movements and systems to contend with the targets identified.

In 1967 General Starbird became manager of the Sentinel (later Safeguard) antiballistic missile (ABM) system, a position he held until his retirement in 1971. Under his leadership, this system was successfully tested at Vandenberg Air Force Base in California by the firing of intercontinental ballistic missiles that were located at radar/missile installations on Kwajalein Island in the Pacific. The system was being deployed in the United States to protect U.S. Minuteman missile fields near Grand Forks, North Dakota. Following the ABM treaty in 1972, however, the United States terminated all deployment of its ballistic missile defense system.

Although Dodd Starbird's thirty-eight years of commissioned military service ended in 1971, his service to the United States continued. He was named director of the newly created Department of Defense Office of Test and Evaluation, and in 1975 President Ford appointed him assistant administrator for national security in the Energy Research and Development Administration. When this organization was integrated into the new Department of Energy in 1977, President Carter named him acting assistant secretary for defense programs.

In 1980 Dodd Starbird finally retired from government service, forty-seven years after pinning on his second lieutenant's bars. Any one of the many positions he held during his last two decades in public life would have been a fitting capstone to a brilliant career. Yet to a man so dedicated to public service, each assignment represented another opportunity to serve his country.

As one of the U.S. Army's most outstanding engineers, General Starbird received many honors, including four Distinguished Service Medals, two Legion of Merit Awards, two Bronze Stars, commendations from the Atomic Energy Commission, and election to the National Academy of Engineering in 1973. But perhaps his greatest achievement was earning the respect of his military and civilian colleagues and subordinates.

Alfred Dodd Starbird—general, engineer, manager, and leader—was one of the finest citizens America has produced. As the West Point Society said when presenting him with the prestigious Ben Castle Award for outstanding service to his country, "He was a man for all seasons, and for all tasks."

Robert E. Stewart

ROBERT E. STEWART

1915–1983

BY GORDON H. MILLAR

Robert e. stewart, a leading agricultural engineering researcher and a central figure in the development of agricultural engineering education, died on November 13, 1983, at the age of sixty-eight. From 1968 until 1980, he was a professor at Texas A&M University and was named distinguished professor emeritus in 1981.

His contributions to the broad field of agriculture and to agricultural engineering are recognized by every serious researcher in the United States and in many other countries. He was a strong leader, a talented educator, and a prolific writer. His principal research was in the area of animal environmental stresses and regulation. Moreover, his work has been applied to substantially improve the animal-based food production capabilities not only of the United States, but also of India and Australia, countries in which major improvements in the food supply attest to his perceptiveness as well as to the accuracy and detail of his research.

Robert Stewart was born in Carthage, Missouri, and received a B.S. (1948), an M.S. (1950), and a Ph.D (1953), all from the University of Missouri. In 1970 he was presented with the University of Missouri Honor Award for distinguished service in engineering.

Robert Stewart is survived by his wife Bonnie; a daughter, Lillian Carl; two sisters; and two grandsons. He was devoted to his family, and despite the demands of his profession and the worldwide scope of his research activities, he always found enough time to participate in family activities.

He was a past president of the American Society of Agricultural Engineers. Prior to joining the Agricultural Engineering Department of Texas A&M as distinguished professor, he was chairman of the Department of Agricultural Engineering at Ohio State University.

Robert Stewart served on the Board on Agriculture of the National Research Council for two three-year terms. He was also past chairman of the Engineers' Joint Council on Engineering Interactions in Biology and Medicine. He was elected to the National Academy of Engineering in 1978.

Bob was very active in developing technical information leading to better and more economical dairy and meat production and was the author of numerous publications. In 1983 he received the Cyrus Hall McCormick Medal from the American Society of Agricultural Engineers for "exceptional and meritorious engineering achievement in agriculture."

More than anyone else, Bob Stewart anticipated the trend in modern agriculture toward raising agricultural animals in engineered environments. Early in his career, he recognized the importance of the environment and, using sound engineering approaches, established criteria for agricultural structures and the methodology for controlling the animal environment. He ranks very close to the top of those in the agricultural professional world devoted to the study of environmental physiology.

Despite his scientific and intellectual depth, Bob Stewart never forgot the fact that without engineering applications the science of agriculture would not reach its full contribution potential. He maintained close associations with the American Society for Engineering Education and the National Society of Professional Engineers. Robert Stewart sustained an active career in engineering and was a registered engineer in several states.

Bob was both a scientist and an engineer, and he will be

greatly missed by his colleagues, his associates, and so many of his students. Just before his passing, he served as a member of the National Academy of Engineering Agricultural Peer Committee, which was organized to bring qualified agricultural engineering candidates into the academy as members. Although he could not travel, he served on the committee with great perception, wisdom, and talent. As a result of his work, several agricultural engineers are now members of the National Academy of Engineering.

The nation and the world are better off for Robert Stewart's scientific and engineering contributions, which will be enjoyed by grateful populations in the many years ahead.

James Stratton

JAMES HOBSON STRATTON

1898–1984

BY WILSON BINGER

JAMES HOBSON STRATTON, retired brigadier general in the U.S. Army Corps of Engineers and partner in the engineering and architectural consulting firm of Tippetts-Abbett-McCarthy-Stratton in New York, died of congestive heart failure on March 16, 1984, at the age of eighty-five. Thus ended a noteworthy professional engineering career, marked by General Stratton's direction of a number of major civil and military engineering projects.

Stratton was born in Stonington, Connecticut, on June 7, 1898; he attended public schools in Paterson, New Jersey, where his family had subsequently moved. After the outbreak of World War I and the declaration of war by the United States, Stratton enlisted in the National Guard; shortly thereafter, however, he was discharged to enter the U.S. Army Military Academy at West Point. Upon graduation, he transferred to the Corps of Engineers.

During his pre–World War II years with the corps, Stratton was assigned to various district engineering offices. It was during these tours that he became acquainted with the importance of soil mechanics in the design and construction of earth dams and later with the construction of military airfields. More than any other engineering officer at that time, Stratton acted as a catalyst to incorporate the young science of soil mechanics into the project development activities of the corps.

James Stratton encouraged engineers to develop their skills and, through his leadership and expertness, provided them with an example. His work had a major impact on the design and construction of dams at Denison, Texas; Franklin Falls, New Hampshire; and Conchas, New Mexico; and of the locks and dams on the upper Mississippi River. In addition, he assumed a major role in the design and construction of the airfield and flood control works at Caddoa, Colorado, including the John Martin Dam.

At the onset of World War II, James Stratton was assigned to the Office of the Chief of Engineers. In this capacity, Stratton was given responsibility for the engineering, planning, and design of those facilities related to the extensive military construction program that had devolved upon the corps—as well as the responsibility for the somewhat curtailed Civil Works Program. As the selected representative of the chief of engineers, James Stratton participated in the initial engineering-related planning of the landing operation on the north coast of France in 1944.

In September 1943 he was assigned to the European theater of operations as a G4 in the Communications Zone; he was stationed in London until being assigned to France in July 1944. For his wartime services, General Stratton was awarded the Legion of Merit (1944) and the Distinguished Service Medal (1945). As the end of hostilities neared, he returned to the United States for an assignment as assistant chief of engineers. In this role he was responsible for reactivating the Civil Works Program of the corps, which played an important part in reducing unemployment following the end of the war and the demobilization of the armed forces.

With the passage of Public Law 280, the seventy-ninth U.S. Congress provided for a study of the future Panama Canal. Consequently, in early 1946 Stratton was named special engineering assistant to the governor of the Panama Canal and placed in charge of the investigation and study of the Isthmian Canal. Years later, the results of these preliminary studies established an invaluable basis for the more comprehensive Sea Level Canal Studies program.

General Stratton's position of special engineering assistant served far more than merely an administrative or even an executive function, for his leadership role of managing a group of 150 engineers and geologists was a highly technical assignment. General Stratton had the vision, creativity, and attention to detail to ensure that the Panama Canal study was thorough, well grounded in the technology of the time, and supported by complete investigations in geology, soil mechanics, hydrology and hydraulics, economics, urban planning, and military and naval sciences.

He completed this duty in mid-1948. His final active duty assignment was as the New England division engineer at Boston, Massachusetts, following which, in 1949, after thirty years of service, he chose to retire with the rank of brigadier general.

Stratton then joined the engineering and architectural consulting firm in New York that had been founded many years before by his West Point classmate Theodore T. Knappen. After the death of Knappen in 1951, the firm's name was changed to Tippetts-Abbett-McCarthy-Stratton. As a partner, Stratton was responsible for many of the firm's major dam projects; for a number of highway, port, harbor, and airport construction projects; and for numerous feasibility studies, all of which were successfully completed in many of the fifty countries in which the firm was active. He retired from the firm in January 1967.

Following his retirement from military service, General Stratton was active in community affairs and for seven years was a member of the board of education in Englewood, New Jersey. He was also a member of the Special Curricula Committee, which was appointed to advise the dean of the Department of Civil and Sanitary Engineering at the Massachusetts Institute of Technology (MIT) regarding courses of study for enrolled undergraduates. In addition, for three years General Stratton served as a member of the board of visitors, which met annually to advise this same MIT department on substantive matters significant to the fulfillment of the purposes for which MIT had been established.

Among his technical publications was an article on military airfields, published in 1945 by the American Society of Civil Engineers, for which Stratton was awarded the society's Arthur Wellington Prize. He was also a contributing author to the *Handbook of Applied Hydraulics*, edited by Calvin Davis, and *American Civil Engineering Practice*, edited by Robert W. Abbett.

Stratton was a member of Theta Xi fraternity at the Rensselaer Polytechnic Institute, and he was a Mason. His professional society affiliations included the Society of American Military Engineers, the American Society of Civil Engineers, the Boston Society of Engineers, and the American Institute of Consulting Engineers. He was elected to the National Academy of Engineering in 1981. General Stratton held professional licenses in eighteen states.

In addition to his personal professional accomplishments, Stratton provided firm leadership to his associates. He was particularly generous in the encouragement, guidance, and support of younger engineers, to whom Stratton believed in giving responsibility. When he himself was in his sixties, he said to a friend in his firm, "What's wrong with the world is that the leaders are old men, and I mean men of my age!"

John G. Trump

JOHN GEORGE TRUMP

1907–1985

BY LOUIS SMULLIN

J OHN GEORGE TRUMP, a pioneer in the scientific, engineering, and medical applications of high voltage machinery, died on February 21, 1985. Married to the late Elora Trump, John left three children: John, Karen, and Christine.

At the time of his death, John Trump was professor emeritus at the Massachusetts Institute of Technology (MIT) in the Department of Electrical Engineering. He was also senior consultant for the High Voltage Engineering Corporation, the company he founded in 1946 and where, until 1970, he served as chairman of the board and then, until 1980, as technical director.

John Trump was born in New York City on August 21, 1907. He earned a B.S. in electrical engineering from the Polytechnic Institute of Brooklyn in 1929 and an M.S. in physics from Columbia University in 1931. In 1933 he received a D.Sc. in electrical engineering from MIT, where he became a research associate in that same year, an assistant professor in 1936, and a professor in 1952. Trump formally retired in 1973, although he continued his active research program as professor emeritus until 1980.

John Trump came to MIT to work with Professor Robert J. Van de Graaff in what was then the new field of super-high voltage generation and applications. "Van's" main interest was in the application of his new electrostatic generator in the field of nuclear physics. John Trump had two main interests: the insulation of super-high voltages in vacuum and compressed gases and the biological applications of high voltage radiation. These wide-ranging biological applications included the treatment of cancer by megavolt (Mev) X-radiation and electron beams, extensive pioneering studies of food preservation by electron beams, and the treatment of sewage and sludge by 2-Mev electron beams.

With grants from the Godfrey M. Hyams Fund, Trump and his young assistants designed and built an air-insulated megavolt generator that was installed at the Huntington Memorial Hospital in 1937. It was large and awe inspiring. On wet days, the generator crackled and sparked or just died, but the conspicuous advantages of its megavolt X-ray therapy soon became clear. The greater penetration depth of these radiations, compared to lower energy X-rays, permitted more deeply seated tumors to be treated with minimal damage to adjoining tissues.

In 1938, with continued funding from the Hyams Fund, the team began the design of a new, compact 1.25-Mev generator that would be insulated with compressed gas. This particular machine was installed in the George Robert White Hospital of the Massachusetts General Hospital, where it remained in active use for sixteen years. Trump then undertook the building of a 1.75-Mev machine for the American Oncological Hospital of Philadelphia—until World War II intervened, that is, and the machine was taken by the U.S. Army for use in the Manhattan Project.

During World War II, Trump interrupted his high-voltage career to work on microwave radar in the MIT Radiation Lab. He served for a time as field services director and was then posted to the British branch of the Radiation Lab. In 1944 he was named director of the lab and given the responsibility of working directly with the Eisenhower Military Command. At the liberation of Paris, Trump rode into the city with General Eisenhower and immediately began to set up the Paris branch of the Radiation Lab.

His diary of this period is fascinating reading, especially for those of us who remember the significance of H2X, Oboe, Loran, MEW, SCR 584, and other sets of initials from the alphabet soup of the day. For his wartime service, John Trump received a Presidential Citation and the King's Medal for Service in the Cause of Freedom.

After the closing of the Radiation Lab in 1946, Dr. Trump quickly picked up the threads of his previous high-voltage research. He formed the High Voltage Engineering Company to put electrostatic high voltage machines to work. Van de Graaff generators were soon in use all over the world with a wide range of applications, including those in physics research, the sterilization of surgical instruments, the cross-linking of polymers, and the radiography of welds and castings.

Trump's main efforts and interests, however, remained on the MIT campus, where he initiated a long series of experiments, supported by the Natick Laboratory of the Army Quartermaster Corps, in the preservation of food by high voltage radiation. There was also a continuing train of experiments on the bactericidal and viricidal effectiveness of high voltage radiation. Much new work was done on compressed gas insulation, but his most noteworthy contributions were in the treatment of cancer by radiation.

Dr. Trump and his staff began a systematic study of the problems of delivering radiation to deep tumors without destroying the intervening healthy tissue. From their research came an improved technique of rotating the patient 360 degrees about the tumor site, so that the radiation beam entered the body from all directions but focused on the tumor. The team also developed techniques for static and dynamic beam shaping to protect healthy tissues. This work led to a cooperative twenty-five-year research venture with the Lahey Clinic: the setting up of a treatment facility in the MIT High

Voltage Lab, where patients were routinely treated under the joint supervision of Trump, his staff, and the Lahey Clinic physicians. Ultimately, more than ten thousand patients were treated.

Until 1950 nearly all high-voltage radiation therapy was done with X-rays generated by the impact of a high-voltage electron beam against a gold target inside a vacuum. In a 1940 paper, Trump, Van de Graaff, and Cloud had suggested using direct high-voltage electrons because of the uniquely different way they penetrated matter.

Although X-rays are absorbed more or less uniformly as they traverse the body from the skin inward, high-energy electrons produce very little ionization until their energy falls below a critical value. They then do all of their ionizing within a very short distance and almost never extend beyond it. The first clinical test of this new technique was made in 1951. The technique offered an ideal way to treat many superficial malignancies, and soon after its initial use, it became a standard method of treatment.

Dr. Trump began his last major effort in 1976. Like all concerned citizens, he was offended by the dumping of millions of gallons of barely treated or raw sewage into our harbors and waterways. His calculations showed that a 2-Mev electron radiation system compared favorably with chlorine treatment on an economic basis, had the additional advantage of destroying many viruses, and appeared to dissociate PCBs and similar compounds into less noxious forms. With National Science Foundation support, Trump and his associates built a pilot plant at the Deer Island Sewage Plant in Boston Harbor. In addition, based on the valuable electron radiation data produced at the Deer Island plant, a commercial sewage treatment plant has been built for the greater Miami area.

John Trump was truly a pioneer in the field of high voltage engineering and high voltage machinery and in the medical applications of high energy radiation. He was the author or coauthor of more than one hundred papers and the recipient of many honors from numerous engineering and medical societies. John Trump was elected to the National Academy of Engineering in 1977. The latest award bestowed upon him was the National Medal of Science, which was presented posthumously in February 1985.

His mixture of personal technical work and quiet leadership produced many important discoveries. John Trump will be missed by his worldwide circle of colleagues and friends.

HERBERT D. VOGEL

1900–1984

BY HARRY E. BOVAY

Herbert d. vogel, one of the world leaders in professional engineering and one of the most creative minds in the area of engineering progress, a retired brigadier general in the U.S. Army Corps of Engineers, a former chairman of the Tennessee Valley Authority, and a former engineer adviser of the World Bank, died on August 26, 1984, at Walter Reed Army Medical Center, in Washington, D.C.

General Vogel was born in Chelsea, Michigan, in 1900 and lived in Washington, D.C., at the time of his death. After graduating with a B.S. from the U.S. Military Academy at West Point in 1924, he obtained an M.S. in civil engineering from the University of California in 1928, a doctorate in hydraulic engineering from the Berlin Technical University the following year, and a professional civil engineering (C.E.) degree from the University of Michigan in 1933. During World War II, General Vogel served in the South Pacific.

Herbert Vogel married Loreine Elliott, daughter of Mr. and Mrs. Eugene Elliott of Washington, D.C., on December 23, 1925, while he was stationed at Fort Humphreys (now Fort Belvoir). Their close and happy marriage produced two sons, Colonel Herbert Davis Vogel, Jr., and Richard Elliott Vogel. Colonel Vogel, Jr. (Ret.), is also a graduate of the U.S. Military Academy and is now vice-president of Merrill Lynch Pierce Fenner & Smith Incorporated, and his brother Richard is an attorney. General and Mrs. Vogel were enjoying four grandchildren at the time of his death. Mrs. Vogel, a lovely and active lady, fully supported Herbert in his endeavors for fifty-nine years.

Active in military and professional engineering matters throughout his career, General Vogel retired from the army in 1954 as division engineer of the U.S. Army Corps of Engineers' Southwestern Division. During this portion of his career, he contributed to the control of large waterways by proving and exploiting the validity of hydraulic models, a contribution that brought about a revolution in engineering concepts. The use of these models was prompted by the country's need to find methods of controlling the Mississippi River and its tributaries to prevent recurrences of the disastrous floods of 1927.

Major General Charles G. Holle (Ret.) stated that General Vogel

attended the Berliner Technische Hochschule, graduating with the degree of doctor of engineering. Next he followed duty with the Mississippi River Commission in Vicksburg, Mississippi, to create the U.S. Waterways Experiment Station, which has become so well-known and highly regarded, worldwide. Full credit of the prestige of the WES is due to General Vogel having been the first director, 1929–1934, for the sound establishment and orientation of it, and for his expert counseling as the WES developed during the subsequent years.

Major General K. D. Nichols (Ret.) also contributed to the facts in this memorial, adding the following:

As a result of his early initiative, Vog combined his intelligence, engineering knowledge, superior judgment, fierce loyalty to his profession, high professional standards, sensitivity, and humor to become one of the world's outstanding hydraulic engineers, respected by his host of friends and associates worldwide.

Once the U.S. Waterways Experiment Station was constructed and in operation, Vogel and his colleagues opened new areas of research and convinced authorities of the reasonableness of using new methods and techniques for solving the problems involved in the control of the Mississippi River and other sizable waterways. Their work required the use, for the first time, of extensive, small-scale models of large rivers. Although these models had some vertical distortion (because a very small horizontal scale had to be used), they were nevertheless useful for waterway control, and new techniques and methods were developed through these models that went far beyond the European concepts.

Indeed, the U.S. Waterways Experiment Station has become a model for practical hydraulic research institutions around the world and is now the most complete and active installation of its kind anywhere. It has been visited by thousands of people from all over the globe. In addition, during the past fifty years, hundreds of problems relating to all parts of the United States and many foreign countries have been brought to the experiment station for study. Millions of dollars have been saved as a result of its work, and major hydraulic structure design improvements have been made.

General Vogel was appointed chairman of the Tennessee Valley Authority (TVA) by President Dwight D. Eisenhower, a position he held until 1963. During his nine years as chairman, he had executive responsibility for the operation of the largest electric power system in the United States. During this period, the capacity of the system was more than doubled; it was supplying electric energy to an area of over eighty thousand square miles.

TVA is responsible for the unified development of natural resources over an area of forty-one thousand square miles and for the development of navigation and flood control of the Tennessee River System. Herbert also served as both president and consulting engineer of the Tennessee River and Tributaries Association.

George H. Kimmons, retired manager of TVA's Office of Engineering Design and Construction, wrote:

During one's career there is always one person who stands out above all the others. For me that person is General Herbert D. Vogel. He was respected by his associates for his achievements and leadership abilities. Not only was General Vogel an outstanding engineer and a great Army officer, he was also one of the most likeable men with whom I have ever had the pleasure of working. I worked directly with General Vogel during his term as chairman of the board of the Tennessee Valley Authority and later when each of us was serving as a member of the Permanent International Association of Navigation Congresses.

As an engineering adviser to the World Bank from 1963 to 1967, General Vogel contributed greatly to the success of the bank, which relies largely on the successful engineering of its projects. He also served in an ex officio capacity as an engineer member of the bank's working party for the Indus Basin Project during its construction, which required many trips to Pakistan. His influence was felt in the supervision of a dam site study and in the authorship of a work entitled "Water and Power Resources of West Pakistan."

In his practice as a consultant and founder of Herbert D. Vogel and Associates (1967 to 1984), his attributes of creative thinking and leadership were highlighted. For example, during this time, he presented papers at several meetings of the Permanent International Association of Navigation Congresses that defined the U.S. position on inland navigation problems. This position included the exchange of planning and engineering technologies with developing countries and their relationship to improving maritime ports and inland terminals. In more recent years, he expressed the view that the entire watershed of the Potomac River should be developed with a view to meeting the long-range water needs of the Washington metropolitan area.

An authority on water and soil conservation and flood control, General Vogel authored numerous papers and articles on hydraulic models, river and harbor engineering, and the development and operation of large electric power systems. As a result, his professional efforts have had a large and beneficial impact on society. His small-scale river model testings for waterways have provided viable solutions to otherwise unsolvable complex problems; they have also saved millions of dollars in addition to improving and adding increased safety features in hydraulic structure designs.

Because of the proof provided by the experiment station as to the validity of models, engineers today do not build large, expensive hydraulic structures until they are first tested on a small-scale basis. Model tests have saved untold millions of dollars in construction costs and have prevented further heavy losses of life and property resulting from disastrous flooding.

A planner, builder, and former director of the U.S. Waterways Experiment Station in Vicksburg, Mississippi, Vogel also served as lieutenant governor of the Panama Canal Zone. He was a member of both the Mississippi River Commission and the Board of Engineers for Rivers and Harbors and served as chairman of the Arkansas-White-Red River Basins Interagency Committee.

His many awards and honors include the Distinguished Honorary Graduate Award of the U.S. Army Engineer School; the Colon Alfaro Medal; the Knight of the Grand Cross (Thailand); the Distinguished Alumnus Award of the University of Michigan; the Award for Meritorious Service to the Engineering Profession of the Year 1967, given by the Consulting Engineers Council; and the Liberation and Independence Medals of the Philippines. General Vogel was also selected in 1972 as the Elected Occupant of the George W. Goethals Chair of Military Construction, Army Engineer School at Fort Belvoir, Virginia.

In 1972 he was also cited by Joint Resolution No. 250 of the House of Representatives and the Senate, State of Tennessee. He received the Knight of the Golden Circle Award of the Army and Navy Club of Washington and the President's and Honorary Member Award of the American Society of Civil Engineers in 1979. General Vogel's military decorations included the Distinguished Service Medal and the Legion of Merit.

His memberships were extensive and impressive. He was elected to the National Academy of Engineering in 1977. He was an honorary member of the Public Works Historical Society and the Society of American Military Engineers; a fellow of the American Consulting Engineers Council; and an honorary member of the Engineers Club of Pennsylvania. In addition, General Vogel was a member of the Royal Society of Arts in London, the Permanent International Association of Navigation Congresses, the International Commission on Large Dams, and the National Society of Professional Engineers.

In reviewing General Vogel's accomplishments, Major General Charles Noble (Ret.) completed his tribute by stating:

Never one to retire from the business of humanity, Dr. (General) Vogel died with his boots on, serving to the end the profession he loved. He left behind a loving wife and family and thousands of professional and personal friends. His funeral service at Arlington Cemetery was the occasion for a large assemblage of the most distinguished and famous crowd of professionals and high-ranking service personnel, friends, and West Point classmates, a crowning tribute to the selfless life of a great soldier, engineer, and public servant.

Howard Vollum

CHARLES HOWARD VOLLUM

1913–1986

BY WILLIAM R. HEWLETT

CHARLES HOWARD VOLLUM was an Oregonian to the core. He was born on May 31, 1913, in Portland, Oregon, where he not only spent his entire childhood but also obtained his education. He received his B.A. in physics from Portland's Reed College in 1936.

Howard Vollum made some of his most notable contributions to science and engineering during World War II as an officer of the U.S. Signal Corps. In early 1941 he was assigned by the Signal Corps to work on problems involving accurate fire control radar at the Air Research and Development Establishment in England. In recognition of his work while with the Signal Corps, he was awarded the Legion of Merit in 1945 by the U.S. government. Later, for the quality of his subsequent work on a precision mortar locator while stationed at the Evans Signal Corps Laboratories in Belmar, New Jersey, he was awarded the Oak Leaf Cluster of the Legion of Merit.

One of the abiding interests of Howard Vollum's civilian life was in the cathode-ray oscilloscope. In fact, he designed and built one on his own in the 1930s, shortly after cathode-ray tubes became commercially available. It was this personal project that helped him obtain admission to Reed College. While he was still a student at Reed, he built a second, although still primitive, oscilloscope that proved useful in testing audiofrequency amplifiers.

In 1946 he returned to Portland in retirement from active military service. In January 1946, along with M. J. Murdock, he founded Tektronix, Inc., in Portland. Vollum became the company's first president and chief engineer. Following Howard's early interests, Tektronix focused on the field of oscillography. During the company's first forty years, its sales volume grew from a meager few thousand dollars during the first year to an annual volume of roughly $1.4 billion.

Interestingly, when Vollum founded Tektronix, he hoped for little more than to offer employment to thirty or forty Oregonians. During the forty years between the company's founding and Vollum's death, however, Tektronix expanded and grew fantastically so that it now has more than twenty thousand employees worldwide.

Howard Vollum's early contributions to Tektronix included the development of the Type 511 oscilloscope, which, in effect, revolutionized oscilloscope design; the Type 512, which was the first direct-coupled high-gain oscilloscope; the Type 104 generator, which was the first to use square waves for transient testing of scopes; the oscilloscope plug-in unit, a device that, by permitting a scope to accept interchangeable units, gave the user the effect of several instruments in one; and finally, the design of the Tektronix cathode-ray tube.

Until his death on February 5, 1986, Howard Vollum continued to participate actively in running the company. At the time of his death, he was vice-chairman of the board. Under his direction, Tektronix won the distinction of becoming the dominant company in the field of oscilloscope development. Indeed, in part because of his contributions, Howard Vollum saw the oscilloscope become the universal instrument in the electronics industry, where it is used for a variety of research, development, and maintenance functions.

Howard Vollum was constantly concerned about the technical aspects of the company's products. He insisted upon a combination of innovation and quality. Many concepts integral to modern-day oscilloscopes are traceable directly to his work.

In his own quiet way, he contributed much to the Portland area and to the state of Oregon that he loved so much. For example, he set up a foundation to channel the corporate donations of Tektronix into innovative programs. He selected projects that perhaps did not have great public appeal but that were all the same characterized by considerable leverage and great benefits to society. He served as a trustee or board member for Reed College, the University of Portland, the Oregon Graduate Center for Study and Research, the St. Vincent's Medical Foundation, and the Oregon Health Sciences University.

In addition to the Legion of Merit award from his own country, Howard Vollum received the Award of the First Officer of the First Order of the White Rose, presented by the Government of Finland. He also received the Medal of Achievement Award from the Western Electronics Manufacturers Association, the Distinguished Service Award of the University of Oregon, the Howard N. Potts Medal of the Trandlin Institute, and the Morris E. Leeds Award of the Institute of Electrical and Electronics Engineers, of which he was also a fellow. He was elected to the National Academy of Engineering in 1977.

Howard Vollum received a number of honorary degrees from institutes of higher education. These included the doctor of science degree from the University of Portland and from the Oregon Graduate Center, the doctor of laws degree from Lewis and Clark College and from Reed College, and the doctor of humane letters from Pacific University.

His later innumerable institutional honors, however, should not obscure Howard Vollum's greatest contribution, which was in the field of engineering: the perfection of the precision oscilloscope.

EDWARD C. WELLS

1910–1986

BY EDWARD H. HEINEMANN

Edward c. wells was one of the last of the "old time engineers." He was truly a chief engineer who understood all the parts of an airplane and usually conceived and directed the design of the entire airplane himself.

Because we were approximately the same age and had similar responsibilities at two competing companies, the Boeing Company and Douglas Aircraft, I came to know Ed and his accomplishments very well and to respect his work greatly. He was an excellent engineer, and under his direction, many of the world's finest airplanes were born. Among them were the Boeing B-17, B-29, B-47, and B-52, as well as the commercial models 707, 727, 737, 747, 757, and 767.

Mr. Wells began his career with Boeing in 1931. He retired as a senior vice-president in 1972, but continued as a company consultant and member of the board of directors until 1978, when he resigned from the board.

As assistant project engineer on the 299 (the forerunner of the B-17), Mr. Wells was responsible for the wing flap system, the largest ever considered until that time. Sophisticated flap systems have been a trademark of Boeing airplanes for forty-five years, beginning with the 299 in 1934.

Mr. Wells received fifteen patents for inventions, most of them for innovations in mechanical and flight systems. For example, he led the engineering efforts that made the B-29 the outstanding bomber of its day. The B-29's basic engineering advances included pressurized body (first introduced on Boeing's 307 Stratoliner in 1938), centralized fire control, power turrets, and dramatic increases in bomb load capacity and effective range.

Wells was made chief of Boeing's Preliminary Design Unit in 1936 and chief project engineer in charge of military projects in 1938. In 1939 he became assistant chief engineer, and in 1943 he was named chief engineer. He became vice-president and chief engineer in 1948.

In 1961 Mr. Wells was named vice-president and general manager of the Military Aircraft Systems Division. This division and the Transport Division were merged to become the Airplane Division in 1963. He became vice-president for product development in 1966.

Ed Wells was widely recognized and honored for his work in aviation. In 1942 he received the Lawrence Sperry Award from the Institute of the Aeronautical Sciences for "outstanding contributions to the art of airplane design." He was named "Young Man of the Year" by the Seattle Junior Chamber of Commerce in 1943, and in 1944 he received the Fawcett Aviation Award for "the greatest single contribution for the scientific advancement of aviation" during the year.

During World War II, Mr. Wells was a consultant to the secretary of war. Later, he was a member of the Research and Technology Advisory Council for the National Aeronautics and Space Administration, a member of the President's Special Task Force on Transportation, and a member of the Defense Science Board. In 1978, because of his significant contributions to aeronautics, Mr. Wells was elected an Elder Statesman of Aviation by the National Aeronautics Association.

Born in 1910 in Boise, Idaho, Mr. Wells graduated with "great distinction" and Phi Beta Kappa honors from Stanford University's Engineering School in 1931. He received an honorary doctor of laws degree from the University of Portland in 1946 and an honorary doctor of science degree from

Willamette University in 1953. He was a life member of the Willamette University board of trustees.

During the 1969–1970 academic year, Mr. Wells took a partial leave from Boeing to serve as a visiting professor in the Department of Aeronautics and Astronautics at Stanford University. He served on advisory boards for Stanford, the University of Washington, and the University of California at Los Angeles.

Mr. Wells was elected to membership in the National Academy of Engineering in 1967. He was also a member of the Society of Automotive Engineers, the American Association for the Advancement of Science, the American Society for Engineering Education, and the American Astronautical Society; he was an honorary fellow of the American Institute of Aeronautics and Astronautics (AIAA). He was president of AIAA's predecessor organization, the Institute of the Aeronautical Sciences, in 1958.

He received the Daniel Guggenheim Medal in 1980 for his "outstanding contributions in the design and production of some of the world's most famous commercial and military aircraft." In 1981 he was elected a fellow of the Society of Automotive Engineers "for exceptional contributions to the advancement of automotive technology." In 1985 he received the Tony Janus Award in recognition of his "outstanding contributions to the development of complex aerospace systems and significant accomplishments in the design and production of a long line of the world's most famous military and commercial aircraft."

Mr. Wells died on July 1, 1986, and is survived by his wife Dorothy; a daughter, Mrs. William (Laurie) Tull of Etna, California; a son, Edward E. Wells of Aurora, Colorado; two grandsons, John and Eric Benjamin; and two sisters, Mrs. William Geer of Bellevue, Washington, and Mrs. William Ketteringham of Sun City, California.

Stanley D. Wilson

STANLEY DeWOLF WILSON

1912–1985

BY RALPH B. PECK

STANLEY DeWOLF WILSON, international consultant in geotechnics and cofounder of Shannon and Wilson, Inc., and the Slope Indicator Company, died on November 17, 1985, of complications resulting from a particularly virulent form of malaria that he had contracted on a consulting assignment in West Africa three weeks earlier.

Stan Wilson was born in Sacramento, California, on August 12, 1912. He attended Sacramento Junior College from 1930 to 1932 and for the following nine years was employed as an engineer for the California Division of Highways. After the attack on Pearl Harbor, he joined the U.S. Army Corps of Engineers, which assigned him to study civil engineering at the University of Minnesota. Later, while he was attached to Fort Belvoir, the corps assigned him to attend the course in airfield engineering under Professor Arthur Casagrande at Harvard University. Wilson so impressed his teacher that Dr. Casagrande persuaded the corps to extend his stay, to allow him to instruct subsequent classes of airfield engineers and to help prepare a soil identification manual for the corps to use for construction of airfields in forward combat zones.

Following his discharge as a first lieutenant, Wilson remained at Harvard where, despite his lack of the usual prerequisite of a baccalaureate degree, he earned an M.S. in civil engineering and rose to the rank of assistant professor in the Graduate School of Engineering.

In 1953 the trustees of Harvard decided to discontinue the program in soil mechanics. The following year, Stan joined with his Harvard colleague William L. Shannon to form the Seattle consulting firm of Shannon and Wilson, Inc. The firm developed into one of the world's leading engineering organizations specializing in geotechnical engineering. In 1978 he retired from active participation in the firm but continued to serve it as a staff consultant while pursuing his own active international consulting practice.

At Harvard, Wilson developed portable miniature equipment for performing moisture-density tests on soils for airfields and, at the suggestion of Karl Terzaghi, devised and built the first model of the slope indicator, an instrument for measuring soil displacements in the interior of soil masses. This device satisfied an important need in the study of existing or incipient landslides and in determining the deformations in dams and in soils around excavations and tunnels. To manufacture this device and other geotechnical laboratory and field equipment, much of which he invented or developed himself, he became a cofounder of the Slope Indicator Company, which developed into an international leader in its field.

Stanley Wilson's practice was characterized by his fundamental knowledge of physics and mechanics, coupled with his ability to measure forces and deformation of soil masses under field conditions. Fully capable of using or developing applicable theory, he was a master at solving engineering problems by the interpretation of quantitative field observations against a background of theory.

A pioneer in soil and rock dynamics, he was largely responsible for devising practical means for estimating ground motions of missile installations under the loading of nuclear blasts and for evaluating the suitability of the Titan and Minuteman sites selected by the U.S. Air Force. He substantially advanced our knowledge of the response to earthquakes of earth dams, slopes, and foundations and was the principal U.S. Corps of Engineers investigator of the landslides caused by the Alaskan earthquake of 1964.

Stan Wilson's greatest area of interest, however, was in the design and behavior of earth and rockfill dams. Among the major dam projects on which he served as consultant are the Karnafuli and Tarbela dams in Pakistan; the Tres Marias and Furnas dams in Brazil; the Akosombo Dam in Ghana; the Infiernillo, Malpaso, and many other dams in Mexico; the Gardiner Dam in Canada; the Bandama River Project in the Ivory Coast; the Lesotho Highlands Water Project; the Uribanti-Caparo Project in Venezuela; the Colbun Hydroelectric Project in Chile; and the seismic evaluation of the High Aswan Dam in Egypt.

In the United States, his consulting activities involved the Brownlee and Oxbow dams in Idaho, the Mammoth Pool Project in California, the Muddy Run and Seneca pumped storage projects in Pennsylvania, the Ludington pumped storage reservoir in Michigan, and the stability problems at the Libby Dam site in Montana.

Stanley Wilson gave generously of his time to young engineers and was a regular and frequent lecturer at the University of Illinois and at the University of California at Berkeley. He was also an affiliate professor at the University of Washington. In addition, he contributed more than sixty technical papers and served on numerous advisory boards to the U.S. Army Corps of Engineers, the Nuclear Regulatory Commission, and the National Research Council.

He was an honorary member of the American Society of Civil Engineers (ASCE) and the Mexican National Society of Soil Mechanics. He was a member of Sigma Xi, the American Society for Testing and Materials, the Boston Society of Civil Engineers, the Consulting Engineers Council of Washington, the Harvard Society of Engineers and Scientists, the International Society of Soil Mechanics and Foundation Engineering, the U.S. Committee on Large Dams, the Associación Argentina de Géologia Aplicada a La Ingenieria, and the

American Institute of Consulting Engineers. In 1967 he was elected to the National Academy of Engineering.

The American Society of Civil Engineers awarded him the Walter L. Huber Research Prize (1961), the Arthur M. Wellington Prize (1968), the Karl Terzaghi Award (1978), and the Rickey Medal (1985). He was the Karl Terzaghi Lecturer of ASCE (1969), the State-of-the-Art Reporter on Earth and Rockfill Dams at the Seventh International Conference on Soil Mechanics and Foundation Engineering at Mexico City (1969), and the Miles Kirsten Lecturer at the University of Minnesota (1983). For his contributions to the Corps of Engineers, he was awarded the Outstanding Civilian Service Medal (1973).

The topics of his numerous publications ranged from investigations of the laboratory and field behavior of soils and rock and the means for observing them to a wide variety of practical soil displacement applications. One of his most influential publications, a monograph written with Raul J. Marsal of Mexico on "Current Trends in Design and Construction of Embankment Dams," was prepared in 1979 for the International Commission on Large Dams and the Geotechnical Division of ASCE.

Those who knew him best appreciated him for more than his technical competence. In the words of one of his fellow consultants who had worked with him often in the field:

Stan reveled in these field visits—often made by small plane, helicopter, jeep, and a fair amount of climbing. There was no hill too steep, no shaft too deep, no swinging foot bridge too narrow to stop Stan from making his inspection. I don't ever recall hearing him say, "I think I've seen enough." He wanted to see all the soils being used in the dam, all the lab tests being run, all the results being obtained, and to observe the contractor's operation in preparing the foundation, placing the fill, and, in particular, the compaction of the fill for the dam embankment. Stan entered into frank but always courteous discussions with the field engineers, lab engineers, or the designers about any point of concern.

Although he traveled extensively, he was devoted and attentive to his family. He and his wife Margaret, to whom he had been married forty years at her death in 1983, were active supporters of the Seattle Symphony. Their three children and five grandchildren were a cohesive unit in which he took great pleasure and with whom he spent many lively times at home or at the family retreat, a cabin near Cle Elum.

George Winter

GEORGE WINTER

1907–1982

BY ANTON TEDESKO

Gᴇᴏʀɢᴇ ᴡɪɴᴛᴇʀ was born on April 1, 1907, in Vienna, Austria, and died November 3, 1982. At the time of his death, he was Class of 1912 Professor of Engineering Emeritus at Cornell University.

An engineer, teacher, researcher, and industry consultant, George Winter became chairman of Cornell's Department of Structural Engineering in 1948. He served in this position for twenty-two years, during which time he brought international distinction to himself, to the department, and to the university. He was a member of several international engineering groups, was fluent in four languages, and maintained friendships worldwide.

George Winter grew up in Vienna during a time of great cultural and intellectual activity. As a youth, he was exposed to and influenced by what went on in the worlds of science, art, literature, drama, and music. The Vienna intellectual climate contributed to his well-rounded education. After studying engineering for a year in Vienna, he moved first to Stuttgart and then to Munich, where he received his diploma engineer degree from the Institute of Technology in 1930.

In his first job, he worked on the construction of the first building that was built higher than permitted under the conventional building code of Vienna. In July 1931 George Winter and Anne Singer were married, and in April 1932 they journeyed to Russia, where George secured a position in structural design and construction under Russia's first Five-Year Plan. He also held a teaching assignment at the Mining Institute in Sverdlovsk.

Their son Peter was born in August 1934. Because the Russia of the purges was not a place in which the Winters wanted to remain, they returned to Austria in early 1938. Winter was then offered a fellowship at Cornell University, and in August 1938 he enrolled at Cornell as a doctoral student in structural engineering. Two years later, he received his Ph.D. and became a staff member at Cornell, a position he retained throughout his life.

George's entry into the research field of steel structures was timely. An expanding market for thin steel structures had created a demand for rational standards of design. In addition, Cornell's Dean Solomon Cady Hollister had obtained support from the industry to conduct the required research. His educational background and experience in engineering practice provided him with the correct perspective for this type of design-oriented research program.

His work led to the publication of the first edition of the *American Iron and Steel Institute Specification for the Design of Cold-Formed Steel Structural Members* in 1946. Most of the research and writing of this code, and of many subsequent editions, can be attributed to George Winter. The code became the generally accepted international standard in the field.

As an outgrowth of his work in thin steel structures, George Winter also became deeply involved in the writing of standards for heavier steel construction, serving for many years as a key member of the American Institute of Steel Construction Specification Committee. He was also chairman of the Column Research Council.

His research contributions in the steel area included investigations of the buckling and postbuckling strength of thin-walled shapes, the effects of cold-forming, and ductility effects, as well as torsional and flexural buckling. In addition to his contributions in cold-formed steel and structural steel design, Winter's interest in reinforced concrete structures spanned his entire professional career. His reinforced concrete research centered on such topics as long-term deflections, microcracking, progressive fracture and failure, and inelasticity and strength.

He devoted much time and energy to the revision and improvement of the Building Code of the American Concrete Institute (ACI), providing leadership for the introduction of a rational approach to structural safety involving load and resistance factors. For twenty-eight years, until his death, Winter was a member of the ACI Building Code Committee and repeatedly the chairman of one of its subcommittees. His influence on the development of reinforced concrete designs was further extended through his efforts as coauthor of the fifth through ninth editions of the book *Design of Concrete Structures*.

Although George Winter exercised great influence on many aspects of structural engineering research and practice, perhaps his greatest impact was in his role of teacher. He was curious to know the basis of every idea when it was stripped down to its roots, and he could explain complex ideas simply and clearly. He demanded much of himself and of others in his quest for improvement.

As Professor Floyd Slate put it in the preface to a commemorative volume published at the time of Winter's retirement in 1975, "The atmosphere which he consistently created in the classroom was exhilarating: the clarity, the stimulation, the thought-provoking questions, the personal interactions, the sincerity, the dedication—all of these things and more made his teaching both a challenge and an excitement." This same commitment to excellence and to nurturing the ability to think critically extended to his work as thesis adviser to his many graduate students. Winter taught many engineers who have gone on to become leaders in the structural engineering profession.

His presence was felt far beyond Cornell's College of Engineering. He played a central role in the intellectual life of the university, particularly in the arts and sciences, through which he maintained many friends. George Winter was a strong supporter of music, and he took an active interest in the musical well-being of the Cornell community. He served on and chaired the Faculty Music Committee and was chairman of the Friends of Music at Cornell.

He was a long-time member of the Andrew D. White and Herbert F. Johnson museums and of the Cornell Library Associates. Prehistoric archaeology was another interest George pursued for many years. He was a member of the American Archaeological Institute and participated in the Smithsonian Archaeological Expedition to Egypt in 1966.

Winter was elected to membership in the National Academy of Engineering in 1970. He served on the Committee on Membership for three years, and he also served on a committee of the technical panel of the National Research Council's Advisory Committee to the Department of Housing and Urban Development. As a member of this committee, he prepared a critique of the criteria developed by the National Bureau of Standards, which NBS subsequently changed.

George Winter was named an honorary member of the American Society of Civil Engineers and of the American Concrete Institute. He received three national awards from the American Concrete Institute: the Wason Research Medal for Research (1965), the Henry C. Turner Medal (1972), and the Joe W. Kelly Award (1979). He also received three national awards from the American Society of Civil Engineers: the Leon S. Moisseiff Award (1948), the Croes Medal (1961), and the E. E. Howard Award (1981).

In September 1982 Winter received the prestigious International Award of Merit in Structural Engineering from the International Association for Bridge and Structural Engineering, "in appreciation of his outstanding contributions in research and teaching of structural engineering." He was also awarded an honorary doctorate from his undergraduate university, the Technological University of Munich.

He was the author or coauthor of more than eighty technical papers, many of which dealt with the results of his research. He also served as visiting professor at the California Institute of Technology, the University of Michigan, the University of California at Berkeley, and the University of Liège. He lectured at the universities of Glasgow, Bristol, and Cambridge in the United Kingdom.

His professional accomplishments were many, but his first love was his family. The Winter family enjoyed spending vacations in the Alps, mountaineering with or without skis, or at their summer home on Mount Desert Island in Maine.

George Winter is survived by his widow, Anne Winter, of Ithaca, New York, and West Tremont, Maine, and by a son, Peter Michael. Peter is professor and chairman of the Department of Anesthesiology at the University of Pittsburgh and lives in Pittsburgh with his wife and two children.

George Winter was unique in being able to excel in so many roles—first and foremost, as a teacher who nurtured critical thinking, but also as a researcher, an author, a member of professional committees, a developer of building codes, and a leader in engineering education and campus cultural life. He greatly expanded the horizons of his students, colleagues, and friends.

APPENDIX

Members	Elected	Born	Deceased
Stuart L. Bailey	1973	October 7, 1905	August 11, 1984
Jack A. Baird	1971	May 27, 1921	May 23, 1986
Robert A. Baker, Sr.	1967	May 31, 1907	December 8, 1982
Thomas Baron	1977	February 15, 1921	May 20, 1985
Richard E. Bellman	1977	August 26, 1920	March 19, 1984
Maurice A. Biot	1967	May 25, 1905	September 12, 1985
Raymond L. Bisplinghoff	1965	February 7, 1917	March 5, 1985
Hans H. Bleich	1978	March 24, 1909	February 8, 1985
Hendrik W. Bode	1964	December 24, 1905	June 21, 1982
Donald B. Broughton	1976	April 20, 1917	December 2, 1984
Adolf Busemann	1970	April 20, 1901	November 3, 1986
Robert W. Cairns	1969	December 23, 1909	January 27, 1985
Edward J. Cleary	1967	June 16, 1906	March 31, 1984
F. Allen Cleveland	1980	January 31, 1923	August 12, 1983
Norman A. Copeland	1977	August 16, 1915	April 30, 1984
Stanley Corrsin	1980	April 3, 1920	June 2, 1986
Luigi Crocco	1979	February 2, 1909	November 19, 1986
A. Earl Cullum, Jr.	1970	September 27, 1909	January 31, 1985
Peter V. Danckwerts	1978	October 4, 1916	October 25, 1984
Marcel Dassault	1976	January 22, 1892	April 18, 1986
Walter S. Douglas	1967	January 22, 1912	March 15, 1985
Thomas B. Drew	1983	February 9, 1902	May 5, 1985
Pol E. Duwez	1979	December 11, 1907	December 31, 1984
Phillip Eisenberg	1974	November 6, 1919	December 16, 1984
Elmer W. Engstrom	1964	August 25, 1901	October 30, 1984
Vivian F. Estcourt	1981	May 31, 1897	May 11, 1985
Phil M. Ferguson	1973	November 10, 1899	August 28, 1986
J. Earl Frazier	1978	July 4, 1902	January 1, 1985
King-sun Fu	1976	October 2, 1930	April 29, 1985
Wilfred M. Hall	1983	June 12, 1894	November 5, 1986
John D. Harper	1971	April 6, 1910	July 26, 1985
Albert G. Holzman	1984	October 28, 1921	May 1, 1985
Stanley G. Hooker	1981	September 30, 1907	May 24, 1984
Frederick J. Hooven	1979	March 5, 1905	February 5, 1985
Olaf A. Hougen	1974	October 4, 1893	January 7, 1986
Herbert E. Hudson, Jr.	1978	September 21, 1910	September 13, 1983
Jerome C. Hunsaker	1967	August 26, 1886	September 10, 1984
Tamaki Ipponmatsu	1978	April 29, 1901	January 24, 1985

Members	Elected	Born	Deceased
George W. Kessler	1969	March 1, 1908	July 25, 1983
Edward W. Kimbark	1979	September 21, 1902	February 8, 1982
Thuston E. Larson	1978	March 3, 1910	March 21, 1984
Harold B. Law	1979	September 7, 1911	April 6, 1984
George M. Low	1970	June 10, 1926	July 17, 1984
Hans A. Mauch	1973	March 6, 1906	January 20, 1984
Robert C. McMaster	1970	May 13, 1913	July 6, 1986
Theodore J. Nagel	1973	December 20, 1913	January 14, 1986
Herbert M. Parker	1978	April 13, 1910	March 5, 1984
Joseph M. Pettit	1967	July 15, 1916	September 15, 1986
Hyman G. Rickover	1967	January 27, 1900	July 8, 1986
Gerard A. Rohlich	1970	July 8, 1910	September 16, 1983
George J. Schroepfer	1981	September 7, 1906	March 11, 1984
Donald B. Sinclair	1965	May 23, 1910	August 24, 1985
Alfred D. Starbird	1973	April 28, 1912	July 28, 1983
Robert E. Stewart	1978	May 4, 1915	November 13, 1983
James H. Stratton	1981	June 7, 1898	March 16, 1984
John G. Trump	1977	August 21, 1907	February 21, 1985
Herbert D. Vogel	1977	August 26, 1900	August 26, 1984
C. Howard Vollum	1977	May 31, 1913	February 5, 1986
Edward C. Wells	1967	August 26, 1910	July 1, 1986
Stanley D. Wilson	1967	August 12, 1912	November 17, 1985
George Winter	1970	April 1, 1907	November 3, 1982

ACKNOWLEDGMENTS FOR
THE PHOTOGRAPHS

HANS HEINRICH BLEICH, by Foto-Life Studio, New York, N.Y.

NORMAN ARLAND COPELAND, by Willard Stewart, Inc., Wilmington, Del.

STANLEY CORRSIN, by James Karmrodt Lightner

MARCEL DASSAULT, by Henry Pessar, Paris, France

THOMAS BRADFORD DREW, by Fabian Bachrach

PHIL MOSS FERGUSON, by Christianson Leberman House of Portraits, Austin, Tex.

JOHN EARL FRAZIER, courtesy of Observer Publishing Company, Washington, Pa.

STANLEY GEORGE HOOKER, courtesy of Rolls Royce Limited

JEROME CLARKE HUNSAKER, by Bara Photographic, Inc., Hyattsville, Md.

HYMAN GEORGE RICKOVER, courtesy of U.S. Naval Photographic Center, Washington, D.C.

GERARD ADDISON ROHLICH, courtesy of University of Wisconsin, Madison, Wis.

ALFRED DODD STARBIRD, courtesy of U.S. Army Audio Visual Agency, Washington, D.C.

JAMES HOBSON STRATTON, by Fabian Bachrach

HERBERT D. VOGEL, by Harris & Ewing, Washington, D.C.

STANLEY DeWOLF WILSON, by Richter Photography, Seattle, Wash.

369